The Texas Revolution and
the U.S.–Mexican War

ALSO BY PAUL CALORE
AND FROM MCFARLAND

Land Campaigns of the Civil War (2000; paperback 2012)

The Causes of the Civil War: The Political, Cultural, Economic and Territorial Disputes between North and South (2008)

Naval Campaigns of the Civil War (2002)

The Texas Revolution and the U.S.–Mexican War

A Concise History

Paul Calore

McFarland & Company, Inc., Publishers
Jefferson, North Carolina

Maps are by the author

LIBRARY OF CONGRESS CATALOGUING-IN-PUBLICATION DATA

Calore, Paul, 1938–
The Texas Revolution and the U.S.-Mexican War : a concise history / Paul Calore.
         p.   cm.
Includes bibliographical references and index.

ISBN 978-0-7864-7940-5 (softcover : acid free paper) ∞
ISBN 978-1-4766-1485-4 (ebook)

1. Texas—History—Revolution, 1835–1836.
2. Mexican War, 1846–1848.   I. Title.
F390.C25 2014   976.4'03—dc23   2014007933

BRITISH LIBRARY CATALOGUING DATA ARE AVAILABLE

© 2014 Paul Calore. All rights reserved

*No part of this book may be reproduced or transmitted in any form
or by any means, electronic or mechanical, including photocopying
or recording, or by any information storage and retrieval system,
without permission in writing from the publisher.*

On the cover: *Storming of Chapultepec—Quitman's attack* (September 13, 1847)
in the Mexican-American War; hand-colored lithograph; original size of painted area:
16½" × 10¾"; originally published in George Wilkins Kendal and Carl Nebel:
The War Between the United States and Mexico, Illustrated
(New York: D. Appleton and Company, 1851)

Printed in the United States of America

*McFarland & Company, Inc., Publishers
Box 611, Jefferson, North Carolina 28640
www.mcfarlandpub.com*

Contents

Preface 1

1. Austin Colony to the Convention of 1833 3
2. Santa Anna and the Politics of Mexico City 17
3. Gonzales, Goliad, and Fort Lipantitlán 30
4. The Siege of Béxar 41
5. The Battle of the Alamo and the Goliad Massacre 53
6. The Battle of San Jacinto and the Pastry War 67
7. The Republic of Texas and Its Quest for Statehood 80
8. Prelude to War 89
9. The Battles of Palo Alto, Resaca de la Palma and Monterrey 102
10. A Shift in Strategy and the Battle of Buena Vista 115
11. The Western Campaigns 123
12. The Battles of Veracruz and Cerro Gordo 137
13. Scott's Drive to Mexico City 148

Epilogue 163
Notes 173
Bibliography 175
Index 177

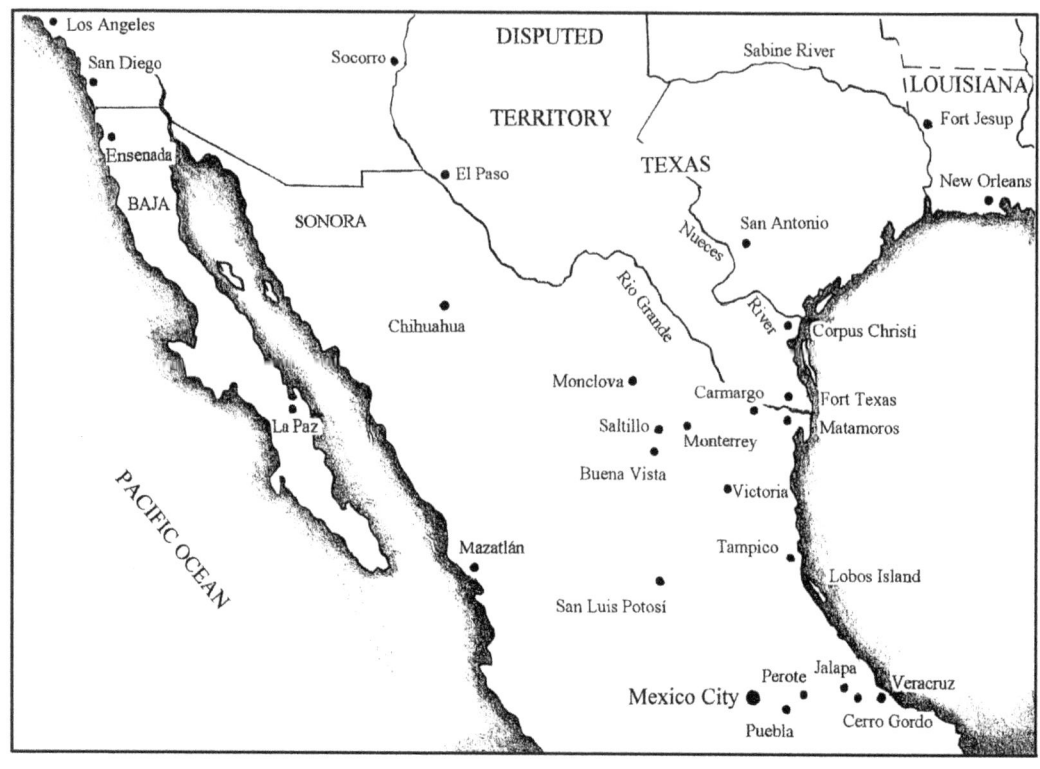

Mexico and Texas

Preface

As all enthusiasts of U.S. history know, the antebellum years of 1800 to 1860 were an incredibly fascinating period in the nation's past. The country experienced such historical events as the dreadful curse of slavery, the innovations in railroad travel, the War of 1812, the Missouri Compromise, the rise and fall of abolitionism, the Underground Railroad, the rise of Manifest Destiny, the introduction of protectionism, the opening of the West, the Indian Removal Act, the growth of the Industrial Revolution, and the election of Abraham Lincoln, just to mention a few.

To the chagrin of some people, however, the commemoration of the American Civil War over the years since, although warranted, has to a large degree overshadowed two other significant events that took place during the antebellum years. Specifically, they were the fight for Texas independence, a conflict that not only awakened the spirit of the American people but also triggered the U.S.'s first battlefield confrontation in a foreign country, and the second significant event: the U.S. war with Mexico.

These two chapters in American history were uniquely instrumental not only for expanding the United States geographically but also for establishing a new and exciting foundation for the development of its social, political, and cultural diversification.

This book recalls the political growing pains of two countries from 1835 to 1848, the sacrifices they made, the suffering they endured, and the selflessness of the human spirit, all for causes both sides believed were just.

Since obtaining her independence from Spain, Mexico had been a country tottering on the brink of political and economic collapse. Political instability in early independent Mexico resulted in an uncertain economic policy, no public programs for development, and, most important, violence and general disorder. Politicians gained and lost power frequently in a game of musical chairs. As a result, many economic policies changed drastically from one year to another or were quickly reversed, and those involving public programs were never enforced. The only solution by the various political factions was to overthrow the government they chose not to agree with. But to compound the difficulties, urban riots, demonstrations, assaults, and rural rebellions usually accompanied the frequent changes of governments.

Along with the political and economic turmoil bred from a series of corrupt, contradictory, and opportunistic leaders, Mexico's difficulties were compounded by the inherent problems of a country with too little to offer its citizens and too large an area for effective governance.

It was in this chaotic climate that America's fascinating saga with Mexico began.

As the Mexican government struggled to resolve her financial problems, an attempt to strengthen the country's economy was made with the introduction of empresarios, or agents responsible for settling colonists on free grants of barren land, in hopes of improving the economy of that region by their efforts at farming and ranching. The settlers, mostly southern Americans, came by the thousands to establish homesteads in Mexico on land that one day would be called Texas.

The early chapters of this book recount an intriguing story of the birth and growth of the empresario system in Mexico, the resourcefulness of the settlers, their achievements, and their struggles against a corrupt Mexican government obsessed with their removal from Mexican society. Once welcomed as fellow countrymen, after a time the colonists were considered to be enemies of the state and treated with merciless reprisals. As they struck back for a political cause they believed in, hundreds of raw, untrained, and determined frontiersmen gathered together in a volunteer army to challenge the might of the Mexican army in the so-called Texas Revolution. These efforts are highlighted herein.

Several later chapters recount the success of the Texans in gaining their independence and sovereignty as the newly formed Republic of Texas, a declaration fiercely resented by the Mexican government. And ten years later, the U.S. war with Mexico was triggered as a consequence of Texas annexation as the twenty-first American state and further instigated by military clashes at the Rio Grande border. Whether the war was politically motivated by the United States to carry out the principles of Manifest Destiny or by the Mexican government to take back Texas, the land "stolen" by the United States is still hotly debated to this day.

The U.S. war with Mexico, fought for just 21 months, is documented in the last three chapters, beginning with the western campaigns and continuing through the battles that led to the ultimate drive into Mexico City itself.

My hope is that readers of this work will learn two very important points: to appreciate the many hardships and sacrifices made by Texans who sacrificed their lives for the political freedom they believed in and for the right of self-determination, and to understand that the struggle to win the war with Mexico not only added over a half-million square miles to the United States, land destined to unleash a vast wave of western expansion, but also introduced a wide degree of diversification to the country, a cultural experience that ultimately benefited everyone.

1

Austin Colony to the Convention of 1833

For Moses Austin, once a wealthy industrialist and the founder of the U.S. lead-mining industry, times were getting much tougher. His story begins in 1783 when as a 22-year-old he became a partner with his brother in a dry-goods store in Philadelphia. Brought up as a Connecticut Yankee, Austin was so encouraged by the success they were having with the business that he decided to expand, to increase his participation in the entrepreneurial world on his own, and, more important, with plans for raising a family, to earn a much better income. Accordingly, he pulled up stakes and moved to Richmond, Virginia, where he opened a second business.

Settling down in Virginia was a satisfying time for the young man, especially after he briefly returned to Philadelphia in 1785 to marry his sweetheart of two years, Maria Brown. He knew his in-laws were quite wealthy as owners of an iron mine in Richmond, a fact that not only impressed young Austin but also provided the impetus for him to succeed financially as they had. Wanting to provide his wife and any future children with the lifestyle she was accustomed to, Austin worked hard at his mercantile business and saved as much money as he could afford.

In June of 1789, Austin's wife gave birth to their first child, Anna Maria. As in all families, it was a very happy moment for the Austin family, but unfortunately the joy they experienced would be very brief. After only one month of life, Anna died, as did little Eliza three years later. With enough savings put aside, in 1789 Austin visited an abandoned lead mine in present-day Wythe County, Virginia. At that point he became convinced that he would try his hand in the mining business as his in-laws had done before him.

With additional financing from his brother and others he bought the lead mine and shortly after expanded its potential by adding a shot tower, smelting furnaces, blacksmith shops, and other enhancements. In fact, so extensive was his program to develop the mine and the surrounding area that the small village he built near the mine was called "Austinville." And when he received a generous contract to cover the roof of the Virginia capitol building in sheet lead, he imported highly experienced smelters and miners from Great Britain to increase the company's expertise. However, as any business would, Austin's mining operation began to fail when his expenses increased faster than his income.

Determined to succeed in the mining business, Austin traveled in the winter of 1796 with his family to Missouri, where in two years he bought another mine that impressed him a great deal. It was called Mine Au Breton. Meanwhile, his brother was left to look after the mine in Virginia, which was eventually seized and resold by the state.

By this time the Austin family included Stephen F., born in 1793, and Emily, born in 1795. James would arrive in 1803.

Two years later, once the family was resettled in their newly built home, called Durham Hall, after his birthplace of Durham, Connecticut, Austin decided to shift his business sense into high gear. He applied and received an empresario contract from the Spanish authorities. According to the terms of the contract, he was granted a parcel of adjoining land and in return he was obligated to reestablish the lead mine and smelting business and to make all the necessary improvements to the land to settle 30 families. His grant was for 7,153 arpents (a unit of measurement used by the Spanish in Missouri, one arpent = .8507 acre) or about 6,000 acres of land.[1]

To satisfy the conditions of his contract, Moses Austin began by sinking the first mine shaft and installing the first reverbatory furnace west of the Mississippi, a furnace in which heat was radiated from the top of the furnace onto the material being treated below. He then had a number of lots surveyed, and along with several hired hands and about 50 of his slaves laid out a town square and built a post office. This construction work continued with the building of a courthouse, distilleries, a jailhouse, a store, a blacksmith shop, and several other structures that formed the beginnings of the present-day town of Potosi, Missouri.

For the next several years his business flourished and he became a very wealthy man, amassing a fortune of over $150,000, a very hefty sum in the early nineteenth century.

However, in the financially depressed environment following the War of 1812 the ensuing economic downturn resulted in the typical debilitating business nightmare: significant decreases in production contracts and unavoidable increases in debt. Orders for such commodities as cannonballs and shot, as well as sheet and bar lead, had fallen off considerably.

Undeterred, after leaving the Potosi mine in the hands of his son Stephen, Moses became a co-founder of the Bank of St. Louis, the first bank west of the Mississippi River. As luck would have it, in Austin's case bad luck, in 1819 he lost most of his fortune when land values plunged and many of the banks failed, including the bank he founded. In fact, in February of 1820 Moses wrote to his son James that he had lost a considerable amount of his investments, especially from his stock in the bank of St. Louis, and that he would not save more than $15,000 after everything was settled.

Although he suffered incredible losses of both his wealth and his businesses, Moses Austin was not a man easily discouraged. Even at 59 years old, he still displayed the motivation, grit, and drive of a much younger man as he contemplated his next business venture. Abandoning the mining industry where he had already established his legacy, Austin decided to use the knowledge he had gained as an empresario in Missouri to apply for a similar but larger settlement contract. This time he would go to Mexico, specifically the territory adjacent to the state of Coahuila, popularly referred to as Spanish Texas or, in the native language, Spanish Téjas. If he could obtain the approval from the Spanish authorities not only would it help him recover from bankruptcy, but it would also make him the first empresario to colonize this very remote and hostile territory in northern Mexico.

But first he had to ride some eight hundred long miles to San Antonio de Béxar, or simply Béxar, on horseback, not only to apply for the land, and lots of it, but also to obtain permission to solicit Anglo-American families to settle on it.

Moses left home in the spring of 1820 and rode to his son Stephen's house in Little Rock, Arkansas. It was here that Moses came down with malaria, which kept him confined until November. Finally fit enough to resume his journey, Austin bid his son farewell and headed for Texas on horseback with $50 in his pocket, some clothing, and accompanied by one of his son's slaves who had to endure the trip riding a mule.

Unfortunately, the bitter cold, snow, and rainy weather in Béxar was terrible that December when Austin arrived from Missouri. And to make matters worse, despite all the planning he went through and all the hopes he had for a brighter future, he was unable to convince the governor of Spanish Texas, Lt. Col. Antonio María Martínez, on the merits of his plan. Unfortunately for Austin, at the time the local authorities were having problems with a filibuster by the name of James Long who believed Spanish Texas should belong to the United States despite the agreement reached by the Adams-Onís Treaty, a treaty that ceded Texas to Spain in 1819. To follow up on his claim, Long raised a small group of armed followers and pledged to take by force what the American politicians failed to do for the good of the country. As a consequence of this nuisance, the commandant of the eastern province, Gen. José Joaquín de Arredondo, ordered the governor to dismiss Austin's request and to demand he leave Béxar or face arrest. Not one to cross his superior, especially the likes of Arredondo, Martínez ordered Austin to leave town immediately.

Although he was disappointed over this seemingly arbitrary rejection, Austin remained optimistic when, by chance, as he was returning to his lodging he encountered an old friend of his he first met in New Orleans years ago. It was Baron de Bastrop, a well-known Louisiana land developer who, fortunately, had direct access to the governor. After explaining the situation he was in, Austin decided to ask his well-placed contact to intervene on his behalf. It turned out to be the best decision he ever made. They returned to the governor's office and convincingly persuaded Martínez to reconsider the plan and its value to the economic growth of Spanish Texas. The day after Christmas of 1820 Austin's request was approved by the governor and forwarded to General Arredondo for acceptance.

For decades the northern frontier of Mexico, a desolate and economically stagnant region, was populated with a very small number of native Mexicans. Even when government incentives were offered, the number of people inhabiting Spanish Texas amounted to only several thousand. One of the persuasive deterrents for nearly everyone to settle there was the savagery of the Indians who continuously patrolled the area searching for their next victims. The Comanche, Apache, Karankawa, and Tonkawa tribes, among others, were notorious for their nighttime raids. They would kill the men, steal the horses, and mercilessly take the women and children back to their camps for some unspeakable horror that awaited them. However, Austin's settlement plan, which he called his "Texas Venture," appealed to the authorities because it offered an excellent way to bring more people, more skills and more money into this poorest section of the country. It also had the potential to promote the growth of their economy, and at the same time the plan would provide more armed men to defend the region against the Comanche and the other tribes. It was a win for everybody.

After taking all this into account, on January 17, 1821, General Arredondo approved Austin's petition, allowing him to settle three hundred families. But, as always, there were several conditions. Since Mexico did not protect the freedom of religion, the settlers had to be Catholic, which was never enforced; they had to respect the king and constitution of Spain, be honest and upright men of character, and cultivate the land within two years or forfeit their grant.

When Governor Martínez received word of the approval he directed the local head postmaster, Josef Erasmo Seguín, who was also acting as the governor's agent, to notify Austin of the good news.

Moses Austin was extremely elated over this fortunate turn of events and wrote to his son Stephen, "I now can go forward with confidence and hope and pray you will Discharge your Doubts as to the Enterprise.... Raise your Spirits Times are changing a new chance presents itself."[2]

But soon his joy would all be changed by another dose of bad luck.

It seems his health had begun to deteriorate during the ride back from Béxar, the result of the dreadful weather he was exposed to for many weeks. With his illness clearly getting worse and Austin sensing his life draining away, two days before his death at the home of his daughter, Emily, Austin made a deathbed request to his wife which she recalled in a letter to Stephen. "[H]e called me to his bedside," she wrote, "and with much distress and difficulty of speech begged me to tell you to take his place and if god in his wisdom thought best to disappoint him in the accomplishment of his wishes and plans formed, he prayed him to extend his goodness to you and enable you to go on with the business in the same way he would have done."[3] On June 10, 1821, the "Grandfather of Texas" died of pneumonia before he ever had a chance to fulfill his dream. Moses Austin now lies in his tomb at the Potosi City Cemetery.

At the time, his son James was attending school in Kentucky and Stephen, who was helping his father launch this new venture, was in Natchitoches, Louisiana, where he joined up with Seguín, who was still acting as the governor's agent. Along with several others, they expected to accompany Moses on an inspection tour of the vast territory granted to him in the contract. It was during the preparation for this tour that on July 10 Austin learned of his father's death. Consequently, to carry out his father's deathbed request Stephen abandoned his desire to remain a lawyer and began a new and more challenging career as an empresario in their so-called Texas Venture.

His first priority was to get his father's contract reauthorized. And to accomplish this technicality Austin and Seguín traveled to Béxar to meet the governor, arriving in August of 1821.

At the meeting, not only did Governor Martínez reauthorize the land grant, he also discussed the terms for distributing the parcels of land. Since the concept of attracting outsiders and settling them on Mexican soil was a relatively new idea to the authorities in Béxar, a formal law regulating the costs, fees, and criteria for land distribution did not exist at the time. In that regard, Austin had mailed a proposal beforehand to the governor whereby he would offer land in quantities of 640 acres for the head of a family, 320 acres for his wife, 320 acres for each child and 80 acres for each slave he owned. The only cost to the colonists would be a 12 ½ cent per acre service charge payable to him for his services as empresario in managing the colony. It was a proposal Governor Martínez readily endorsed. In addition, the governor stressed that Austin should inspect the coastal plain between the San Antonio and Bravo Rivers as soon as possible in order to locate an appropriate site of his choosing for the colony.

Relieved that the project was back on track, Austin and Sequín arrived in the vicinity of the Colorado River in September along with their guides Manuel Becerra, who was also a civil judge and one of Austin's land grantees, and three Aranama Indians. After several days of examining the vast amount of pristine wilderness, some two hundred thousand acres, the enormous tract of real estate he selected extended from the point where the Lavaca River flows into Matagorda Bay northeastward approximately 120 miles along the Gulf Coast to the vicinity of Galveston Bay, then inland from those two points covering an area of about fifteen thousand square miles.

To satisfy the terms of the contract, however, now Austin had to attract and then convince three hundred Anglo-American families that by settling in Spanish Texas they would be provided with the means to build a more productive future. Without doubt, in spite of the Indian problems, giving away large tracts of land for free had to be a great incentive for the families looking to start a new life on their own land. In the United States; for instance, a minimum of eighty acres was selling for $1.25 an acre payable upfront.[4] However, under Austin's contract the settlers' only cost was the 12 ½ cents an acre service charge. Another attraction was that no formal agreement between Mexico and the United States existed at the time that allowed American creditors to collect debts owed by the settlers. Therefore, the settlers who defaulted on their American loans, some possibly facing debtors' prison, could set up a homestead in Spanish Texas without having to worry about those creditors.

His first step to attract potential settlers was to travel to New Orleans, where he posted an advertisement of his land deal and settlement terms and invited one and all to experience a new lifestyle in Mexico. To Austin's surprise, the response was overwhelming.

In less than three months a majority of the colonists were signed up and were ready to move in once Austin had their property surveyed. Some of the families were financially well-off, looking to start a new life in a different environment, whereas a few families wanted a safe haven to hide from creditors and to begin life over again and others just wanted to move out west for reasons known only to them.

But despite having his land grant approved and settlers waiting to settle, quite unexpectedly he was informed by Governor Martínez that there were potential problems that could impact the future of his contract.

After an 11-year fight to free Mexico from Spanish control, on September 27, 1821, Gen. Agustín de Iturbide marched his victorious army into Mexico City. Begun in 1810, it was the final event that brought to an end the long struggle for Mexico's independence from Spain. Expected to be the beginning of a joyful period in Mexican history, it was instead a period of unrelenting turmoil, instability, and political revolts.

Ironically, the timing could not have been worse for Austin. Since Mexico gained her independence just as he was carrying out the final stages of his colonization effort, Austin was now faced with two problems. The first arose because Austin's land grant in Spanish Texas was approved by the Spanish government. But since the Mexicans now controlled the government, Spanish Texas was to be referred to as Mexican Texas and the approval for the land grant had to come from the Mexican authorities. In addition, nothing would be done on this matter until new immigration laws were enacted by a new congress. Likewise, the second problem was over Austin's proposal for acreage distribution and fees in the land grant. Since the rates were not approved or authorized under any formal Mexican colonization law, Austin's contract was placed on hold until Mexico issued her own immigration guidelines.

As a result, Austin would have to wait until a new congress as well as a new head of state was chosen to approve a general immigration law before he could receive another judgment on his colonization contract. And that was not going to happen anytime soon.

It took about eight months, but finally, on May 19, 1822, the congress overwhelmingly confirmed General Iturbide as the first emperor of Mexico and on July 21 his coronation was held at the Mexico City cathedral.

Eight months later, in spite of all their problems with Iturbide and the way he was managing the new government, the so-called rump congress, which was the remnants of the prior congress, was able to pass the Imperial Colonization Law. The new act specified, among other rules, that settlers engaged in farming were entitled to at least one labor of land, which amounted to 177 acres. Those who were cattle ranchers would be eligible to receive one league, or 4,428 acres, some of which included riverfront acreage. Of course most families claimed their occupations were a combination of both farming and ranching to receive a larger parcel of land. Also, settlers were free of taxes for six years and were to pay only half the taxes for the following six years, and children of slaves would be freed at the age of 14. In addition, empresarios were entitled to receive about 67,000 acres of land for every two hundred families they settled. Meanwhile, Austin was still collecting the 12½ cents service charge as well.

And so, in February of 1823, with the bureaucratic red tape finally broken Austin received the news he was waiting for—his colonization plan had been reviewed and was approved. Delighted that he was back in business, Austin resumed his efforts to encourage those with a pioneering spirit to settle in Mexican Texas.

Unfortunately, Iturbide's mismanagement of government affairs, his aversion to any form of dissention with his policies, and his mistreatment of the opposition, among a host of other factors, could no longer be tolerated by the political factions that are always prepared to overthrow a wayward government. Consistent with Mexico's history in dealing with political leaders who fall out of favor, there were demonstrations and revolts, then Iturbide was forced to step aside, and finally he was exiled to Italy.

Beginning in October of 1824, one of the first significant acts of the new government, now administered by Pres. Guadalupe Victoria, was to repeal Iturbide's Imperial Colonization Law. Although this appeared to be another huge setback for Austin, by virtue of his strong lobbying efforts he managed to persuade the new government to

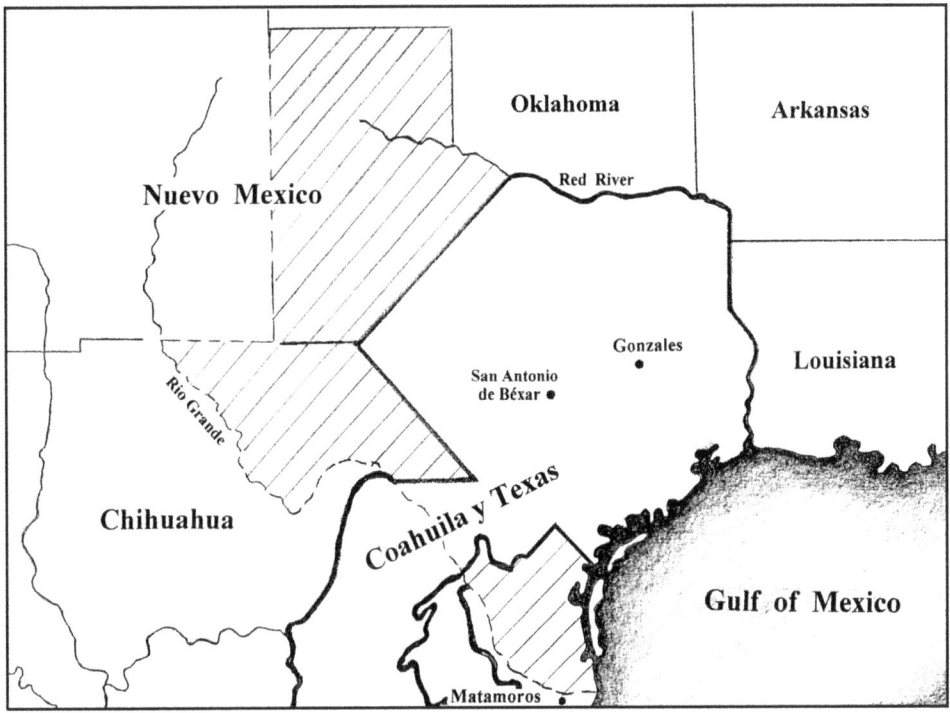

Coahuila y Texas

issue a special decree that permitted him to retain the terms of his contract as mandated under Iturbide. Also, since the adjacent territory to the north of Coahuila called Mexican Texas did not have representation in the Mexican congress, one provision of the new constitution combined the state of Coahuila and Mexican Texas to form the state of Coahuila y Texas, with its capital at Saltillo. Nine representatives would be seated from Coahuila and three from Texas.

At any rate, Stephen Austin was now the empresario of "Austin Colony," a village about a hundred miles inland on the Brazos River. He also founded San Felipe de Austin, which boasted at the time of having around 50 cabins, a hotel, a couple of saloons, a blacksmith shop, a post office, and several stores. In fact, it would be his capital, the administrative and political center of his colony.

While Austin was organizing the construction in San Felipe the congress in Mexico City was still busy revising the immigration laws. To annoy the settlers in Coahuila y Texas even more, in 1825 the congress placed the burden of administering public lands in the hands of the applicable state. By virtue of this ruling, Austin's contract now had to impose a onetime expense of $127 a league title fee payable to the land commissioner and a one-time payment of $30 to the state, which the settler had to pay within six years.

This new colonization law issued by Coahuila y Texas also retained the payment of sixty-seven thousand acres to the empresario payable after he settled two hundred families, a provision that caused many families to refuse paying Austin the 12½ cents service charge.

It wasn't long before Austin learned that many of his colonists had a problem with the service charge they were paying him. Apparently, the provision that granted the empresario over sixty-seven thousand acres of land hit a raw nerve with his colonists. Since he was being rewarded with all this land, they complained, why should they continue to pay him the service charge?

To resolve that issue, the settlers filed a complaint with a legal official in Béxar and won their case. Not to be outdone, however, in retaliation Austin convinced the land commissioner to split the $127 title fee with him and then charged each settler an additional fee of $50 per league in accordance with an ambiguous provision of the new law.

Although Austin Colony was the first settlement in Texas, it certainly wasn't the only one. Actually, in 1825 there were three other smaller settlements established from land grants. One was started by Green DeWitt, named DeWitt Colony, with the town of Gonzales as its capital. It was a small settlement on the banks of the Guadalupe River that had a population of 75 settlers in 1826. The second and predominately all–Mexican colony was populated with about 40 Tejanos, or settlers who were of Mexican origin, and was called "De Leon Colony" by its empresario, Martin De Leon. A third contract was awarded to Haden Edwards, but it was revoked by President Victoria in 1826 over title disputes with the local Mexican residents. Eventually some 24 empresario contracts were issued, each with varying degrees of success.

By 1825 the first 297 families were already settled onto their new homesteads in Austin Colony, 69 of which owned a total of over four hundred slaves. (Three hundred and seven titles were actually issued, since some grantees held more than one title.) They came by wagon, by horse, by foot, and even by boat from New Orleans to the port cities of Brazoria and Matagorda. But come they did, in what became known as the most successful colonization movement in U.S. history. Known as the "Old Three Hundred," these first settlers were mostly farmers of British ancestry coming from Louisiana, Alabama, Arkansas, Tennessee and Missouri. Like most pioneers of that period to establish their homesteads the colonists were a hardy and tough crowd. They were able to withstand the rigors of traveling in all kinds of weather for hundreds of miles in ramshackle wagons, eating whatever they could forage from the land, and willing to accept the work and harsh conditions required to begin a new life, not to mention having to endure the mental strain from not knowing when an Indian raid would occur.

Recognizing what appeared to be a seemingly never-ending throng of potential settlers looking to move into the colony encouraged Austin to expand his landholdings. Over the following four years Austin was kept busy managing Austin Colony as well as investing in additional grants. In fact, by 1829 Austin held three new settlement contracts issued in 1825, 1827, and 1828 respectively for an additional nine hundred families, all living prosperous and productive lives.

Meanwhile, as the growing number of Americans migrating into Texas began to attract the attention of the authorities in Mexico City, the White House was also keenly interested in this area. Pres. Andrew Jackson was well aware that Texas was presently inhabited by over twenty thousand Americans and their slaves. He also knew that Austin Colony consisted of a large number of thriving farms and ranching communities under the management of Stephen F. Austin and that it boasted of having a constitution, elected

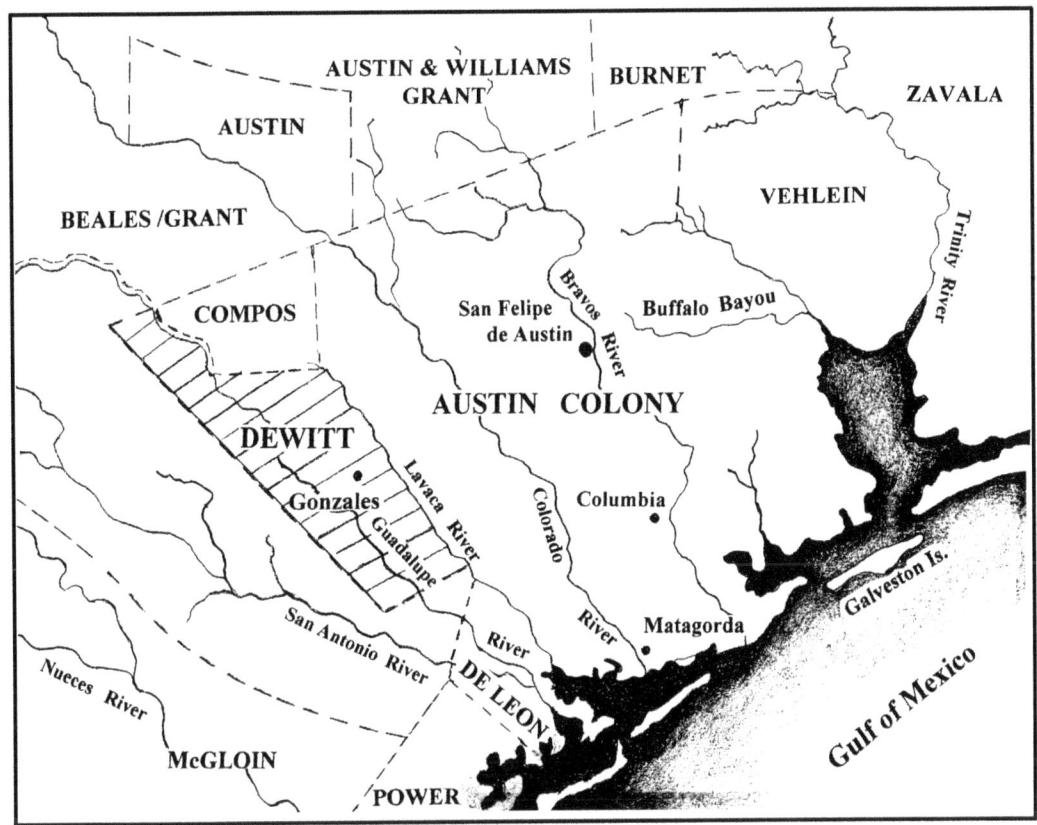

Texian Settlements

militia officers and justices of the peace, civil and criminal codes, an appellate court, schools, and even a well-respected armed security force.

As a result, President Jackson began to show an interest in purchasing a large tract of barren land in Texas. "Texas was necessary, Jackson said, for the security of the great emporium of the west, Neworleans [sic], and that great god of the universe had intended the great valley [of the Mississippi] to belong to one nation."[5] The president was convinced that if Texas ever gained her independence the congressional fight to annex her would be shameful, considering the outcry he expected from the antislavery northerners. For that reason Jackson favored purchasing the land outright by making an offer the Mexicans couldn't refuse.

Southern politicians saw Jackson's effort to purchase Texas as a tremendous opportunity to not only further the spread of slavery but also expand southern interest in national politics. Considering the impact the purchase of Texas would have on the southern economy as well the enormous political ramifications it would bring, southern aristocrats took a keen interest in this issue.

Taking advantage of the financial problems being experienced in Mexico after she gained her independence, Jackson thought the timing was perfect for diplomatic discussions on the Texas deal. Accordingly, instructions were forwarded to Joel Poinsett, the U.S. Minister in Mexico City, to initiate talks immediately on a land deal and to negotiate for a boundary at the Rio Grande. In addition, as a deal sweetener an offer of $3 million was authorized even though Jackson was prepared to go as high as $5 million if that became necessary. However, at the end of 1829 the new Mexican president, Vicente Guerrero, didn't quite see it that way. He was highly insulted that the United States was interfering in Mexican internal affairs and demanded Poinsett's recall. As a result, from that point on relations between the United States and Mexico grew steadily worse. To get the Texas deal back on track, several months later the U.S. chargé, Anthony Butler, was tasked to reopen the Texas talks and, as Jackson instructed, to improve the relations with the Mexican government. Butler was also authorized to use his own discretion in spending U.S. funds if it accomplished their objective.

In Justin H. Smith's book *The Annexation of Texas*, Butler is described as "personally a bully and swashbuckler, ignorant at first of the Spanish language and even the form of diplomacy, shamefully careless about legation affairs, wholly unprincipled as to methods, ... and totally scandalous in his conduct ... in brief, he was a national disgrace."[6]

Contrary to Jackson's analysis of Mexico's political environment, the timing could not have been worse. With the Mexicans living up to their reputation for engaging in presidential musical chairs, President Guerrero was deposed in a rebellion by his vice president, Anastasio Bustamante, who then had Guerrero executed. Bustamante subsequently assumed the presidency on January 1, 1830, the third Mexican president in six years.

Although political chaos in the extreme was hardly anything new in Mexico City, Butler managed to arrange two meetings with the foreign minister but again to no avail. In fact, the negotiations over Texas had become so drawn-out, frustrating, and difficult that Butler was forced to consider a stronger measure, namely, one that President Jackson himself had alluded to in a discreetly veiled suggestion in 1829—bribery. At the time, Jackson said, "I scarcely ever knew a Spaniard who was not the slave of avarice, and it is not improbable that this weakness may be worth a great deal to us, in this case."[7] Jackson also told Butler that he was authorized to use his own "discretion" in spending the money as long as it was kept secret and succeeded in acquiring Texas. Both men knew that in Mexico bribery was an accepted form of doing business, and in this particular case Butler thought its use was diplomatically implied by Jackson.

However, Butler absentmindedly informed the president via a letter he failed to encode that he was contemplating a $200,000 bribe to close the Texas deal as the president had once suggested. Unable to control his emotions, Jackson was outraged when Butler reminded the president of the instructions he had received. The president not only fiercely denied that he ever suggested such an unseemly tactic but also stated his vehement resentment of the insinuation that the office of the president of the United States had authorized such corrupt behavior. Butler stayed on for a few more years, only managing to get an agreement for a new joint commission to survey the U.S.–Mexico border. In the end, however, Jackson's bid to purchase Mexican land never materialized.

With all the attention Jackson was giving to this desolate corner of Mexico it didn't take long before government officials in Mexico City became quite concerned over the large influx of Americans coming into Mexico. Ironically, what was once considered a good way to improve the economy and the well-being of the country, especially in

Coahuila y Texas, was now viewed upon with much trepidation. Their paranoia and suspicion led them to believe that one day the United States might attempt a hostile takeover to acquire northern Mexico in order to increase her slaveholding territory, a fear that was proven to be more of a premonition. To buttress their argument, they claimed the Texians consistently refused to assimilate into the Mexican culture, continued their old customs, built their own schools, spoke their own language, and traded mostly with the United States, behavior that only exacerbated the bitter enmity between the Texians and the Mexicans. ("Texian" was the term generally used from 1821 to 1836 to identify an Anglo-American settler in the Texas colonies.)

The more the Texians demonstrated their ability to be self-sufficient, politically stable, and culturally independent from the rest of the state, the more attention the colonies attracted from the Mexican government. Furthermore, the government suspected the Texians were becoming increasingly reluctant to give up their American citizenship to live in Mexico.

In fact, the concern over the growing population of Anglos in the settlements and their apparent autonomy was now coming to a head.

The mounting frustration over a growing population of Anglos and their apparent lack of assimilation forced the new president to take direct action. As a consequence, Pres. Anastasio Bustamante ordered Gen. Manuel de Mier y Terán to review the various Mexican colonization laws that were instituted from 1823 to 1825. Terán's final report resulted in a series of some 18 new laws or articles issued on April 6, 1830, that were principally aimed at the settlers living in Coahuila y Texas. One of the laws called for the enforcement of custom duties while another dealt with the ever-sensitive issue of slavery. Slavery had already been outlawed a year before but with the ever-present turmoil in Mexico City nobody was paying much attention to the goings-on in faraway Texas. Consequently, since the law was never enforced in Texas, it was simply ignored by the slave owners. With this new law, Bustamante now not only demanded the Texians comply with the existing law against slavery but also prohibited further introduction of additional slaves, which would cause the colonists to face military intervention. To evade Bustamante's new ruling, however, the devious colonists simply converted their slaves into indentured servants for life, a maneuver that must have infuriated the authorities in the capital city.

Another law prohibited any further immigration from the United States into Coahuila y Texas, an outrageous ruling that infuriated the Texians. The wording of this law was such that it prohibited the settlement of immigrants in any territory that was adjacent to their native country, an indirect reference to the United States and the Texas border. Even though Austin would gain an exemption of this law for his own colonies and for Green DeWitt's colony as well, the Texians were livid that this fundamental freedom was being stripped away. Other laws included one that rescinded the property tax law, a law that exempted Texians from paying taxes for ten years, and another that called for colonies to have a minimum of 150 people or be canceled.

To challenge these and other laws and to discuss their common goals and actions for reforms, from October 1 to 6 of 1832 a political convention was organized with 55 delegates in attendance. The meeting was held in San Felipe de Austin, the capital of Austin Colony. The delegates represented Texians who resided in 16 colonies besides

Austin Colony, such as those located in Goliad, Béxar, Victoria, and Gonzales. Surprisingly, the two communities with the largest number of Tejanos, Béxar and Victoria, failed to send anyone to represent the Mexican settlers. According to the political chief in Béxar, Ramón Músquiz, the Tejanos felt duty bound to turn down the offer since the goal of the convention itself was a violation of Mexican law. By the same token the Tejanos were quite annoyed that the Anglos were still going to hold the convention even without hearing their own grievances and their own recommendations.

The first order of business was to elect the convention officers. To the satisfaction of the majority of voters, empresario Stephen F. Austin was elected president of the convention, a tribute to his many years of experience dealing with the Mexican authorities. Over the next several days the delegates continued to engage in seemingly endless discussions over not only a wide array of injustices but also the corrective actions the government should take to improve the governing of Coahuila y Texas.

The most controversial items were the resolutions requesting the repeal of the prohibition on immigration from the United States, and a petition that called for the separation of Texas from Coahuila and its formation as an independent Mexican state. In regard to the latter, the Texians were fed up with having only three representatives in the state legislature, because they were always at the mercy of the other nine representatives from Coahuila on matters important to their interests. The documents were then prepared for delivery to the state legislature in Saltillo and to the Mexican congress in Mexico City.

Unfortunately, the political chief, Músquiz, perhaps the most powerful official in Mexican Texas, informed the convention, or perhaps reminded the convention, that under Mexican law the convention was an illegal assembly. Evidently, all grievances had to follow a specific path up the bureaucratic ladder for approval before the local political chief, namely Músquiz, could forward the concerns to the state and to Mexico City. As a result, on November 7 Músquiz nullified everything that was accomplished at the meeting.

At the end of 1832, an arrangement was made with the political chief whereby instead of the Texians submitting the resolutions, the ayuntamiento or city council of Béxar, after obtaining signatures from Goliad, San Felipe de Austin, and Nacogdoches, would submit a nearly duplicate document to the one approved by the convention but this time through the legal channels to Saltillo, the capital of Coahuila y Texas, and to Mexico City. The delegates agreed to this scenario, but there was one condition. If the convention leaders did not hear from the Mexican government within a reasonable amount of time the Texians would hold another convention to declare their independence from Coahuila.

Unfortunately, however, the political landscape had dramatically changed. The legislature moved the capital from Saltillo to Monclova, and if that wasn't enough to keep the Texian resolutions waiting, in December President Bustamante resigned from office. After several months of indecision, Gen. Antonio López de Santa Anna became the new president in April of 1833. However, Santa Anna remained at his hacienda, leaving his vice president, Valentín Gómez Farías, in charge until the end of April.

As a consequence of the resulting turmoil in Mexico City the convention's resolutions were going nowhere. Quickly losing their patience, the Texians called for a second convention to discuss the options for declaring its independence from Coahuila and for drafting their own state constitution.

The Convention of 1833 met in San Felipe de Austin for 13 days beginning on April 1, 1833. Replacing Austin as president by the 56 delegates was William H. Wharton, a man with a fiery temper and reputed to be the designer of the Texas "Lone Star" flag. And as before, no Tejanos were in attendance.

The agenda of the convention was in most respects a duplicate of the previous one except the first day was spent by the delegates voicing their opinions as to why breaking away from Coahuila was justified. It became quite evident that as the grievances continued the consensus pointed to the irrefutable fact that in its present condition the government in Mexico City was in no condition to legislate over any state, let alone Coahuila y Texas. On the second day the convention delegates chose Sam Houston, representing Nacogdoches, to lead the committee that would draft the new state constitution. As a former governor of Tennessee and once a member of the U.S. Congress, Houston was highly regarded for his political experience and his close relationship with Pres. Andrew Jackson. At the conclusion of their deliberations the proposed constitution was based to a large degree on the U.S. version and also included portions from the state constitutions of Massachusetts, Missouri, Tennessee, and Louisiana.

Also accomplished during the meetings was the creation of a new list of resolutions for governmental reform. With a few exceptions the revised list reflected the previous document from the first convention. And last but not least was the most significant document of them all, a new petition requesting that Texas be allowed to split from Coahuila and be granted separate statehood. One thing was for certain. If that request was denied or not responded to, the drafted constitution was totally meaningless.

Before the convention adjourned it was decided to send Austin, Dr. James Miller, and Erasmo Seguín, the local Tejano leader, to Mexico City with the list of resolutions and the petition. Although Seguín, or for that matter any other Tejano, did not attend the convention, the mere fact that a leading Tejano was shown to be involved, if only for the delivery, was thought to be a good political move to attract the Tejano community's support. Austin ended up going alone, however, when Dr. Miller thought he was needed more in Coahuila to treat people caught in the cholera epidemic. And when Austin went to Béxar to inform Seguín of his being selected, he said he was unable to go. As a loyal Tejano he was still incapable of defying Mexican law.

Austin arrived in Mexico City on July 18, 1833, just as the cholera epidemic struck. Not immune to this dreaded disease, Austin managed to get through it, as did the congress, which was shut down to wait out the epidemic. With much time to contemplate his surroundings, Austin became increasingly discouraged and fed up with the state of affairs that always seemed to exist in Mexico City. It wasn't just the timing of the epidemic that bothered him but now also the wild and distorted street rumors he was hearing such as how the Texians were about to start a revolution to gain statehood and that the Texians thought the Mexican government was too weak and could easily be persuaded to yield to Texians' demands. Totally exasperated over the attitude of the Mexican people, Austin wrote to his brother-in-law James F. Perry, "I have had much more respect for them than they deserve."[8]

As he waited for the congress to reconvene, in October Austin learned from his sources that the Texians refused to wait any longer for a response to their requests and were calling for a third convention. Inexplicably, Austin absentmindedly wrote a letter to a council official in Béxar suggesting that all the councils meet and form a new state government of their own. However, with the political chief out of town the letter was read by a lower-level official who had it delivered to the governor of Coahuila y Texas, who, in turn, relayed the information to Mexico City. To make matters worse, when Austin finally met Vice President Farías he became somewhat frustrated during their discussions and insisted that if Texas was not granted statehood she would obtain it by herself. Obviously, the vice president was outraged over this threat that, at least to him, sounded very much like Austin was suggesting he was about to foment insurrection. To compound Austin's plight, when Farías also read the letter Austin wrote he ordered his arrest for treason.

Immediately responding to the vice president's orders, the army apprehended the empresario in Saltillo on January 3, 1834. He was imprisoned in an old Dominican monastery with no official charges filed against him, with no court appearances, and held behind bars for virtually all of 1834. After he was released in December on bond, he was restricted to Mexico City until July 1835. As he languished in his small jail cell, Austin wiled away the time writing letters, one of which reflected the torment he felt. "I have been true and faithful to this government and nation," he wrote, "have served them laboriously; have tried to do all the good I could to individuals and to the country; have been a philanthropist, and I am now meeting my reward. I expect to die in this prison."[9] Austin's imprisonment however, may not have been a legitimate criminal case but, as some suggest, a means to keep Austin out of circulation while Santa Anna put his next military maneuver into motion.

Santa Anna's first reaction to all the wild talk and dissention among the Texians was to send his aide, Col. Juan Almonte, to Texas and secretly collect intelligence about the attitude of the people and the plans the Texian leaders might have for a future revolt against his government. At the same time, anticipating the possibility of further trouble, especially from what he read in Austin's letter, Santa Anna thought it prudent to reinforce Capano, the strategic port on the Gulf Coast and the entry point for his supplies. To accomplish this mission, however, he needed to seize several transport ships that were tied up in Matamoros, a vital port on the Rio Grande. Not leaving any stone unturned, as a precaution to prevent interference with his plan he thought it wise to keep Austin under wraps while the expedition to seize the ships was being carried out. In July 1835, once the ships were under way to the docks of Capano with their cargoes, Austin was released. From Mexico City, Austin traveled directly to Gonzales.

Independence from the state of Coahuila, however, still remained elusive.

2

Santa Anna and the Politics of Mexico City

As you may recall from the previous chapter, it was the first of April when 56 Texian delegates met in San Felipe de Austin to begin their Convention of 1833. Desperately attempting to reform the way the Mexican government was dealing with the settlers, they met to prepare three documents—a list of resolutions, a petition that requested Texas be allowed to split from the state of Coahuila and be admitted as a separate and independent Mexican state, and, last, a draft of their state constitution in the event the authorities in Mexico City approved the petition.

In Mexico City, however, another significant event was also taking place that very day. The Mexican congress officially declared Gen. Antonio López de Santa Anna the new president of Mexico, a position previously held by Anastasia Bustamante. Santa Anna was a military officer who would play a major role in the military and political history of Mexico for more than a quarter century. Without question, any discussion about the early history of Mexico would not be complete without first mentioning the military and political exploits of Santa Anna, the "Napoléon of the West"—and there were many.

One of seven children, Antonio de Padua María Severino López Santa Anna was born in Jalapa, a small town near Veracruz, in 1794 to a middle-class Creole family. A so-called mountain-town, Jalapa (or, to some, Xalapa) was known for its abundance of beautiful flowers of all colors and a variety of delicious fruits, in all likelihood a product of the town's location in a tropical forest where the stifling humidity had to be endured nearly year-round. In spite of this unpleasant discomfort, living in Jalapa was extremely desirable because it seems the high altitude prevented the dreaded yellow fever, popularly referred to as the *vomito*, from spreading into that location.

While growing up under the rule of the Spanish Crown, Santa Anna became enamored by the glamour of the Spanish troops as he watched them each day marching through the town square of Veracruz, the port city where he grew up, dressed in their colorful uniforms and plumed helmets. The young lad was soon taken in by the pageantry of it all. Consequently, in 1810, at a mere 16 years of age, he became a cadet in the Fijo de Vera Cruz infantry regiment under the command of Col. Joaquín de Arredondo. The regiment was permanently garrisoned at Veracruz and consisted mostly of locals who were immune to the diseases that affected that area.

The timing could not have been more fitting for the young soldier eager to experience the adrenaline rush of combat. At a parish church two months later, the fiery revolutionary priest Fr. Miguel Hidalgo y Costilla called for an army of insurgents to overthrow the Spanish colonial government, for the death of all Spaniards, and, most important, for independence from Spanish rule. And so it was from the pulpit that morning that his cry lit the spark that ignited the Mexican War of Independence, a war that would endure for 11 years.

As a fresh recruit in the Spanish army garrisoned in Veracruz, Santa Anna soon received a taste of how the Spaniards dealt with Mexican insurgents when he was assigned to help put down a bloody Hidalgo uprising against Spanish authority. However, other than several minor skirmishes, his participation in the major campaigns of the war was peripheral at best. Without doubt, his most valuable experience was gained from fighting Indians in the internal provinces, where he received an arrow wound, and from his participation in border skirmishes against American gringos and filibusters. Indelibly etched in his psyche, however, was the violence and cruelty he witnessed firsthand of Arredondo's mass executions of nationalist rebels, as well as the mutilations and beheadings during the so-called Gutiérrez-Magee Expeditions and the Battle of Medina, lessons he would never forget. Quickly climbing through the ranks, when he reached his early twenties he was promoted to captain, a commission he proudly displayed by the three white lace stripes on the sleeves of his uniform.

Santa Anna's arrogant attitude and his sweeping ideas soon caught the attention of Gen. Ignacio Cincúnegue, serving as the interim governor of Veracruz. As a result, Santa Anna's growing prominence in the region was looked upon with disdain, jealousy, and suspicion by his immediate superiors, especially Col. José Antonio Rincón, the chief of the Veracruz garrison. Because of this uneasy relationship, Santa Anna was convinced that discrimination played a major role in his failure to gain a command responsibility for defending Veracruz. Troubled by this perceived biased treatment, Santa Anna simply circumvented the chain of command. In fact, one of his character traits was his ability to use his persuasive charm to gain the help from officials of higher authority to intervene on his behalf. As it turned out, it was this modus operandi that enabled him to receive his cherished first command in 1818 over the objections of his immediate commander.

Evidently, Santa Anna wrote a letter to Viceroy Juan Ruiz de Apodaca describing his lofty ideas and how he planned to implement them. At the same time, Santa Anna also complained that he was being prevented from bringing his ideas to fruition by his commanders. Touched by his dilemma, a sympathetic Apodaca sent instructions to General Cincúnegue that resulted in awarding Santa Anna the command of a militia unit as well as adding more tension to the already-strained relationship with his superiors.

Now his consistent string of victories as commander of a one-hundred man militia unit in Veracruz over insurgent agitators earned him well-deserved praise and a glowing reputation. These successes, of course, only added fuel to the growing animosity from Colonels Cincúnegue and Rincón.

During one of Santa Anna's many raids, a ruthless Mexican insurgent was captured. Instead of granting the prisoner an opportunity to repent, as was usually the practice, Santa Anna ordered his execution by a firing squad. When Cincúnegue reported him to the commanding general in Mexico City and charged him with a breach of discipline, Santa Anna immediately, and without permission, traveled to Mexico City to win the support of Viceroy Gen. Pascual Liñán, who remarked to Cincúnegue that in his opinion Santa Anna's young age may have caused his overzealous behavior, but nevertheless he considered him quite extraordinary. To the frustration of Colonel Cincúnegue, the charge against Santa Anna was, of course, dropped and Santa Anna was returned to his unit to implement his latest plan to capture the most notorious insurgent of them all, Gen. Guadalupe Victoria. Not surprising, the elusive leader of the insurgents was a master of evading capture and he demonstrated it once again to Santa Anna.

In 1819, one of Santa Anna's benefactors, General Liñán, was appointed to replace Cincúnegue as interim governor of Veracruz. A change in Veracruz leadership also meant a change in Santa Anna's career. He was appointed to lead an effort to plan, rebuild, and resettle several abandoned towns. Santa Anna was granted the power to distribute the land and the authority to organize the committees, select the appropriate size of each piece of real estate, and assist in the construction of the buildings, including the shops. Above all, he set up the governments and ran several of the communities himself. These settlements included the towns of Medellín, Jamapa, San Diego, and Tamarindo, with a combined population of nearly six hundred families.

The following year, however, Santa Anna was replaced when complaints from the residents began to be heard about how he had forced them to work on military officers' quarters without pay and to build a large yard for him to corral his cattle. Also there was talk about Santa Anna's brutal treatment of some individuals for minor offenses, how his friends were suspected of stealing merchandise from the shops, and how some settlers lived in fear of him.

Although he was admired for his charisma, Santa Anna was the kind of man who could easily manipulate people to advance his own military and political agenda. His vanity was second to none, and against his enemies he could be extremely cruel and heartless. At the same time, his personal demeanor could be dignified and attractive. He was tall and slender, dashing to the extreme in full dress regalia, and his manner captivating, attributes that captured the attention of many senoritas and deservingly earned him the reputation of being a first-class womanizer. Although he became the hero of the army, a brave soldier and a shrewd politician, he was also a shameless opportunist who was alternately loved and hated throughout his life.

During Mexico's war for independence, for instance, Santa Anna was a dedicated follower of Gen. Agustín de Iturbide and his royalist philosophy and on Iturbide's behalf fought strenuously against those who advanced the movement for Mexican independence from Spanish rule. It was a battle between the royalists, who were in favor of a Mexican monarchy, and the insurgents, who preferred an independent Mexico under a republican form of government. In this regard, Santa Anna's unmitigated allegiance to the monarchy and especially to General Iturbide was quite important to him since he knew the prospects for achieving his own objectives were quite favorable in this setting.

General Iturbide's ultimate goal was to resist the forces seeking independence from

Spain and to establish a monarchy in Mexico ruled by none other than Spain's King Ferdinand VII. However, when political forces in Spain began to weaken the powers of Ferdinand and even to threaten the monarchy itself General Iturbide began to have second thoughts about resisting the movement for Mexican independence. With the prospects of a failing monarchy in Spain, Iturbide was forced to revise his plan for persuading Ferdinand to rule Mexico. Considering the political upheaval taking place in Madrid, Iturbide now thought the best chance for attracting a deposed Ferdinand to rule Mexico would be if Mexico became independent.

After General Iturbide received support from insurgent leader Gen. Vicente Guerrero at a meeting on February 24, 1821, they undertook a monumental reversal in the conduct of the war. On that day, they officially joined forces and introduced their "Plan of Iguala." Also known as the "Plan of the Three Guarantees," it effectively sought to transfer royal leadership from Madrid to Mexico City. The plan was based on three goals. It called for Roman Catholicism to be the official religion of Mexico, for social equality for all social and ethnic groups, and, most significantly, for a declaration of Mexico's independence from Spain as a constitutional monarchy. Iturbide's new goal was to make sure that Mexico would be governed by either Ferdinand VII, any willing conservative European prince, or a Creole (a person of pure Spanish ancestry) appointed by the Mexican congress. Six months later the Treaty of Cordoba was signed by Iturbide and the Spanish viceroy, which in effect ratified the plan. And persuaded by the promise of Mexican independence, insurgent leader Gen. Guadalupe Victoria also agreed to support the plan.

The coup de grace that dramatically brought the war to a close came on September 27, 1821. Welcomed by ecstatic crowds, Iturbide marched his victorious Army of the Three Guarantees into Mexico City and proclaimed the independence of Mexico, ironically a scenario he was fighting against for years. Amid the boisterous celebratory mood of the Mexican citizens and displays of red, white, and green bunting, on the following day the Declaration of Independence of the Mexican Empire was signed. Although an irate congress in Madrid refused to acknowledge the treaty, the fact that the Spanish viceroy signed it was good enough for Mexico to consider her independence valid and final.

General Iturbide had now reached the summit of his ambitions. He was wined and dined and celebrated countrywide as the hero of Mexican independence.

Meanwhile, news of Iturbide's Plan of Iguala reached Santa Anna in Veracruz on March 5, 1822, just days before he took his regiment to Orizaba, a small town about 90 miles due west. Without many details of the plan, he was not very enthusiastic about it.

At Orizaba, he confronted insurgent troops led by Gen. José Joaquín de Herrera for six days. While garrisoned in a convent during this time, Santa Anna had a chance to consider the ramifications of Iturbide's new agenda and how it would affect him personally. After some soul-searching, Santa Anna underwent a change of heart as well and decided not only to support Iturbide's new plan but also to change sides and to join forces with Herrera, the very man he was presently fighting. Of course Herrera's promise of a promotion to colonel if Santa Anna defected was certainly persuasive enough for him. Later that month, on his way back to Veracruz, he met the insurgent leader who had eluded him for some time, none other than Gen. Guadalupe Victoria, the principal leader of the independence movement. At their meeting, in a gesture of upmost respect and humility Victoria, with a deep bow, offered his services to Santa Anna. Always scheming for personal advantage, however, instead of accepting the offer, Santa Anna turned his own command over to Victoria while assuming a subordinate position under Victoria. With this move, Santa Anna guaranteed that his switch to the cause of independence would not be questioned by anyone. His philosophy changed from wholeheartedly supporting a monarchy for Mexico to enthusiastically supporting her independence under the leadership of Victoria.

At any rate, in 1822 Santa Anna was promoted to commander of the Jalapa garrison. Once a mere militia commander, he was now the ranking military officer in his hometown. Almost immediately it became obvious to Santa Anna that to protect Jalapa and to sustain his army he needed money, and lots of it. The only place he could get the 12,000 pesos he wanted was from the local government. Although the town council could offer only half that amount, Santa Anna's usual persuasive arm-twisting enabled the council members to come up with the full amount. It would not take long before everyone learned that Santa Anna's way was always the only way.

When the partying was over in Mexico City and the banners were taken down for another day, the new reality came into view. Iturbide found himself faced with the task of organizing a new government. His first step was to appoint himself the president of a Provisional Government Junta, an interim legislative body of some 33 to 36 members that would rule until a new congress was established. Their primary task was to find a suitable leader for the country. But who would it be? Iturbide's original plan was to offer the crown to Spain's Ferdinand VII, who, it appeared, could possibly be deposed in a coup. But when Ferdinand was able to rebuff the challenge to his throne and to regain power, he refused the overture, as did everyone else of European royal pedigree. Puzzled by this unexpected circumstance, the Mexican capital was in an enormous state of confusion.

According to most historians, since Mexico lacked anyone of royal lineage to assume the reins of power it remains unclear whether Iturbide decided to take the crown for himself to satisfy his inflated ego, which seemed most likely, or it was a choice made at the insistence of the people. All the same, Iturbide had the foresight to include among the possible candidates someone chosen by the Mexican congress of Creole ancestry, a class in which he belonged.

And so:

> On the night of the 18th of May, 1822, the people and the garrison of the capital proclaimed Iturbide the emperor of Mexico.... [A]s if by magic, the entire capital was in a blaze of light; the public square and private edifices were magnificently illuminated; the buildings were decorated with banners, and the balconies were filled with the most respectable inhabitants; every countenance seemed joyful, and the universal shout ascended—"Long live Agustín the First." The streets presented a compact of human life; the city garrison, officers of the army, the leading citizens of the metropolis, and many distinguished men from different sections of the country, thronged the vicinity of Iturbide's residence, and united in general acclamation. Not a murmur of disapprobation was heard from any source.[1]

Some reports claim Iturbide polled the crowd of adoring supporters to see whether they preferred a monarchy or a republic. When the crowd's reply favored a monarchy Iturbide took this information to the provisional congress and asked for their approval.

That month his title was confirmed, and with all the appropriate pomp and ceremony for such an auspicious occasion Iturbide was crowned Agustín I, constitutional emperor of Mexico, on July 21, 1822. As for Santa Anna, on August 14 he was promoted to brevet lieutenant colonel.

However, Iturbide's reign would be a short one.

The relationship between the emperor and the rump congress was extremely strained from the very beginning. Congressional opponents who still championed a republican form of government were routinely arrested and imprisoned. When this failed to stifle his enemies, he closed down the congress and created a new junta to replace it, which effectively eliminated the representation and voices of the provinces in governmental affairs, and as a final rejoinder to suppress criticism he censored the press as well. Also, as the economic conditions continued to degrade Iturbide was unable to cover government expenses.

To help counter this revenue shortfall, he imposed a very unpopular 40 percent tax on the wealthy. Nevertheless, despite the many hardships his country was suffering, his own personal lifestyle remained luxurious and extravagant, a scenario not going unnoticed by the people. Santa Anna, however, as was his usual tactic under these circumstances, praised the emperor for how everyone would benefit under his leadership. And as expected, as a reward for being such a loyal supporter, Iturbide promoted Santa Anna to the rank of brigadier general. Of course, also trying to court General Iturbide's sister at the time may have helped a little as well.

Finally, for the new emperor time had run out. Of all his indiscretions, the final straw was Iturbide's attitude toward the provinces. They were fed up with his obvious indifference and belittling behavior that left them politically isolated from the central government in Mexico City. And as history has shown, in Mexico political revolts were a standard operating procedure and an unwritten law for dealing with an unpopular leader and Iturbide, despite his new royal pedigree, was no exception.

Without his patron, Santa Anna, true to his opportunistic principles, abandoned his loyalty to Iturbide in favor of advancing his own political agenda or, at the very least, for self-preservation. In fact, Santa Anna would become one of the principal leaders opposing the reign of Iturbide and a loyal follower of his previous enemy and now his best new friend, Gen. Guadalupe Victoria, a committed supporter of a Mexican republic and a strong candidate to become the first president of Mexico.

What followed was the customary revolt by the politically influential military, led by none other than Santa Anna, who was by now a full-fledged member of the Victoria coalition. By signing the so-called Plan of Casa Mata, they declared their intentions to overthrow Iturbide and to replace the monarchy with a republic, a government that was guided by a written constitution. It was a declaration also agreed to by Gen. Vicente Guerrero, who was once another of Iturbide's closest supporters.

With political dissention over Iturbide's mismanagement of the government reaching a crescendo, on March 19, 1823, Iturbide was forced to abdicate after the Mexican congress nullified their election of Iturbide as emperor. And as if that weren't enough, he was charged with treason and ordered exiled to Italy.

Following a brief stay in Livorno, he and his family were forced to move once again, this time to England, when Spain began to pressure the local authorities to banish him from the country. In England, Iturbide wiled away his time writing his autobiography, but still the indignities he had suffered from those he felt were responsible for his downfall and for the tremendous damage they caused to his legacy must have weighed heavily on the former war hero and emperor. Iturbide was a proud man, and despite his shortcomings, he saw himself as a man who had faithfully served the people of Mexico not only in the military for over 15 years but also as its political leader.

Meanwhile, his most dedicated supporters continued to report how conditions in Mexico had worsened. Still, all their attempts to persuade him to return home were seemingly to no avail.

Finally, when he heard rumors that Spain was contemplating an effort to retake Mexican territory Iturbide was convinced that he had no choice but to return to his beloved country as its liberator once again.

However, the Mexican congress had a standing order that called for his execution if he ever returned. It seems the national congress had decreed that "in case he should attempt to land in the country in any capacity whatever, he should be declared an outlaw ... and the authorities should punish him as such."[2] Iturbide claimed it was a declaration he was unaware of.

Upon his arrival in Mexico with his family and a friend, he was met by the governor of Tamaulipas, who pretended to greet him warmly. Following the initial welcoming formalities, Iturbide was quickly arrested and without a trial sentenced to death. On July 19, 1824, the man who was once venerated as a national hero and crowned its first emperor was executed by a firing squad. According to a bystander, "he adjusted the bandage upon his eyes, knelt down, and receiving two balls in the forehead and two in his heart, fell dead."[3] Fourteen years later, when cooler heads prevailed, his remains were interred in the Mexico City cathedral with full honors.

With the removal of Iturbide from office another provisional government was established consisting of a three-member triumvirate, which included Gen. Nicholas Brávo, Pedro Celestino Negrete, and Guadalupe Victoria.

To alleviate further government instability and to answer the unrelenting call for a federal republic, on October 2, 1824, General Victoria was declared the first president of Mexico. Two days later the Constitution of 1824 was ratified, a document that transformed the country from a monarchy into a federal republic. It was a constitution highly praised by the Texians because it gave considerable rights to the independent states. Called the United Mexican States, the country now consisted of 19 states and four territories.

The following year Santa Anna displayed his self-serving ways once again by marrying 14-year-old Inés de la Paz García, a marriage mostly consummated out of convenience. She was born into a very wealthy Spanish family who offered a very generous dowry, a financial benefit Santa Anna could not resist. Since Santa Anna was a philanderer extraordinaire, his romantic interest in his wife was rather superficial. Nevertheless, they raised four children and resided in the sprawling hacienda called Manga de Clavo, on an enormous cattle ranch Santa Anna bought with the dowry.

Upon his taking office it quickly became apparent to President Victoria that the government was faced with severe financial problems, the result of the devastating war for independence from Spain. As president and responsible for rebuilding the Mexican economy, he opened trade routes, received foreign aid from the British government, and attracted foreign investments into the country through mining operations. Despite these and a myriad of other difficulties confronting him, some of Victoria's other accomplishments included the establishment of the national treasury and formation of a naval force.

The strongly felt animosity toward anything Spanish was so deeply rooted in the psyche of the Mexican government, however, that the Spanish-born people residing in Mexico were also a problem for the government to deal with. Arguably, his most controversial measure, therefore, was the "General Law of Expulsion," passed in 1827, which mandated the removal of all foreigners from Mexican soil but chiefly Spaniards.

Knowing the unsavory reputations of his contemporaries for gaining power, President Victoria should have watched his compatriots more closely.

The coup began at the end of Victoria's presidential term in 1829 when Gen. Vicente Guerrero lost the presidential election to Manuel Gómez Pedraza, one of Victoria's ministers. The final outcome of the election was not based on a popular vote by the people but instead was left to the Creole representatives of each state legislature. Each of the 19 legislatures could cast one vote for president.

Supposedly, Guerrero, who was the underdog, made an agreement with Santa Anna before the ballots were counted. If Guerrero lost the election, Santa Anna would start a revolt against Pedraza and his supporters. In return, Guerrero would make Santa Anna his minister of war. On that note, Santa Anna proceeded to lobby each of the town councils in favor of his candidate, but to no avail. Pedraza won the election by three votes, and that's when the trouble began. Since the voice of the people had not been heard, a huge outcry from the citizens joined in the revolt. At one demonstration, Santa Anna demanded that Guerrero be made the president, declaring that he was the candidate the people clearly preferred.

Three days later, news arrived that Pedraza had resigned and fled for his life when the army shelled the National Palace under the orders of no one less than Guerrero, Gen. Santa Anna, and politician Lorenzo de Zavala. It seems this entire episode persuaded Pedraza to renounce his victory, at which time the Mexican congress dutifully annulled the election and in April of 1829 awarded the presidency to Guerrero.

Meanwhile, in Spain during the summer of 1829 a number of Spaniards were in an uproar over President Victoria's "General Law of Expulsion." This was the statute that called for the removal of all foreigners from the country. In reality it was designed to rid the country of Spanish-born people despite the fact that, according to Harold D. Sims in his book *The Expulsion of the Spaniards from Mexico, 1827–1829*, the estimated six thousand Spaniards living in Mexico constituted only a mere .08 percent of the total population of 8 million. Even though bribery, family status, and politics all played a part in determining who would stay and who would leave, in the end only about a quarter of the Spanish population remained. Consequently, this act proved to be a devastating blow to the Mexican economy.

Evidently these angry groups of exiles from Victoria's expulsion order were, for some reason, anxious to return to Mexico and were demonstrating wildly in the streets of Madrid. To bolster their complaint, the frustrated schemers began to spread false and inflammatory information that indicated the Mexican people wanted a return of the monarchy.

From the very beginning of this expulsion order, Ferdinand VII was highly offended that the Mexican government was evicting hundreds of his people. And at the time he vowed to take whatever action was necessary to punish Mexico for condoning such a terrible law. Now, 18 months after the law was issued, it was still creating a great deal of commotion in the capital city of Spain.

Needless to say, already outraged over this whole affair, the king was easily persuaded to order an armed intervention into Mexico and to return her to the Spanish Crown.

To begin their campaign to strip Mexico of her newly won independence, a Spanish fleet arrived from Cuba on July 26, 1829, with roughly four thousand hardened Spaniards aboard, many of whom were exiled activists. Led by the flagship *El Soberano*, under the command of Gen. Isidro Barradas, a valued favorite of the king, the fleet of 20 ships sailed into the Pánuco River. Two days later, they landed at Cabo Rojo on the southern outskirts of Tampico, where the troops disembarked. Following a reconnaissance of the immediate area that morning the Spanish army was ordered into formation. Smartly attired in their colorful uniforms, they began their march to Tampico, one of Mexico's strategic coastal ports. Meanwhile, alerted to the Spanish invasion, the citizens of Tampico fled to Altamira only five miles away.

After setting fire to Fort de la Barra, a fortification located on the Pánuco River, General Barradas and his troops marched into the abandoned city of Tampico, where he established his headquarters.

The military officer ordered by President Guerrero to intercept the invading army was General Santa Anna. With the Spanish invasion of his beloved homeland now under way, the 35-year-old general was provided with a superb opportunity to further enhance his patriotic image and his political standing. Consequently, on August 9 he and his vice commander, Gen. Manuel de Mier y Terán, eagerly boarded their artillery and the approximately fifteen hundred men on a fleet of borrowed vessels and departed Veracruz for Tampico. General Terán, a graduate engineer and former director of the National School of Artillery, was considered by most one of the most competent and dedicated officers in the Mexican army. Meanwhile, the cavalry would ride overland and meet the army at the Pánuco River.

In the early morning hours of August 20, Santa Anna's fleet arrived near Tampico. When he learned that General Barradas was some 70 miles from his position, he decided he would pay a call on his opponent. But, resisting the urge to attack immediately Santa Anna decided to delay his attack until later that evening. The assault certainly surprised the Mexican garrison and was maintained for several hours, but in the end it had very little effect except perhaps to tell the Spaniards that Santa Anna had arrived. Resumed on the following morning, the twenty-first, the spirited and bloody assault lasted only four hours before the Spaniards wisely called for a cease-fire. At this point Santa Anna thought General Barradas was about to surrender, but instead he discovered that Barradas was not in Tampico at all but had gone on an expedition into the interior with three thousand of his men. In so doing he left only roughly one thousand troops to garrison the city. Strangely enough, as Santa Anna negotiated with Spanish colonel José Meguel

Salomón, General Barradas returned with his troops and interrupted the proceedings. Santa Anna was not only surprised over this sudden development; he was also caught in a terrible bind. Barradas's forces had blocked Santa Anna's escape route to make a quick retreat and he was vastly outnumbered to stay and fight. During a break in the negotiations, he dispatched one of his officers to return to headquarters and to return with a forged letter stating that reinforcements had just arrived. In a stroke of genius, in a ruse Santa Anna showed Barradas the forged letter, which was enough to convince him that Santa Anna was commanding an overwhelming number of troops and that it would be to his disadvantage to call off the talks. Consequently, instead of ordering an attack, which Barradas knew he couldn't do anyway since most of his men were sick, Barradas suggested they continue the negotiations the next day and in the meantime both sides would return to their previous positions, which, of course, Santa Anna agreed to do.

Contemplating his strategy at his camp, Santa Anna recognized he had the advantage of field position, a circumstance he intended to exploit to the fullest. Therefore, over the days ahead he was reinforced with additional troops and he prepared his army for a siege by placing twenty-six hundred troops and four pieces of artillery in range of the city. Then, at a given signal, his artillerists commenced to lob shells into Tampico.

Meanwhile, as Tampico was being bombarded, General Terán marched some nine hundred troops to Fort de la Barra and seriously attacked the vastly outnumbered Mexican defenders and forced them to surrender.

With his fortifications being bombarded, his supplies cut off, no chances to get reinforcements from Fort de la Barra, no food or clean drinking water, and most of his men suffering with yellow fever, a common occurrence for outsiders at this time of the year, on September 11, 1829, General Barradas had little choice but to agree to the terms of a surrender.

Santa Anna's popularity soared like never before. By his successful defense of Mexico's newly won independence his position in Mexico's history was now solidly established. Everywhere the "Savior of the Motherland" traveled, he received the accolades of a thankful nation.

When news of Santa Anna's accomplishment arrived that night the mood was brilliantly stated by journalist Guillermo Prieto and documented in *Santa Anna of Mexico* by Will Fowler. "The city awoke at an unearthly hour in the middle of the night to the roar of the cannons, the pealing of bells in all of the churches, the splendid lights that lit up the most far away cabins and the highest of palaces, the cheers, the immense rejoicing of all the classes of society. Barradas has surrendered, shouted the newspaper boys as they ran in all directions; people who did not know each other embraced; the shopkeepers, in their doorways, uncorked bottles and toasted with whoever passed by; the reveilles sounded; the fireworks lit up the sky and there were times that the [expression of] pleasure sounded just like a storm."[4]

In Mexico City, however, although President Guerrero participated in honoring his general, privately he held a deep dislike for Santa Anna. In that regard, instead of rewarding Santa Anna with a position in his administration, he appointed him the military governor of Yucatán. Deeply disappointed over this unwanted assignment, in November Santa Anna retired his commission and moved to his hacienda of Manga de Clavo in Veracruz, where he became the governor and spent his leisure time gambling and enjoying cockfighting, his two favorite vices.

While Santa Anna was engaged in Tampico, presidential wannabes were active once again. Pres. Vicente Guerrero had previously dispatched his vice president, Gen. Anastasia Bustamante, to Jalapa as a precautionary maneuver to prevent any further incursion from Spanish forces. However, true to form, in December Bustamante took advantage of this opportunity. After just eight months in office, Guerrero was overthrown by his political opponents and forced to flee. Declaring Guerrero unfit to govern, Bustamante then assumed the presidency in 1830 and ordered the search for and kidnapping of the former president. Early the following year, Guerrero was lured aboard a ship where he was betrayed by the captain for 50,000 pesos, court-martialed, convicted of treason and executed by firing squad on February 14, 1831.

Since 1821 it was common and accepted political practice in Mexico for army generals to fight other generals for presidential power. And so the tradition continued in 1832 when Guerrero loyalists, who were seeking revenge for their assassinated hero, staged a revolt against Bustamante led by the impetuous General Santa Anna and his army. Not one to shy away from political revolts, Santa Anna returned from Manga de Clavo in January after being invited by Guerrero sympathizers to lead the revolt. The fact that Guerrero was Santa Anna's daughter's godfather may have influenced him as well.

Reacting to this affront on his presidency, Bustamante temporally delegated his duties to his vice president so that he could take the field and fight the arrogant and insubordinate rebels attempting to take away his presidency. Following a series of battles against Santa Anna and others, to end the conflict Bustamante signed the Agreement of Zavaleta, resigned the presidency, and was exiled to France. With Bustamante out of the picture and Santa Anna back in favor, the Mexican congress elected Santa Anna, the "Hero of the Motherland," to the presidency in April of 1833.

As president of Mexico, General Santa Anna, a young and highly motivated officer, was now at the pinnacle of his political career. Calling himself the "Napoléon of the West," he knew his craving for power and wealth had finally been achieved. He saw himself as the man in charge and more important, the man who would change the face of Mexico from a federalist model to a centralist system. Men of his character, however, invariably strive for more and more authority and indulge in more and more lavish extravagance, traits that in the end only contribute to poor judgment, unflinching arrogance, and the disregard for responsibility, all attributes that ultimately lead to their downfall.

What made Santa Anna so unique was his unremitting involvement in scores of political revolutions during the course of his career. Even during his 11 non-consecutive terms as president over 22 years, he was seldom able to remain in Mexico City for any length of time to fulfill his oath of office. Instead, presidential responsibilities were routinely delegated to his vice presidents while he either answered yet another call from some new trouble spot or chose to retire to his various haciendas. In truth, it was Santa

Anna's ego. He enjoyed the attention and the notoriety of carrying the title of president as well as receiving the acclaim from battlefield victories. But the boring day-to-day business of shuffling paper and haggling with politicians was something he preferred to leave to someone more suited for that side of the business. For instance, from April 1833 to February 1836 Santa Anna spent less than one year sitting in the office as El Presidente. In this fashion, Santa Anna and his vice presidents would alternate the duties of the presidency. In fact, when he was elected in April he chose to remain at home rather than attend the inauguration. He finally arrived for work several weeks later and even then stayed for only 18 days.

Therefore, one of his first actions as the new president was to delegate his responsibilities to his second in command, Valentín Gómez Farías, supposedly due to illness but in all likelihood to relax at his hacienda and enjoy his favorite sport of cockfighting.

In Mexico City, the vice president had to deal with a radical administration and a radical congress. Almost immediately he created a tremendous backlash from the Catholic hierarchy, and the army as well, when he and the congress implemented two major reforms. As an advocate for the separation of church and state, the church was instructed to restrict its sermons to strictly religious matters and that mandatory tithes were now prohibited. Also, among other decrees, the church had to relinquish its hold on education. In this regard, the National University of Mexico was closed because its faculty was composed entirely of priests. Farías also reduced the size of the army because he considered it too influential. With passage of these rulings, a firestorm of complaints arose almost instantly from the church and other groups against Farías and subsided only when Santa Anna agreed to return to Mexico City to straighten the matter out.

Upon his return, and in accordance with his Plan of Cuernavaca, Santa Anna rescinded all the laws enacted during the tenure of his vice president, the university was reopened, the congress was dissolved and all the bureaucrats who put the reforms into operation were dismissed. He also replaced his vice president with his minister of war, Gen. Miguel Barrágin, and in June of 1834 replaced the radical congress with politicians who supported his centralist ideology.

With these radical moves, Santa Anna had laid the groundwork for his dictatorship. It was during this time as well that the congress launched the so-called Seven Laws, an edict that allowed the president to close congress, suppress the Mexican Supreme Court, and fix the presidential term at eight years. In addition, it replaced the independent state-governing bodies with "departments" headed by military governors responsible only to Santa Anna. And if that weren't enough, militias were terminated and the administration centralized all government power in Mexico City. But worst of all, it was also during this time that the centralist congress pushed through legislation that replaced the federalist Constitution of 1824.

Although Santa Anna repeatedly said he had no influence over doing away with the previous system and that he was never present when his centralist congress passed these laws, he nevertheless wholeheartedly supported the congress and was certainly responsible for their actions and the actions of his administration.

In reality, this was the beginning of Santa Anna's efforts to change the government of Mexico from a federalist system to a centralist one and the beginning of a conflict and power struggle between the central government and the former states. These changes also added fuel to the growing dissatisfaction over Mexican policies the Texians were striving to separate themselves from.

The Texians refused to be governed by an administration they saw as injurious to their welfare. Their response to the new legislation was to take matters into their own hands, to send a clear message to Santa Anna that they were willing to fight to the last man for the independence and freedom of their communities. They passionately supported the Constitution of 1824 because it limited the power of a central government and gave more liberties to the states. Not long afterward, the Texians began to form Committees of Correspondence and Safety in each affected area to provide information and to coordinate anti-centralist activities. The parent committee resided in San Felipe de Austin, the Texian capital. Besides Coahuila y Texas, other states as well rebelled against Santa Anna's changes. Such states as Durango, Yucatán, and Zacatecas, for instance, were openly demonstrating against the new dictator and his government for terminating the state militias.

But Santa Anna was not a person who took criticism kindly. His sick acquiescence toward inflicting retribution on anyone opposing his ideology was clearly illustrated in May of 1835. Upset over the new law that abolished local militias, the governor of Zacatecas overruled the law when he reminded the citizens that despite Santa Anna's ruling, in his opinion the state government had the right and the power to decide when to keep and how to use its militia.

Learning of this disrespect to his authority, Santa Anna left the comfort of his hacienda to personally direct the punishment that he would order to make an example of these people and to show others what to expect if they failed to support his ideology. In his shameful reprisal, he used no fewer than three infantry divisions, ten pieces of artillery, and one thousand cavalrymen to conduct a 2:00 a.m. attack. In two hours the "battle" was over and nearly three thousand prisoners were taken by government forces. Once the rebellious militia was defeated, Santa Anna showed his gratitude to his troops by allowing them two full days of lawlessness. They were free to loot, to rape, and to kill without any consequences for their actions. According to reports that followed, more than two thousand innocent people were killed and the rich silver mines of Zacatecas were heavily looted. To share in the spoils himself, Santa Anna had wagons of silver bars delivered to his hacienda. News of this atrocity would soon spread throughout Coahuila y Texas, which not only inflamed the anti-centralist sentiment but also created a hatred for Santa Anna in Zacatecas that would last as long as he lived.

Gradually, Santa Anna began to receive reports of unrest and demonstrations opposing his government from every other corner of Mexico. States such as Nuevo León, Tamaulipas, Guanajuato, Jalisco, and Querétaro were all protesting the injustices of the new centralist constitution. Despite the increasing tensions, however, Santa Anna remained just as determined to suppress any and all attempts to oppose his presidency and his ideology.

3

Gonzales, Goliad, and Fort Lipantitlán

Despite the bold threats made by Santa Anna, most of the Texians were of one voice in their opposition to his dictatorial rulings and the acquiescence of his loyal soldiers. The Texians were fanatical supporters of the Constitution of 1824, the equitable freedoms of an independent Texas, uncompromising believers in the right of self-determination, and steadfast in their willingness to fight an armed revolt if necessary to accomplish their goals.

The Texians seeking independence from Coahuila were not just the colonists from Austin Colony. Texians from the other settlements were also becoming more involved in the movement.

One such settlement belonged to Green DeWitt, a veteran of the War of 1812 and the son of a prominent Kentuckian. Captivated by the accomplishment of Moses Austin, DeWitt petitioned the Spanish government for a land grant as well, hoping to capture similar success to that enjoyed by the Austin family. With the assistance from Stephen F. Austin, DeWitt was able to secure his empresario contract in April of 1825, a contract to settle four hundred families on land adjacent to Austin Colony. His settlement was called DeWitt Colony, and his capital, Gonzales, was named after Don Rafael Gonzáles, the provisional governor of Coahuila y Texas in 1825. DeWitt was given six years to fulfill his contract, which he failed to do before it expired. After ten years only about 160 families were living in Gonzales, growing cotton and corn and raising cattle, cows, hogs, and horses.

By 1835 most of the people living in Gonzales were loyalists who still continued to maintain their abiding support for Santa Anna. But recently, after picking up bits and pieces of news from travelers passing through the town, the people had been becoming quite alarmed about the growing dictatorial powers of the president, the dissolution of the legislature of Coahuila y Texas, the terrible incident at Zacatecas, and particularly the repeal of the 1824 Constitution, all of which were making them question their loyalty to him and his centralist administration.

Nevertheless, there was one thing they all agreed upon. They shared a lingering hatred of Santa Anna's troops ever since one of their own citizens was severely beaten by a Mexican soldier for little or no apparent reason. According to witnesses, the soldier used the butt of his musket as a club to batter the poor fellow into a bloody heap, and all with no obvious justification. It was an act of brutality that quickly altered the opinions of the colonists and instilled a deep resentment of the Mexican army in general. And as fate would dictate, in the days ahead the people of Gonzales were about to confront their hated adversary, a military detachment from San Antonio de Béxar.

Although the September incident with the Mexican soldier was an isolated one, the frequent Comanche raids were more serious and kept the settlers in a constant state of anxiety. Even though no deaths were reported as yet, the mere presence of the savages made life in Gonzales an extremely apprehensive one. If they didn't steal the horses, they would loot the houses of the settlers' meager possessions or the general store of their favorite foods and merchandise. One of the worst of these attacks came in 1826 when the Indians burned Gonzales to the ground. The town was soon rebuilt, and at the request of DeWitt in 1831 the political chief for the Department of Béxar, Ramón Músquiz, agreed to loan the town a small bronze eight-pounder cannon to use for self-defense against any future Indian raids. Also, on the receipt, DeWitt agreed to return the gun when asked to do so.

However, in September 1835, after four years, Músquiz advised Col. Domingo de Ugartechea, the commandant in Béxar, to call for the return of the gun. It was mutually agreed that to leave this weapon in the hands of the Texians was unwise at this time, particularly while widespread political unrest over Santa Anna's centralist policies dominated Coahuila y Texas. The colonel even alluded to the possibility that the gun could be used against them in a letter he wrote to his superior, Gen. Martín Perfecto de Cos.

Without further delay, Colonel Ugartechea ordered a military spokesman, along with a five-soldier escort, to visit Gonzales and to request the immediate return of the canon. In Gonzales, however, when the alcade (mayor) was told he had to return the gun his first response was to call for a meeting of the town's citizens. Following their discussions a vote was taken that flatly rejected the return of the gun, a decision duly relayed back to the authorities in Béxar.

After the alcalde, Andrew Ponton, had some time to reflect on his rather brusque response to Ugartechea's agent, he decided it was best if he explained his actions to the authorities in Béxar. Consequently, to ensure the reason behind his refusal to give up the gun was fully understood, on September 26, 1835, he wrote a letter to Músquiz that simply explained that the people of Gonzales needed to retain the gun since the problem with the Indians still existed.

In reality, Ponton knew the gun was relatively useless in a firefight and he also realized that refusing to return the old, diminutive cannon was not the real issue; the standoff had now developed into a matter of principle. The cannon was the symbol of the age-old scenario of the oppressed fighting against the dictates of the oppressor. Meanwhile, as a precaution, the women and children were moved together for safety and riders dispatched to other settlements in search of assistance in the event a confrontation developed over this matter.

Needless to say, the response from the alcalde only angered Colonel Ugartechea and made a confrontation with Mexican troops much more likely. As expected, on September 27 about one hundred Mexican dragoons (mounted infantry) under the command of Lt. Francisco Castañeda were dispatched from Béxar with official orders to retrieve the gun. In addition, if any resistance was experienced in this effort Castañeda was authorized to make arrests, but under no circumstances was he to use military force. However, there was one problem, and it was a big one. To reach Gonzales the detachment had to cross the Guadalupe River, which, because of recent rains, was heavily flooded, and to make matters worse, all the boats in that area had been removed.

Lieutenant Castañeda and his men reached the river on September 29. Not only was the swiftly moving river too risky to cross, but a group of 18 heavily armed Texians was waiting on the opposite riverbank to make sure the soldiers didn't try also. The spokesman, Joseph D. Clements, shouted across the river to Castañeda that the alcalde was not present and that he did not have the authority to negotiate with him over the gun. Furthermore, Castañeda and his soldiers would have to wait on their side of the river until the alcalde returned. In fact, it was all a bluff so that any attack by Castañeda would be delayed and at the same time gave the Texians more time to continue soliciting a fighting force from the nearby communities and to plan a strategy.

At that point, Lieutenant Castañeda had little choice but to bivouac for the night on higher ground several hundred yards from the river and to await the return of Ponton to continue the negotiations.

In the meantime, in a show of solidarity expected among the settlers when any one of the settlements was in serious trouble, approximately 150 loyal volunteers arrived in Gonzales, all of them just spoiling for a fight. However, Ponton thought the number of men assembled to this point was inadequate for the potential conflict he expected to occur. To gain additional assistance, a courier was promptly dispatched to San Felipe de Austin and the Lavaca and Navidad River valleys to recruit additional armed supporters.

With a sense of urgency running high throughout the town, a meeting was held and John H. Moore was elected to lead the Texians with the rank of colonel. Also under consideration were Edward Burleson, an Indian fighter and veteran of the War of 1812, James W. Fannin, Jr., a captain in the Bravo Guards, and empresario Stephen F. Austin, who had just been released from Santa Anna's prison. During the course of the meeting the men recognized that their continued resistance could ignite an attack by Castañeda's detachment. So, instead of their waiting for the Mexicans to attack Gonzales, the decision was made to bring the fight to them. As a precaution, the families packed up their possessions and were moved away from Gonzales to a safer location.

The following day the alcalde was still absent, but to avoid an unwanted confrontation at the time the Texians allowed Castañeda to communicate his demands by sending one swimmer across the river with his message. In response to their request for the cannon and to maintain their ruse, the Gonzales spokesman continued to insist that since the alcalde was out of town he was not authorized to deliver the cannon.

The refusals to hand over the cannon may have been quite exasperating for the Mexican commanders to accept, considering the fact that when the gun was originally received by Green DeWitt in 1831 he promised on the written receipt to return it when asked to do so.

Throughout this exchange between the two sides, the tenor of their negotiations was far from being mean-spirited as one would expect. Instead it took on an air of knowing they each had a different point of view, which had to be defended, a form of mid-nineteenth-century political correctness.

While the frustrated Mexican troops wiled away their time waiting for Ponton's return, on the morning of October 1, 1835, after a Coushatta Indian informed Castañeda that the Texians were reinforced to over 150 men, the lieutenant thought it prudent to move his troops seven miles farther upriver where the river was more fordable.

Meanwhile, in Gonzales that very morning the little cannon, which had been buried, was dug up and secured onto a set of wooden wagon wheels. And since there were no cannonballs to be found, assorted scrap metal was cut up, such as chains, horseshoes, et cetera, and pushed down the barrel of the gun. With all their preparations completed, including a sermon by a Methodist minister, around dusk the Gonzales "army" confidently began their trek toward the Mexican camp. Consisting of about 50 mounted men, the cannon, and the men on foot, they proudly displayed their makeshift flag, a banner made from an old dress by Sarah DeWitt, Green DeWitt's wife, and their daughter Evaline, that displayed a black cannon against a white background and which simply read: "COME AND TAKE IT."

Around 7:00 p.m. the Texians began to make their way across a ferry crossing and then proceeded to trudge upriver toward Castañeda's new camp. Arriving in the early morning hours, they hid among the thick cover of the trees adjacent to the camp and waited for the first light. Taking full advantage of Castañeda's failure to set up a picket line, just before dawn of October 2, 1835, the Texians emerged from the woods. Through the heavy morning fog they proceeded to fire blindly on the surprised soldiers still sheathed in their bedrolls. Although several Mexicans returned the fire, it was more of a reflex than out of a desire to cause harm. Soon a contingent of riders was dispatched in a counterattack, but as the Texians retreated back into the thick woods they were forced to turn back. Still unable to clearly see the opposing shooters, both sides entered into a self-imposed cease-fire until the morning sun melted away the remaining fog. With visibility substantially better, around 6:00 a.m. artilleryman James C. Neill placed the little cannon into position and lit the fuse, its ineffective blast merely signaling that hostilities could resume once again.

Despite Ugartechea's orders to resist any engagement, this minor, mostly one-sided skirmish lasted only a few hours before a meeting was arranged between Colonel Moore and Castañeda by an emissary who also attended the affair with an interpreter.

While the men were on horseback in an adjacent field, the meeting began with both sides explaining their differing political views and with Moore repeatedly asking Castañeda to surrender. When the Mexican lieutenant refused to yield to Moore's demands to capitulate, the meeting abruptly ended. Not long after the lieutenant returned to his camp, however, Neill fired their little cannon once again, evidently Colonel Moore's way of getting in the last word.

Varying reports list the casualties at one or two Mexicans killed and one Texian injured when he was thrown off his horse and bloodied his nose. Although it was a relatively insignificant firefight, it marked the opening shots of the Texas war for independence and the first true "battle" of the Texas Revolution. As for the infamous cannon, the gun's ultimate fate still remains quite controversial and much in dispute.

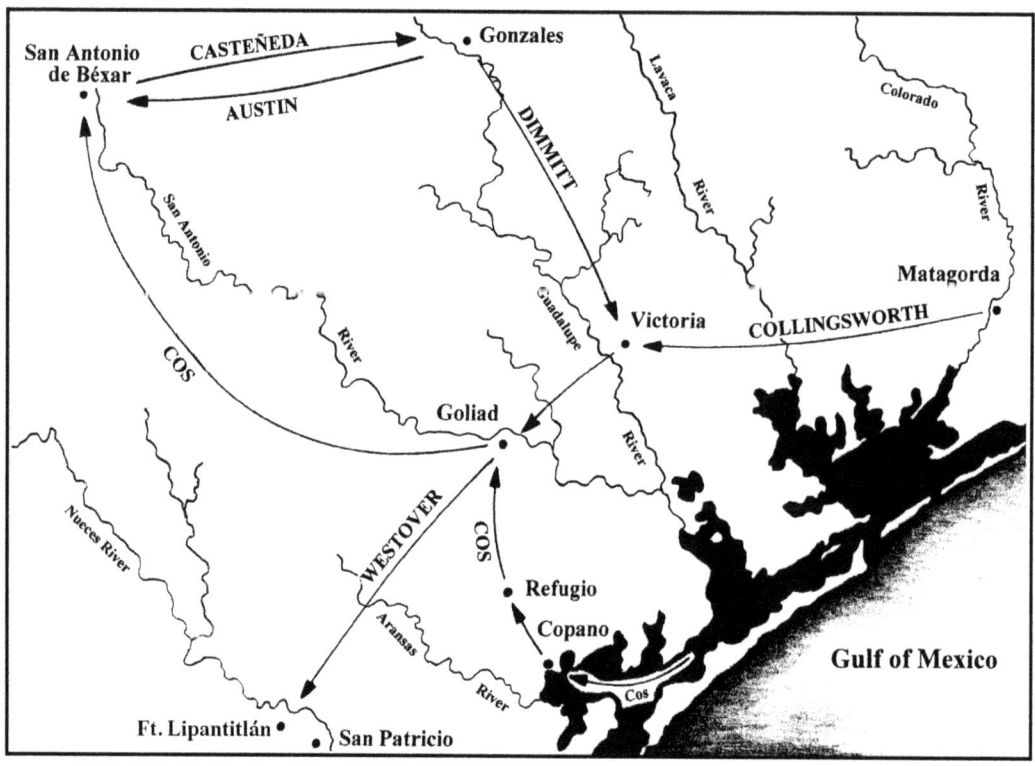

Troop Movements, September to October 1835

On the one hand, the Mexican dragoons sheepishly withdrew from Gonzales empty-handed and resentful of the fact that their orders forced them to confront their humiliation instead of the enemy. On the other hand, the Texians at Gonzales were ecstatic over their first taste of victory. Called the Battle of Gonzales, their success only encouraged them and many others to join in the fight against the Mexican regime.

Two days after the victory Austin left Gonzales and traveled to San Felipe de Austin and reported to the Committee on Public Safety, "War is declared—public opinion has proclaimed it against a Military despotism—The campaign has commenced. The Military have advanced to Gonzales—General Cos has arrived and threatens to overrun the country."[1]

While the fight over an antiquated little cannon may have been just a simple little skirmish, the psychological impact on the Texians was enormous. Drawing first blood dramatically captured the imagination of everyone seeking justice, liberty and a republican form of government. In that respect it was the spark that ignited the Texians to fight for the cause they felt was just.

When word of the Gonzales victory reached San Felipe de Austin and the surrounding regions, scores of volunteers, men emotionally motivated to join a fight, any fight, flocked toward Gonzales. Indeed, the town was inundated with between three and five hundred volunteers ready and willing to help the Texians in their campaign. And swept by "war fever," more were on their way. Although many were young men seeking excitement away from their drab lives, also included were a number of shopkeepers who were willing to close their doors to join in the fight. In fact, it became quite fashionable to put signs on their doors that simply read: "G.T.T." (Gone to Texas). At the same time, even more men silently suffered with the disappointment of not being able to go where the action was. It seemed as if this war fever had suddenly spread throughout Texas as the talk of revolution began to be heard from the pulpits to the dinner tables.

Despite the celebratory atmosphere in Gonzales over their perceived victory, Mexican colonel Ugartechea was not one to easily accept rejection. In a letter to Austin, still at San Felipe de Austin, the colonel threatened to return to Gonzales with an army large enough to impose his will. If the Texians remained adamant in their refusal to return the cannon, he warned, he would have no alternative but to attack in a state of war instigated by the Texian colonists.

When the Texians in Gonzales learned of Ugartechea's threat they sent an urgent communication to Austin imploring him to return. Responding to the plea, on October 10, 1835, Austin returned to the camp in Gonzales and found a marked decline in the morale of the men. There seemed to be little agreement among them on how to proceed with their next attack, an assault on San Antonio de Béxar, and what to do about the threat from Ugartechea. With over three hundred Texians lying around, all chomping at the bit for some action, Austin recognized the problem was a lack of leadership and of organization. Consequently, the following day an election was held to determine who would plan the strategy and set the rules. Although he had no military training whatsoever, without objections the unanimous choice was Austin himself, who was also given the title of general.

Once this democratic process was completed General Austin selected his staff and to a highly reenergized camp announced his first decision—the long-awaited drive toward Béxar would be their response to Colonel Ugartechea's threat.

The Battle of Goliad

In early 1834, while Austin was imprisoned in Mexico City, Santa Anna was deeply involved in a scheme to strengthen his supply route to the interior of Mexico.

Never one to relax his military preparedness, the Mexican president depended a great deal on Copano, a strategic port of entry, to receive his troops and supplies from the Gulf Coast. The cargo off-loaded at Copano would be transferred to riverboats and taken a few miles farther up the Gulf Coast to San Antonio Bay. From there the cargo would travel up the San Antonio River to the most important city in that area, Béxar, the political center of Texas. However, located upriver between Béxar and the Gulf was Goliad, a small, nondescript town of about 25 to 30 inhabitants. Except for the Spanish settlers who were trying to eke out a living there and an old Spanish mission, the only significant feature in Goliad was the Presidio La Bahia, or simply "La Bahia." It was a well-fortified Spanish-built fort on the river's edge, in effect the sentry guarding Santa Anna's supply route from the Gulf of Mexico to Béxar. Any enemy vessel trying to reach Béxar would have to get by La Bahia first. Therefore, it was extremely critical that Copano and Goliad were well defended in order for Santa Anna to continue transporting his troops to the interior and to deliver supplies and equipment for his military campaigns against the Texians.

Therefore, in July 1835 he ordered Col. Nicholas Condelle and two hundred troops to reinforce La Bahia, and in August reinforcements were delivered to shore up Col. Domingo de Ugartechea's garrison in Béxar and the nearby Franciscan mission called the Alamo. In addition, government troops were also stationed at Fort Lipantitlán, a makeshift earthwork on the edge of the Nueces River southwest of Refugio. That garrison protected the only other supply route to Béxar, the supply route from Matamoros.

In addition, to launch Santa Anna's plan to transport goods and equipment to Capano several ships moored in Matamoros were seized. The captured ships were then loaded with troop reinforcements, provisions, ordnance, and supplies under the command of Santa Anna's 35-year-old brother-in-law, Gen. Martín Perfecto de Cos.

General Cos served as Santa Anna's centralist enforcer. With Santa Anna's policies still being criticized by the colonists and at times by violent demonstrations and outspoken rhetoric, Cos was given the responsibility for stamping out all opposition to Santa Anna by whatever means he felt was necessary.

Especially annoying to Santa Anna was the lack of support he was getting from the people living in Goliad. Just as opposed to his centralist's views as many others in Mexico, they had the audacity to vent their displeasure by conducting unlawful demonstrations and speaking out against the policies of his government. Indicative of his lack of tolerance for anyone daring to disagree with him, he felt he had no choice but to deal with these rebellious settlers immediately. Therefore, as an example to others when Colonel Condelle arrived in Goliad he was ordered to arrest the alcalde and to confiscate all their weapons. As extra punishment, on September 20, 1835, Condelle took the menfolk down the San Antonio River, where they were forced to unload General Cos's ships, which had just arrived that day, and to deliver the enormous amount of supplies to the fort with the few oxen and carts they had available. At the same time, he quartered his own troops in their homes.

By this time, Santa Anna, who was at his hacienda in Veracruz, was so exasperated over the disrespectful actions of the people that he ordered General Cos to add even more reinforcements to Goliad as well and to use whatever force was necessary to repress the individuals who were not obeying the country that had adopted them as her own. On that note, Cos was also instructed to drive out all the agitators where he found them and to disarm all of the colonists. Almost immediately, General Cos ran into opposition from practically everyone in an age when owning a horse and a firearm was a matter of survival.

After leaving relatively small numbers of reinforcements in both Copano and the nearby town of Refugio, General Cos, as instructed, headed toward Goliad, where he arrived on October 2 with around four to five hundred troops. The 50-mile march was uneventful considering a group of die-hard federalists had been planning to kidnap him for ransom and to steal the rumored $50,000 in silver bars he had in his possession. (The bars were, in all likelihood, his share of the silver stolen from the mines during Santa Anna's attack on Zacatecas in May.)

However, when General Cos learned about the Mexican confrontation at Gonzales he correctly anticipated the Texians' next move had to be an attack on the garrison at Béxar. Consequently, with the attack on Colonel Ugartechea's garrison imminent, Cos knew it was extremely imperative that he deliver additional reinforcements to him also before the Texians arrived and began their assault.

As Cos scrambled to reorganize his mission, his first priority at the moment was to dispatch a detachment of troops to reinforce Fort Lipantitlán in order to ensure the supply route northward to Béxar was more secure. Once the troops left Goliad to reinforce Fort Lipantitlán, he had to decide what he should do with the tons of supplies he brought with him that were now stored in La Bahia. Since he had to depart sooner than scheduled, the means to transport the supplies and provisions with the army had not yet arrived. Instead he was now forced to leave it all behind under guard of around 30 soldiers under the command of Col. Juan López Sandoval.

On October 5 General Cos, along with Colonel Condelle and his troops, marched out of Goliad with a force of over four hundred troops to help defend Béxar. In General Cos's haste to leave Goliad, however, he made an enormous error in judgment. He failed to leave behind the reinforcements he was tasked to provide for the defense of Presidio La Bahia, a mistake that would have dire consequences for Santa Anna in the near future.

In the meantime, when word arrived in Gonzales that General Cos was preparing to leave Goliad to join forces with Colonel Ugartechea a strategy meeting among the volunteers was held. At this meeting, without Austin, who had left for San Felipe on October 4, they discussed the options available to prevent General Cos from delivering the reinforcements to Béxar. During the brainstorming, the only viable option appeared to be to intercept General Cos before he reached Ugartechea. When most of the Texians refused to risk such a fight, a group of some 40 men decided to leave Gonzales to join the kidnap conspirators who were planning to rendezvous in Victoria. Included in the group were Philip Dimmitt and John J. Linn, who were the chief instigators in the kidnapping scheme from the very beginning but decided to put it off so they could assist the folks in Gonzales.

After traveling about 60 miles, on October 6, 1835, Dimmitt and the others stopped at Victoria, where they ate and got some rest. Soon additional armed Texians began to arrive and more yet from the Texian militia in Matagorda, 90 miles to the east, including its leader, Capt. George Collingsworth, bringing the total to around 125. Collingsworth (or Collinsworth) and his followers came to Victoria to join up with the other conspirators and to recruit additional Texians to help them implement the kidnapping plan. But in the end the central committee at San Felipe de Austin refused to sanction the scheme because of the risks involved, primarily for not having the artillery they would need to support them at the fort.

Three days later, the group of would-be kidnappers learned that General Cos had already left Goliad on October 5 and had taken the silver bars with him. More significantly, they were told that only a token garrison remained in the fort guarding large quantities of supplies. Since their kidnapping plan was disapproved and knowing a mere handful of troops were left behind by General Cos, Collingsworth, who now took charge of the plotters, agreed to implement a new plan. They decided to ride the 25 miles to Goliad, drive out the Mexican troops occupying La Bahia, and take ownership of the vast quantities of supplies warehoused there. Before they left Victoria, 49 members of the group signed the so-called Compact of Volunteers, a document they would offer to the alcalde pledging no harm to the people of Goliad and to protect them from any future attacks by Santa Anna troops.

It was in the pre-dawn hours of October 10 when the men arrived at the outskirts of Goliad. Unfamiliar with the territory, some of the men temporally lost their bearings in the dark and while wandering aimlessly were surprised to meet up with Ben Milam, a veteran of the James Long filibuster expedition who had just escaped from a Mexican prison. Finally reunited with Collingsworth and the rest of the group, the men located several houses where they were able to obtain axes from the locals to chop their way through the thick wooden doors of the fort. Since the garrison was understaffed, Collingsworth and his band confronted very little resistance and easily gained entrance to the interior courtyard.

The Battle of Goliad lasted for only about 30 minutes. There was sporadic musket fire coming from the surprised troops but with little or no effect. Once convinced they would all be killed if they continued to fight, the garrison under Colonel Sandoval quickly surrendered. One Texian was wounded, and varying accounts estimated one to three Mexican soldiers killed and three to seven wounded.

Although the entire Mexican garrison surrendered initially, 20 of the soldiers managed to escape in the darkness and confusion. They all found refuge in Copano and Refugio, where they warned the commanders there that the Texians would soon be advancing in their direction. To the pleasant surprise of the Texians, however, the two small garrisons, the reinforcements left by Cos, evacuated these two very critical positions and consolidated forces with the troops at Fort Lipantitlán. (Present-day Copano is now a ghost town gradually falling into the Gulf.)

With Copano abandoned and by capturing La Bahia, Captain Collingsworth scored a tremendous victory for the Texians, and for three reasons. One, the army under General Cos was now isolated in Béxar, cut off from reinforcements and supplies that would have come directly upriver from the Gulf Coast. And two, since Santa Anna's supply route, the one that was so important to him, was now decimated; he was forced to find a longer overland route to provide men and supplies to his brother-in-law. The last reason was that the Texians inherited a windfall of supplies, equipment, and provisions found at La Bahia. For instance, a few of the items were 175 barrels of flour, three hundred muskets, clothing, blankets, sugar, coffee, whiskey, rum., and several cannons. For Santa Anna, it was indeed a very unfavorable development.

The Presidio La Bahia, the gem of their victories, was now under the control of the Texians. To keep it that way, Philip Dimmitt, a De León colonist, was elected to command the one hundred Texians who would remain at the fort. Following the release of the Mexican prisoners, the rest of the Texians, including Ben Milam, were transferred to Gonzales to join up with the rising number of volunteers. As for the victorious Captain Collingsworth, he returned to Matagorda to recruit more colonists into the Texian army.

Back in Gonzales, Austin was overjoyed when he was told of this victory. With two consecutive wins under their belt, the Texians definitely had the momentum. And with more and more volunteers coming forward, the future of their movement seemed bright.

In La Bahia, Captain Dimmitt's responsibility appeared to be the rather mundane task of distributing the goods left behind by General Cos. Not one to sit idly by while the real action was going on, in mid–October Dimmitt proposed an attack on Fort Lipantitlán, the only available supply link between General Cos and the port at Matamoros, on the Rio Grande. Most important, Dimmitt understood the strategic importance of Matamoros. Therefore, he reasoned, by capturing Fort Lipantitlán the supply route between Matamoros and Cos would be shut down and at the same time Matamoros would be exposed to a future invasion by Texian forces. In addition, freed of Mexican forces, the citizens of San Patricio would be able to elect delegates to the so-called Consultation, a political gathering similar to the Conventions of 1832 and 1833, and to organize a militia for their own self-defense. Despite Dimmitt's recommendation, no response was forthcoming from General Austin.

Taking matters into his own hands, Dimmitt dispatched two of his men to the town of San Patricio, less than two miles from the fort, with messages for the federalist leaders. Unfortunately, to Dimmitt's disappointment, the Mexican soldiers intercepted the men and they were now being held prisoner. The young commander, upset over this revelation, began planning a rescue operation when he read a reconnaissance report that said Mexican troops were gathering at the fort. Concerned the Mexicans were planning to retake Goliad and reestablish their supply link to Béxar, Captain Dimmitt thought it most urgent that he act at once not only to rescue his two men but also to prevent their counterattack on Goliad. Again, without approval of his proposition, at the end of October the Texians, led by Capt. Ira Westover, rode out of Goliad toward Fort Lipantitlán on a more circuitous route than usual. Before they left, however, more bad news arrived when Dimmitt was told his two men had been transferred to Matamoros.

Picking up additional Texians along the way, Westover, now with a force of 60 or 70 men, arrived on the outskirts of the fort in the receding twilight of dusk on November 3, 1835. Shortly before his arrival, however, Westover stopped at a ranch where he learned that a large body of Mexican troops was searching for them, undoubtedly the troops from the fort. With this information in hand, Westover began to lay out his strategy for an early morning assault on the fort when two civilians from San Patricio were spotted in the camp. The men were picked up, questioned, and threatened with charges of aiding the enemy. At this point one of the men, a James O'Riley, offered to persuade the Mexicans in the fort to surrender in return for their release, a deal Westover quickly agreed to. As a result of their deal, Westover and his men gained access to the interior of the fort without firing a shot. Once they were inside, a search quickly located the 27 Mexican troops, all cowering in their wooden huts. The prisoners were rounded up and brought outside the fort, where they were released to cross the Rio Grande to Matamoros after promising not to take up arms for the rest of the conflict. What followed was a search of the fort, where they found two small cannons, about a dozen and a half muskets, several pounds of gunpowder, but not one single cannonball.

The biggest surprise of all, however, was that Fort Lipantitlán was not really a fort after all. Instead, it was just a single embankment of dirt that shielded a bunch of dilapidated huts, all surrounded by a fence. At that point the men spent the night resting in the nearby town of San Patricio before returning in the morning to set the huts ablaze and to destroy the guns.

Later the next day, around 4:00 p.m. as the men watched Fort Lipantitlán disappear into smoke, Westover spotted the main body of the Mexican garrison silhouetted along the horizon. Westover's men immediately took up their battlefield positions among the trees to force the Mexican troops to fight dismounted, and a fierce gun battle ensued in which Westover's men totally dominated the Mexican troops by virtue of the superior accuracy of their Texas long rifles compared to the archaic Mexican Brown Bess muskets. The firefight continue sporadically, but as nightfall overtook the battle a severe storm with torrential rain rolled across the bloodied field. Westover and most of his men abandoned the field and spent the night comfortably cared for back in San Patricio while several Texians stayed behind under cover to keep their adversaries pinned down and to suffer even more without shelter in the rain and cold of that November night.

Returning to the battlefield on the morning of November 5, Captain Westover, now able to observe the suffering wounded on the field, granted permission for his men to treat the enemy troops. Following this compassionate gesture he graciously allowed them all to withdraw to Matamoros. Of the approximately 90 Mexican troops, the casualties were estimated to be around 5 killed and 17 injured. The Texians had only 1 man wounded.

With his mission completed, Captain Westover and his men returned to La Bahia, where they were severely criticized for accomplishing nothing of significance except pardoning the Mexican troops, burning several wooden huts, destroying useless weapons, and leaving the inhabitants of San Patricio to fend for themselves.

Meanwhile, Captain Dimmitt was having a change of heart. His enthusiasm for the Texian fight to resurrect the Constitution of 1824 had waned and his commitment was now focused on complete independence from Mexico, a position completely contrary to Austin's. Angry over Dimmitt's lack of loyalty to the Texian position, Austin felt he had no choice but to remove him from his command. On December 6, 1835, Dimmitt and his men moved on toward Béxar to participate in the siege but arrived too late to join in the final assault. Dimmitt returned to Goliad about a week later and, despite Austin's orders, resumed his command. Also, as a result of the victory over General Cos, Dimmitt wrote and framed a so-called Goliad Declaration of Independence and designed the first Texian flag of independence. It portrayed a muscular arm holding up a bloody sword, which he raised over La Bahia. This display of patriotism angered some Mexicans who, in turn, would later turn Dimmitt's life into a nightmare.

4

The Siege of Béxar

Newly elected to command the Texas volunteer army, on October 11, 1835, Austin issued his first general order, which stated, "A general muster and inspection will take place at 9 o'clock a.m. tomorrow 12th October. The line of march will immediately thereafter be taken up for Béxar."[1]

The following morning the mood in Gonzales was one of anticipation, excitement, and anxiety, all rolled into one. This was the day everybody was waiting for, especially the new volunteers who were itching to get on with the fight. Many had left their homes and their families to do what they felt was their patriotic duty. They all knew that in just the first two weeks of October the Mexican troops had suffered losses at Gonzales, Goliad, Copano, and Refugio. This time, in Béxar as well, General Cos would see for himself how determined they were to fight for their independence from the state of Coahuila.

When all was ready, on a given signal, an estimated three to four hundred men, mostly Texians from the Austin and DeWitt colonies and hundreds of volunteers, rode out of Gonzales toward Béxar, some 70 miles away. They were a motley bunch of ruffians with fewer guns than men, short on powder and lead, with no heavy artillery to brag about, no cavalry, and a very limited amount of rations. Also, it was no secret to them that when they confronted the Mexican army they would be outnumbered and outgunned against a foe who also had more experience and was better equipped with artillery and the intelligence-gathering capabilities of a first-rate cavalry. It was a daunting prospect for some of the men who never pulled a trigger against an enemy soldier. Nevertheless, the one thing they had that the Mexican troops did not have was purpose. Each and every Texian was putting his life on the line for the same specific purpose—to gain a political system that guaranteed they and their families lived in a free and democratic society. This, they rationalized, was their equalizer.

The march was not an easy one for both General Austin, who had to maintain discipline, and the first-time volunteers who were totally offended with having to take orders from their superiors and having to accept various forms of punishment for seemingly arbitrary infractions. Fortunately for them, the advance was virtually uneventful, except perhaps for being reinforced by about a hundred more volunteers who rode 250 miles from Nacogdoches to join in the fight.

Also arriving at this time was the famed adventurer Jim Bowie. At 40 years old, he was widely known for the knife he carried that now bore his name. To others, however, he was somewhat infamous for his involvement in many shady land speculation deals. Since his wife and children had died in the cholera epidemic he had become heavily involved in the Texas Revolution, first as a delegate to the Convention of 1833 and just recently when he joined the army to be in the thick of the fighting.

As the army slowly struggled along, Austin contemplated the possibility that he could be marching right into unseen forces lurking somewhere ahead. To make up for a mounted company he didn't have, therefore, Austin dispatched a makeshift cavalry to scout ahead and determine whether General Cos was aware of their presence and, if possible, the strength of his defenses. The mounted Texians were led by the newly made colonel Ben Milam, a veteran of the battle that captured the Presidio La Bahia in Goliad.

On October 16, the Texians reached Cibolo Creek, only 25 miles from Béxar, where they set up their bivouac. It was during this time that Colonel Milam returned with the news that, in all likelihood, at least from his observations of enemy troop movements, General Cos was well aware of their presence. Now knowing that he was being observed, General Austin thought the time was right to call a council of war to determine their next move.

Following a great deal of lively and heated arguments, they agreed the best idea was to find a way to arrive at a solution satisfactory to both sides without firing a shot. If there was a way to negotiate and avoid bloodshed they should try it. But that meant somehow Austin would have to establish a dialogue with General Cos. Consequently, on October 17 a letter was delivered to the general in which Austin diplomatically called for discussions that could enable both sides to settle their differences. In his response the following day General Cos said he, too, wanted to avoid a war but flatly refused to negotiate with what he called illegal foreigners. The 36-year-old general concluded his answer with a dire warning. If Austin did not bring this incident to a halt Cos would be forced into making an example of the colonies.

This blatant threat from General Cos bothered Austin. So much so that after conferring with his staff he had to decide whether to attack now or institute a siege. First, however, since his present location was too far from Béxar to be effective, he decided he had to move his army closer to his enemy.

As they were still camped out along Cibolo Creek, several days later a meeting was held between Austin, his officers, and a visitor who just dropped by on official business. He was Sam Houston, a former politician who at one time was a U.S. congressman and governor of Tennessee. Houston was now a delegate in the Consultation, which was officially serving as the new Texian Provisional Government.

The Consultation was scheduled to meet for the first time in Gonzales around mid–October to discuss the goals of the Texians, specifically whether to demand independence from Coahuila y Texas or to remain part of Coahuila but to demand the Mexican government return to the Constitution of 1824. However, when the fight over returning the cannon occurred in Gonzales the meeting was postponed. Meanwhile many of the delegates who were already in Gonzales joined Austin's army in the fight against Lieutenant Casteñeda. The Consultation meeting was now going to be held in San Felipe de Austin on November 1, 1835, if there was a quorum. Consequently, on behalf of the provisional government Houston was visiting the camp for two reasons.

Needing a quorum, Houston stopped, first to ascertain whether the group of delegates who were also in Austin's army would be allowed to leave the front lines to attend the meeting. Second, he wanted to determine whether Austin's army was capable of withstanding an assault on the better-trained and better-equipped Mexican forces in Béxar. This was a very critical battle for the Texian nation, he said, and a great deal depended on their beating General Cos, a military officer of relatively vast experience.

Houston's opinion was that Austin's men were not sufficiently trained, were vastly outnumbered, were without blankets and tents, and lacked the necessary discipline to guarantee a victory. To this end, Houston recommended that Austin withdraw from their present position and regroup at Gonzales for reinforcements, the much-needed training, additional supplies, and more organization.

On Houston's first request, with the exception of those delegates who were also staff officers Austin agreed to allow the delegates to leave the ranks to attend the Consultation meeting. On the question of withdrawing his forces for more training, Austin, with the support of his staff, thought otherwise. He knew the amount of passion his men had for this fight, he knew the hardships they had endured that enabled them to be here, and he knew they had the capacity and the spirit not only to fight hard but also to come away the winner despite the disparity in numbers. They were there for a purpose, he explained, and he was not going to back out of it now. Following Houston's departure with the delegates, one Texian remarked, "He has endeavored to discourage our men and alleging the impracticability of taking Bexar."[2]

Two days after the meeting with Houston, on October 27, Austin dispatched a search party of about 90 men to locate a defensible position closer to the city. The search party was commanded by Bowie and Capt. James W. Fannin, Jr., a veteran of the Battle of Gonzales and one of the few in the group who had some formal military training.

At the same time, General Austin and the army pulled up stakes and headed for Salado Creek.

Following along the San Antonio River, about two miles short of the Mexican fortifications the search party found what they considered to be the ideal place for General Austin's headquarters and campsite. Since the main road was so close to this new position, they surmised the army could easily detect any attempt to bring reinforcements and supplies into the fortified city. It was called the mission Purísima Concepción, near the San Antonio River. Convinced of its suitability, Bowie sent word to General Austin to advance the army to this new site. However, as they would soon discover, a campsite so close to the enemy only increased the likelihood that frequent clashes would occur as well.

Not to be outfoxed, the next morning General Cos ordered a small detachment of infantry and cavalry to show his newly arrived neighbors that their presence had not gone unnoticed. The infantry was commanded by Col. Domingo de Ugartechea, who, as you recall, had ordered the return of a loaned cannon that had incited the residence of Gonzales to revolt. His strategy against Bowie was to attack the Texians from the front while the horsemen rode around to the rear, effectively trapping Bowie and his men in the middle.

At around 8:00 a.m. the Mexican troops began the firefight with a volley of indiscriminate firing at the Texians who were lying low along the San Antonio riverbank. Yelling out to the men, Bowie advised, "Keep under cover, boys, and reserve your fire; we haven't a man to spare."[3] Shortly after the small-arms fire, the Mexicans rolled out two pieces of small-caliber artillery and fired with no effect. This was soon followed by a loud and disorganized charge by the Mexican infantry. Fannin and his men, frontiersmen with a sharpshooter's eye, instantly returned fire, stopping the charge in its tracks. Overwhelmed by the deadly fire, the Mexicans were compelled to retreat immediately. This same scenario was repeated twice—small-arms fire, cannon shots, and a surge of troops, only to retreat once again when fired upon. When it became apparent to Colonel Ugartechea that his artillerymen were special targets for the Texian sharpshooters, the use of the small cannons was brought to a sudden halt. At that point, several Texians sprang from the riverbank, captured a loaded cannon, and fired it at the retreating troops.

As the infantry withdrew back toward the city, the Mexican cavalry entered the fray. Because the Texians were surrounded by trees the cavalry played no part in the fight except to fire their small cannon from a safe distance. Once they performed that little responsibility they withdrew from the field as well.

Although it was called the Battle of Concepción, it was more of a skirmish than a battle. It did drive home the point, however, that although the Texians were vastly outnumbered, their superior weapons and keen marksmanship were enough to level the playing field. The fight was between the Mexican smoothbore Brown Bess muskets, with a range of 70 yards, against the Kentucky long rifles, weapons with a range of 200 yards. Despite the heavy fusillade of inaccurate Mexican musketry, only one Texian died. On the Mexican side, around 70 would never see the light of day again.

A half hour later General Austin and roughly five hundred men pulled into their new campgrounds.

Following a reconnaissance of the surrounding area by Colonel Milam, General Austin was surprised that the fortifications confronting him were much stronger than he had anticipated. Consequently, as an ongoing safeguard, daily search parties were dispatched to scour the area and to intercept wagon trains of supplies or reinforcements heading for the enemy's fortifications.

The most important and largest city in Coahuila y Texas, San Antonio de Béxar, or simply Béxar, was located on the western side of a meandering bend in the 60-foot-wide San Antonio River. On the opposite side of the bend, less than a mile away stood the former Franciscan mission called the Alamo. Surrounded by a barren prairie, the city consisted of a dozen or more side streets laid out in a simple crosshatch pattern, all encompassing a large public square located in the city center. One of the two main streets, Soledad Street, ran along the eastern side of the square. The other, Acequia Street, in parallel on the west, cut through the center of the public square effectively, dividing the public square into two halves. Off to one side stood the traditional adobe homes, a church, the priest's house, and several smaller buildings. Additional houses and shops lined both sides of the remaining streets.

The defenses enjoyed by General Cos included breastworks constructed on every street where it entered into the square and at least 10 to 15 pieces of artillery. One large 18-pounder was mounted on the roof of the church, while two redoubts (small stone forts containing artillery), one erected on the eastern side and one on the inside of the city, contained two smaller guns each, and other guns were scattered around the public square as well, not including the six guns mounted on the walls of the nearby Alamo. Also, within the fortified city, General Cos's troop population presently stood at around eight hundred men.

Over the next several days Austin realized he had to do something fast before the bad weather set in. He had two options; either he attacked General Cos now or laid a siege and waited it out. Either choice represented a tough fight indeed. Without heavy artillery, supporting an attack on such strong defenses would only subject his men to heavy losses, something Austin wanted to avoid. Waiting for the enemy to surrender under a siege also had its drawbacks. With the freezing weather setting in and with food and supplies limited, morale and discipline were already beginning to break down.

The men were becoming more and more dispirited and morale had greatly declined. Sickness and desertions were also another problem. It was obvious to the general and his staff that if the Mexican army was allowed to escape they would advance on the colonies as Cos had threatened to do. If that were to happen, all that the Texians had fought for would be lost. This was why Sam Houston reminded Austin at their meeting that the fight at Béxar would be the most critical one of them all. In the end, it was an easy decision to make for Austin. The only option was to place General Cos under siege until the reinforcements and heavy artillery arrived and then attack. Until then, Austin would have to deal with the boredom of his men the best he could. In that regard, he issued a series of rules that he hoped would moderate their behavior. He reminded them of the advice he offered back on October 11 in his first general order when he told them, "The first duty of a soldier is obedience," and, "It is expected that the army of the people altho [sic] hastily collected will present an example of obedience that will do honor to the cause we are engaged in, and credit to the patriots who are defending it."[4] However, many were tough frontiersmen and backwoodsmen unaccustomed to sitting around waiting for something to happen or for someone to tell them they could or couldn't do something. But, Austin rationalized to himself, they were all volunteers who were under no legal obligation to anybody. If they chose to leave they could simply leave. To General Austin, a man with very little military command experience, being a general was not as glamorous as he thought it would be. Deep down, he wished for a genuine army, with formal training, compensation, regulations, and an understanding that they were obligated to respect and obey superior officers. Nevertheless, he suspected when the time came to fight they would give it their all.

On November 1, 1835, General Austin tried once again to negotiate with General Cos rather than fight, with heavy losses of lives on both sides. In this regard, he dispatched a courier under a white flag with a letter demanding that General Cos surrender immediately. General Cos responded by returning the letter to Austin unopened. Understanding that no answer is sometimes an answer in itself, Austin decided to take the bull by the horns. Leaving Bowie, Fannin and their men to monitor the southern sector of the city, Austin took the remaining troops outside the northern edge, where they set up their camp in the vicinity of a lone adobe building called the Old Mill.

Meanwhile, inside the city, General Cos was fully aware that an army much weaker than his own and deficient in every other respect was situated within two short miles of his position. But yet the close proximity of Austin's army was not a cause for General Cos's concern. What bothered him the most was the fact that he was unable to obtain reinforcements and supplies if and when he needed them now that his supply line had been compromised. At the same time, the Texians could rely on the hundreds of fresh Texians who were more than eager to join in the fight. Also, his reputation and the honor of the homeland were at stake, not to mention the reaction of Cos's brother-in-law if his supposedly professional and well-tuned army was driven out of Texas by the likes of inexperienced volunteer soldiers. Therefore, in an attempt to replenishes his forces he dispatched Colonel Ugartechea along with a unit of cavalry to the Rio Grande to seek reinforcements.

Reaching a quorum on November 3, the Consultation meeting in San Felipe de Austin opened their deliberations by electing a provisional governor and a lieutenant governor, as well as electing Houston as commander of the Provisional Army of Texas. Henry Smith, the former alcalde of Brazoria and an outspoken advocate of independence, was elected governor, James Robinson, a land grantee from Nacogdoches, the lieutenant governor, and Sam Houston, now Gen. Sam Houston, was selected to lead the new army. Since the current army was already organized under General Austin, later in the year a new recruiting effort would be launched to form Houston's army in Gonzales. The Provisional Army would be the regular division and would supplement the volunteer force already on hand. There were four enlistment options in the Provisional Army—the Regular Army, the Permanent Volunteers, the Volunteer Auxiliary Corps, and the Texas Rangers. Members of the Regular Army joined for two years, received $24 in cash, eight hundred acres of land, and instant Texas citizenship, but were subject to all U.S. Army regulations. Permanent Volunteers had to agree to stay on until the war was over. The Auxiliary Corps members joined for only six months. They received 320 acres if they joined for one year or 640 acres for two years of service. The fourth option was to be one of the expert riflemen in the Texas Rangers with a salary of $1.25 per day. However, because of personality clashes, incompetence, differing agendas, and internal bickering over policies, the Consultation proved to be ineffective and would be replaced by the upcoming Convention of 1836.

Later that month General Austin learned that he had been elected by the Consultation to serve as one of three commissioners to the United States. In that capacity Austin was to travel to New Orleans to solicit loans and volunteers, arrange credit for munitions and equipment, fit out warships, and try to secure recognition of Texas and annexation from the United States. As a result of this new assignment, Austin had to leave the campaign temporarily, a move that resulted in the November 24 election of a new commander, 37-year-old Lt. Col. Edward Burleson, Austin's second in command. A North Carolina native, Burleson served as a colonel in the Missouri and Tennessee militia and was a veteran of the War of 1812.

Back in the Texian camp, the American troops discovered they were not the only ones having morale problems. In early December of 1835, a discouraged Mexican officer chose to surrender rather than put up with the horrendous conditions he experienced in the city. According to intelligence gathered from him and others, there was a lack of medical care, as well as food and freshwater for both the soldiers and the animals. Evidently, according to the informant it was a condition that was taking a toll on everybody.

General Burleson was very much encouraged by this information. He was convinced that at last the siege was having the desired effect on the fighting spirit of the Mexican soldiers. Because of their growing demoralization, Burleson declared, this was the best time to attack. But to the dismay of the commander, his own men showed very little enthusiasm for doing anything, let alone participating in a gun battle.

Evidently, during the protracted lull that came from waiting for the enemy to surrender the men's lethargy and disinterest had returned in a big way. The cause was principally sheer boredom and inactivity, hunger, and the continued exposure to the harsh weather without proper shelter. This, of course, resulted in increased desertions, increased alcohol consumption, and sickness. And as expected, discipline had substantially decreased, and motivation was nearly nonexistent. Disgusted and fed up with the character of his army, General Burleson decided it would be foolhardy to attack the Mexican fortifications with the officers and men in their present state. The prudent alternative was to simply withdraw to Goliad, where the army could bivouac for the winter. Ben Milam, however, did not agree.

Just returning from a reconnaissance expedition, Colonel Milam became extremely angry when told the new commander had ordered a withdrawal to Goliad. Trying desperately to keep his emotions in check, to the astonishment of the men around him Milam quickly stormed into the general's headquarters. With a respectful tone of confidence and restraint, Milam offered the general a proposition. At 47 years old, Milam was no stranger to combat. An adventurer most of his adult life, he was used to living under unforgiving conditions. Also, he had fought in the War of 1812, served with the filibuster James Long back in 1820, spent time in a Mexican prison, and joined Captain Collingsworth's group at the battle at Goliad.

Clearly gaining Burleson's attention, Milam suggested that if he could rally enough support from the men to invade the city he was willing to lead the assault. Once the battle was engaged, Milam continued, the rest of the men might be motivated enough to join in or be held as reserve. If he failed outright, the army could then withdraw to Goliad as planned with the satisfaction of knowing they had tried their best. Burleson agreed.

Outside the general's quarters, the men quietly assembled, all patiently waiting to hear the results of the confrontation. As Milam exited the general's tent he loudly called out, "Who will follow old Ben Milam into San Antonio?"[5] Of the some six hundred Texians in the camp about half responded in the affirmative. Amid the roaring cheers, the reenergized men gathered for a pre-battle briefing after which they agreed to let Milam lead them to victory in the morning.

In the very early hours of December 5, 1835, the Texians assembled at the Old Mill, a decaying and vacant building located close to their camp just outside the northern end of the city. Following last-minute instructions, Milam divided them into two divisions. One division was commanded by Milam, the other by 36-year-old Col. Francis W. Johnson.

A Virginian from Leesburg, Johnson had contacted malaria in 1826, which, on the advice of his doctor, compelled him to migrate to Mexican Texas to take advantage of the healthier climate. Once in Texas, he became a friend and surveyor for Stephen F. Austin and was a delegate to the Convention of 1832, where he became well known for

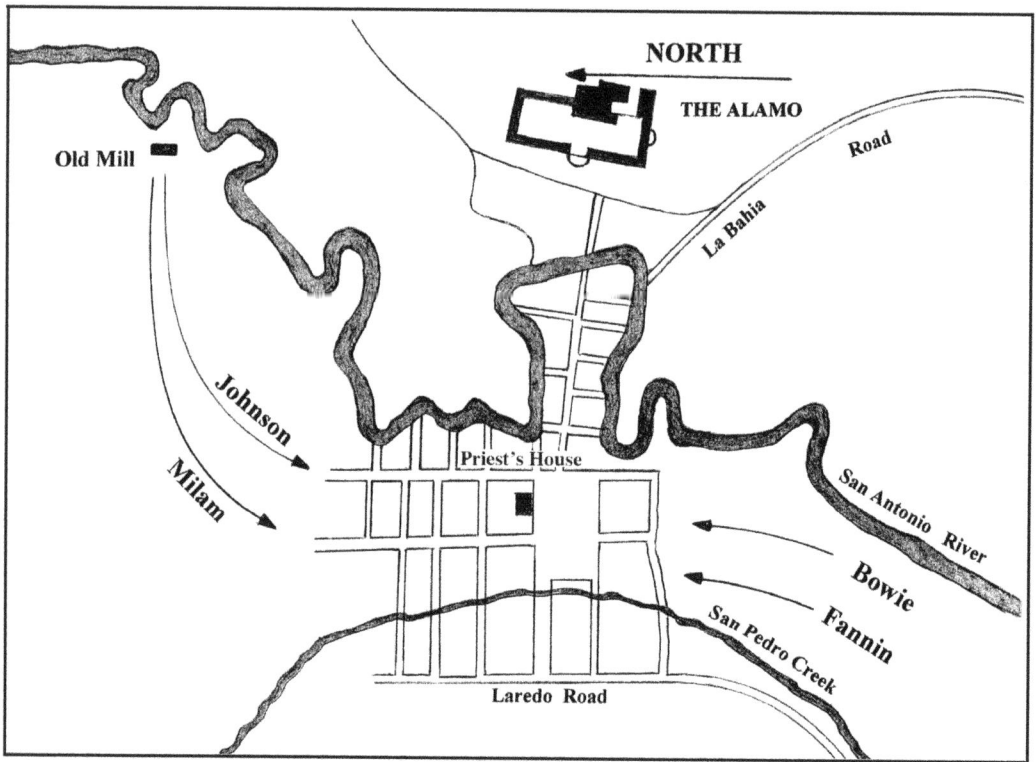

San Antonio de Béxar Campaign

his hot temper and his advocacy for war with Mexico. Since the start of the Texas Revolution, Johnson was a strong supporter of Austin, who selected him to serve as his adjutant and inspector general of the volunteer forces under his leadership.

Each division was responsible for advancing along the two main streets leading into the city. Also included was a makeshift cavalry, Texians on horseback, whose role it was to patrol the perimeter to intercept reinforcements and any attempt by the Mexican troops to escape and to obtain food and grain from the local ranches. And a few miles away, Col. James C. Neill and a small gun crew were strategically positioned within range of the Alamo walls with one small cannon primed and ready to fire. The men in the Old Mill would advance toward the city when they heard the report of Neill's gun.

Meanwhile, in the Mexican garrison, General Cos had little choice but to disburse his troops into purely defensive positions. With the approximately six to eight hundred men at his disposal, most would defend the city while a smaller group garrisoned the Alamo Mission. At the same time, General Cos was anxiously waiting for Colonel Ugartechea, who was expected to return soon from Matamoras with hundreds of reinforcements.

Hunkered down in the darkness, the Texians nervously waited for the sound of Neill's cannon. With the wait seemingly taking forever, the stillness of the night was broken only by the heavy breathing of the shivering men enduring the anxiety of the moment. Suddenly the men sprang into action as the muffled roar of the cannon reverberated from the Alamo grounds. Colonel Neill had sent one round smashing into the wall of the mission with instructions to continue shelling the place until the sound of gunfire could be heard coming from Béxar. The shelling was designed to divert attention away from the Old Mill as the men dashed toward the city and occupied the first houses at the end of the two streets. Milam would advance along Acequia Street while Johnson continued along Soledad Street. Edging their way forward toward the breastworks in the plaza, located about 950 yards ahead, the volunteer army quietly slid along the front of the houses on both sides of each of the two streets. Both divisions were well aware that as they crept closer to the Mexican artillerymen the chances of being spotted increased and at that point all hell would break loose—which it did.

Now under continuous small-arms fire from the rooftops and windows, as well as blasts of canister from the artillery posted in the main square, the Texians were forced to leave the streets for the relative safety of the houses. The Texians were now compelled to advance from house to house, from rooftop to rooftop, and through the walls of adjoining houses. At times they were even required to engage in hand-to-hand combat with the Mexican soldiers occupying the same rooms or the same roof. Fighting in this fashion, day by day, one house at a time, the Texians managed to make their way closer and closer to the enemy forces in the city center. Finally, when the Mexican artillerists behind the barricades and at the closest redoubt came within range of the Texas sharpshooters, the complexion of the battle began to change. As the sharpshooters were picking the artillerists off one by one with the longer-range and more accurate Kentucky long rifles, the cannon fire became noticeably less and the fighting more sporadic. The following day, this methodical advancement continued. Under a steady onslaught of musketry, long rifles, and a borrowed six-pounder, the Mexicans were forced to withdraw their ordnance.

Sensing the time was right for an all-out assault, on December 7, 1835, as Colonel Milam stood outside one of the houses, he was killed instantly by a Mexican sniper firing from his vantage point high in the trees. The death of their leader was a devastating blow to the Texian fighters, one that could have caused the despondent men to abandon the effort entirely. Instead, after voting Colonel Johnson as Milam's replacement the Texians gained a revitalized incentive to avenge his death by renewing their attack with even more resolve. Fighting with sheer adrenaline, the Texians advanced in full force firing at anything that moved until they captured the "Priest House," the last fortified house overlooking the main square. From this position, the remaining enemy batteries were easily silenced.

Although the loss of Colonel Milam weighed heavily on the men, they had a more pressing predicament that kept them awake at night. With ammunition about to run out they wondered how they could continue to fight after Colonel Ugartechea arrived with the Mexican reinforcements. They didn't have long to find out.

The next day, their fears were justified when Ugartechea arrived with around seven hundred reinforcements from Laredo to bolster the Mexican defenses. Considering General Cos had lost a great deal of his army to desertions, the timing of their arrival could not have been better—except for one thing. To everyone's surprise, most of the reinforcements were not soldiers at all but jailhouse prisoners who had agreed to fight only to get their freedom. But, once they were free of their shackles, becoming involved in a gunfight was the last thing they wanted to do. With their newfound freedom before them, the prisoners simply ate most of whatever food was still available. And with little or no resistance, most had somehow slipped through the porous perimeter guard that Burleson had organized and abandoned the field, leaving the remnants of the Mexican army at the mercy of the Texians. Equally discouraging was the fact that when General Cos was informed that the reinforcements were close by he sent two hundred troops to escort them into the city. However, supposedly finding no reinforcements, they quickly deserted. With his army severely decimated by desertions and battle deaths, on December 9 General Cos determined that his defensive lines could no longer withstand the advance of the Texian forces. He had little choice but to redeploy his troops from the city to the relative safety of the Alamo, less than a mile away.

To Santa Anna Cos wrote, "In such critical circumstances there was no other measure than to advance and occupy the Alamo which, due to its small size and military position, was easier to hold. In doing so, I took with me the artillery packs and the rest of the utensils I was able to transport."[6]

Moving his troops into the Alamo was the most logical choice for General Cos since he already had the foresight to prepare for this eventuality. Under the direction of Colonel Ugartechea, work had been ongoing since October to construct defensive works within the old mission.

In the Alamo, the situation had grown extremely desperate. Hearing of a plan Cos had designed for a counterattack, around two hundred cavalrymen, fearing they would soon be surrounded and killed, simply left the mission and rode south toward the Rio Grande. Learning that he had about 70 dedicated troops under Col. Nicolas Condelle still defending the plaza in Béxar, General Cos remarked to his emissary, "Go save those brave men. I authorize you to approach the enemy and obtain the best terms possible. Save the dignity of our Government, the honor of its arms and honor, life and property of chiefs, officials and troops that still remain even though I myself perish."[7] After spending only two days in the Alamo, General Cos, now with only about one hundred experienced regulars in the garrison, ordered his emissary to inform the Texians of his intent to capitulate.

Gladly accepted by Burleson, the 18 terms of the surrender were concluded on December 11, 1835. Included in the terms was a demand that required General Cos to remove his army from the Alamo within six days. And once paroled, Cos and his officers would not resist efforts to reestablish the Constitution of 1824, that the convicts were to be brought back across the Rio Grande, and that they and the cavalry were allowed to keep their firearms and ten round of ammunition. Also, the army was permitted to take one four-pounder and ten rounds of powder and balls.

Four days later, once the formalities of surrender were completed, General Cos and his men withdrew from the Alamo. With their departure, no organized garrison of centralist troops remained in Texas. Losses for General Cos were an estimated 150 casualties; and for the Texians, 35.

With the battle for Béxar over and the Texian army understaffed, any new hot spot required a shift of manpower from one battlefield to another. Also, with no enemy troops left in Texas, many of the remaining volunteers believed the war was over and returned to their homes while others with no homes to go to were potential candidates for whatever assignment came up next. Even General Burleson resigned his command and took leave to be with his family at Christmas.

As for General Cos, when he notified the minister of war of his surrender he was brusquely told to return to his post to redeem his wavering reputation, if he could. And so, over the next several weeks, General Cos and the remnants of his rejected army trudged 250 miles to Monclova to rest and to regroup. He arrived in Monclova, the capital of Coahuila, on January 20, 1836.

With the men at Béxar now considered surplus, the provisional government saw fit to reduce the Texian presence in the town when they ordered Colonel Johnson and Dr. James Grant to take about three hundred of the four hundred idle men from the Béxar garrison. The men were ordered to appear in Goliad and Refugio so they could prepare for the long-anticipated invasion of Matamoros. Consequently, the only troops left to garrison Béxar were a small contingent of about one hundred fresh volunteers whom Colonel Neill would command. Colonel Neill, however, was incensed over this vast reduction of personnel and its blatant blow to his reputation and ego. Incensed over this transgression, in a letter Neill wrote to the governing consul he said, "The clothing sent here by the aid and patriotic exertions of the honorable Consul, was taken from us by arbitrary measures of Johnson and Grant, taken from men who endured all the hardships of winter and who were not even sufficiently clad for summer, many of them having but one blanket and one shirt, and what was intended for them given away to men some of whom had not been in the army more than four days, and many not exceeding two weeks."[8] Considering it impossible to defend the city with so few men, he moved his volunteer soldiers into the Alamo, abandoning the city so many men had died for.

As you recall, the seeds for the invasion of Matamoros were planted when Captain Dimmitt, the commander at Goliad, suggested the move in a letter to Austin two months earlier following the Battle of Goliad.

Although Dimmitt failed to receive a reply to his recommendation to invade Matamoros, the idea gained much interest in the provisional government. It seems several members of the Council, led by Dr. James Grant, a wealthy Scotsman, were instrumental in trying to bring the invasion plans to fruition. There were several reasons the group wanted to invade Matamoros, but perhaps the one that drew their attention the most was the estimated six-figure income in fees the shipping business in the port was earning each month. This was money the Consultation wanted to collect for themselves to finance further programs to incite opposition to Santa Anna. Consequently, the governor of the provisional government, Henry Smith, approved the plan to attack Matamoros and asked their new military leader, General Houston, to command the army that had yet to be recruited. Old Rough and Ready, however, was lukewarm to the idea and in the end wanted no part in it. Still needing a commander for the expedition, after a failed attempt to draw in General Burleson, who had retired his command and gone home following the siege of Béxar, his successor, Colonel Johnson, agreed to lead the expedition. Meanwhile, on the side, James W. Fannin, Jr., newly promoted to colonel in the Regular Army and who fought with Jim Bowie at the Battle of Concepción, was now working for the provisional government, busy recruiting additional troops for the expedition.

Now that he had his troops at Colonel Neill's expense, Grant, along with two hundred of the volunteers, arrived at Goliad around January 10, 1836, to take the supplies stored there for his expedition. When he confronted Dimmitt, who had just arrived back from Béxar several weeks earlier, the situation began to get ugly. Grant, now calling himself the acting commander in Chief of the Federal Volunteer Army, ordered Captain Dimmitt to remove his bloody-arm independence flag from the atop the fort and attempted to commandeer all of the supplies, provisions, and ordnance still remaining at La Bahia. Outraged over the challenge to his authority, Dimmitt removed his flag, resigned his command, and stormed out with about 30 volunteers. From Goliad, Dimmitt and his followers headed to the Alamo to help reinforce Colonel Neill.

And that's when the Matamoros invasion plans began to unravel.

In January, General Houston arrived at the fort in a failed attempt to resolve the problem. Consequently, Grant and his men left Goliad to join up with Johnson and the rest of the men in Refugio. Houston, however, stayed on with Grant and the volunteers and with his unique power of persuasion attempted to convince the men to abandon the expedition. Not long afterward, with all the political infighting and mass confusion over who would command the expedition and who was in charge overall, it was decided to abort the attack on Matamoros completely. Now free from recruiting troops for the Matamoros expedition, in early February 1836 Colonel Fannin and four companies of the Georgia Battalion moved into the vacated La Bahia in Goliad, which he renamed Fort Defiance.

5

The Battle of the Alamo and the Goliad Massacre

By the end of October of 1835 the Texians had become an enormous irritant to Santa Anna. Once welcomed with open arms as citizens of the homeland, they were now considered outside agitators that had to be quickly dealt with.

Lounging at his hacienda, Santa Anna couldn't help but contemplate the fact that in October alone the Texians had challenged Lieutenant Castañeda in Gonzales, captured La Bahia in Goliad, forced the withdrawal of the garrisons from Capano and Refugio, and were now advancing their army to assault General Cos in Béxar. Santa Anna was also reminded that the Texians had made a total mockery of the Mexican law against slavery and about their arrogant insistence to remain autonomous, their obvious unwillingness to assimilate, and their total disrespect for the law prohibiting illegal conventions, not to mention Austin's treasonous intentions as spoken to the vice president. He also remembered how American filibusters had invaded Mexico to establish territorial claims and that Pres. Andrew Jackson had even offered to purchase Mexican land to further extend southern slavery.

Besides the total lack of respect for the Mexican culture, the growing population of Americans in Texas also weighed heavily on Santa Anna's mind. Even though Bustamante had imposed a restriction on immigration from the United States, thousands still poured across the border. It was an edict the administration found difficult to enforce and as a result it was something the Mexicans lost complete control of. By conservative estimates, in 1834 the number of Anglos living in the region was at least four times as great as that of the native Mexicans.

The Mexican president, extremely outraged over these developments, abruptly left the comforts of his hacienda in Veracruz and returned to Mexico City. After formally placing his vice president, Gen. Miguel Barragán, in charge of the executive department, Santa Anna was faced with the enormous task of piecing together an army he could depend upon to eject the Americans from Mexico once and for all. The remote northern provinces were once an area receiving scant attention; now it was about to receive the full wrath of the government's interest. Santa Anna's mind was made up. He was fed up with the Americans and was going to show these cocky and arrogant Texians who the real boss was.

On December 5, 1835, Santa Anna and Gen. Vicente Filisola arrived in San Luis Potosí to begin organizing an all-out advance northward toward Béxar and the nearby mission called the Alamo. Although Santa Anna had several loyal generals who could lead the army, he chose to lead the attack himself. It would provide an enormous and satisfying opportunity to not only drive the Americans out of Mexico but also demonstrate to the Mexican people that he was still the Savior of the Motherland. Coincidentally, this was also the very day Ben Milam and the Texian volunteers first stormed into the streets of Béxar to begin their assault on General Cos and his army.

By now the Mexican troops not only consisted of the die-hard regulars Santa Anna could count on but also many untrained, undisciplined, and untried recruits, reluctant draftees, prisoners "borrowed" to fight for the motherland, the homeless, and a smattering of Indians. Called the Army of Operations, it was underfunded, undersupplied, underclothed, undernourished, underarmed, and trained in accordance with the practices of old and obsolete Spanish tactical manuals.

Nevertheless, in a matter of some three weeks Santa Anna managed to recruit and dress as best he could an army of some six thousand men, both infantry and cavalry, with funds forced from the local governments, the churches, and wealthy families. Despite these drawbacks, as well as having little food and water, scant medical care, antiquated short-range Brown Bess muskets, and unreliable gunpowder, these were the troops Santa Anna was going to risk his reputation on. Conditions were so grim that even before they started the men were told their rations would be cut back to around six to eight ounces of either hardtack or toasted corn bread per day. Also, there was a shortage of feed for the mind-boggling twelve hundred mules the army had on hand to haul the wagons, and two hundred oxen that would pull the supply carts. But, to alleviate their shortages the commanders knew they could always count on the towns they passed through that would "donate" meat, corn, flour, feed, and whatever else the army was in short supply of. And to add to their difficulties Santa Anna had to contend with the women and children who were also present for the marches, evidently an old military custom that allowed the women to serve as cooks, nurses, and foragers. On one hand, the women may have helped when nurses were required to tend to the sick and wounded or to prepare the food. But, on the other hand, they were an understandable distraction the commanders could do little about.

In the course of their stay at San Luis Potosí, Santa Anna called his staff together at his headquarters, where he discussed the troop movements for the upcoming expedition. Santa Anna informed the officers that he intended to divide the army into three divisions.

The first division, led by Gen. Joaquín Ramírez y Sesma, who was in Saltillo with his fifteen hundred troops, cavalry, and artillery, had been ordered to depart on December 7. Sesma's destination was Laredo, about 185 miles to the north. Meanwhile, General Cos, presently at Monclova, would rendezvous with Sesma at Laredo. From there the combined forces would continue on for another 150 miles to Béxar.

Once the remaining troops under Santa Anna and Filisola reached Saltillo from San Luis Potosí, Santa Anna would dispatch the second division under General Filisola.

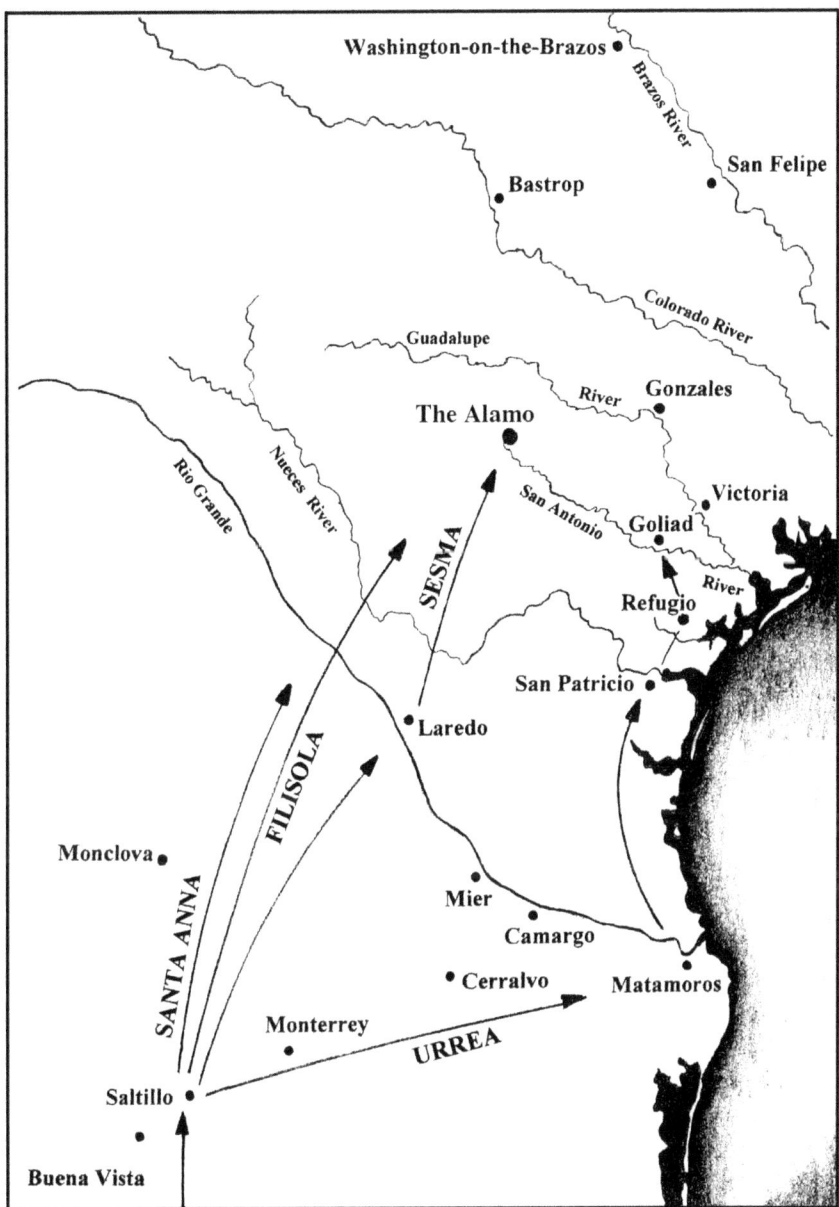

Santa Anna's Drive Into Texas

Being of higher rank, when Filisola arrived in Béxar he was to take overall command of the Mexican forces until Santa Anna personally arrived with the third division, currently around thirty-five hundred men.

Filisola was quite popular in eastern Texas, being an empressario with a contract to settle six hundred Tejano families. And prior to his becoming Santa Anna's second in command, Filisola was the commandant of the Eastern Internal Provinces.

The Army of Operations broke camp and headed northward in late December totally unprepared to face the challenges looming ahead. After reaching Saltillo on January 6, the army rested for around three weeks. During this time most of the men were able to receive some training, General Filisola headed northward toward the Rio Grande, and it gave Santa Anna enough time to recover from an illness. To compound Santa Anna's desperate condition, he learned Fort Lipantitlán had fallen and that General Cos had surrendered Béxar in December, losses that, quite understandably, only added to his growing despair. Although his supply route from the Gulf to the Mexican interior appeared to be lost, at the same time this dire predicament encouraged Santa Anna to strike back at the Texians with even more fervor. His bitterness was motivated not only because he had intended to establish Béxar as his base of operations but also as a matter of personal pride. He now had to avenge the attack on Cos's army and to restore the family honor.

Reeling from their embarrassing thrashing at Béxar and the total loss of their all-important supply route from the Gulf, the authorities in Mexico City could only vent their frustrations by belittling the Texian volunteers as uncivilized backwoodsmen and hunters with no discipline or experience in the art of war.

Adding to the Mexicans' frustration was the belief that hundreds of American adventurers and insalubrious riffraff were continuing to cross the border into Mexico. They were coming to replace the Texians who had left the army thinking the war was over. In fact, Santa Anna was still convinced that the American government was playing a major role in this effort in order to take over the northern territory of Mexico.

Therefore, in an attempt to deter the United States from entering the conflict, at the direction of Santa Anna, Minister of War José María Tornel introduced a unique and ominous circular on December 30, 1835, that warned foreigners, meaning Americans, who were carrying weapons or captured bearing arms against Mexico would be treated as pirates. The phrase "treated as pirates" in this edict was used to point out that all foreign captives would be immediately put to death, as Mexican law allowed for captured pirates.

After Santa Anna agreed with the contents of Minister Tornel's dire warning, its articles would be indelibly embedded in his psyche. So much so that in the months ahead he would proudly display a bright red flag at his battles to let the Americans know they were now considered to be foreigners and would thereby suffer the consequences if captured. In this way Santa Anna intended to shamelessly use these laws as a legal way to deal with the Americans he so despised.

The loss of Capano, La Bahia, and Béxar was a devastating blow to Santa Anna's war effort and a loss he was determined to reverse. While his army advanced to Béxar, to complete the effort to reestablish his supply line he knew he had to win back Capano and La Bahia as well. Consequently, Gen. José Urrea was assigned to lead a detachment of around six hundred men from Saltillo to Matamoros, on the Rio Grande. Urrea would then march along the east coast of the Gulf, passing through such towns as San Patricio, Refugio, and Capano before carrying out his ultimate assignment, the attack and capture of the fort at Goliad.

Once the Army of Operations was ready to travel, at the end of January their march resumed.

Marching to the Rio Grande was not an easy journey for the soldiers, wives, children, or even the animals. It soon became quite evident that the Mexican army's march to Béxar was in itself a disaster. Not accustomed to hours upon hours of arduous marching, the exhausted recruits insisted on moving at their own slow pace. If that weren't bad enough, when the army left San Luis Potosí the men had their rations reduced even more, since a lack of hired teamsters forced the army to leave with only a portion of their supplies. And worst of all, hundreds suffered and many died from dysentery, the result of drinking stagnant water, a horrible situation exacerbated by the absence of doctors who could provide just the basics of medical treatment.

Also adding to their misery was the terrible weather. By the time the second division and Santa Anna's main body reached the Rio Grande in the middle of February of 1836, hypothermia began to take its toll from the men's having to march, eat and sleep outdoors in the freezing temperatures and nearly two feet of snow. In fact, the winter of 1835–36 was the worst anyone had experienced in this part of the country. Confronted with blizzard conditions, the army came to an abrupt halt. And with hardly any decent shelter, they all suffered tremendously. Many died, especially the Indians from the Yucatán, who were not accustomed to the cold temperatures.

When the weather ceased to be a problem, it was the Indians. Raids by the Comanche and the Apache for food and supplies became serious enough to warrant a detachment of Mexican troops to maintain constant surveillance of the surrounding region. Finally, as hunger began to dictate the behavior of the troops, foraging expeditions became routine. Private homes and farms were great sources of food supplies and draft animals. Soldiers stopped often to steal coffee, grain, corn, flour, et cetera, as well as cattle, hogs, horses and mules.

Despite the suffering from the harsh winter weather, the marching across the desert region in the searing heat, the Indian attacks, the lack of food and freshwater, the sicknesses, the four hundred deaths, and all the other hardships, the march continued northward. For this reason the elitist Mexican officials believed that despite the stylishly dressed Mexican soldier's suffering extreme hardships and limitations, their tenacity, fortitude, and superiority would make the inexperienced, unrefined, buckskinned, and apathetic American backwoodsmen no match for them.

While Santa Anna's forces gradually made their way toward Béxar, several of the Texians thought it prudent under the circumstances to withdraw from the Alamo. Although evacuating the mission was in hindsight the wisest thing to do at the time, not everyone agreed, especially Col. James C. Neill, who was still in charge of the one hundred or so Texians garrisoned there. Instead, living up to the existing expectations of a brave and patriotic officer, Neill decided that his troops would remain in place to defend the old mission. Neill and his men saw the Alamo as the key to the defense of Texas and wanted to make their stand not only to defend the Alamo but also to defend the sanctity of their honor. Although he succeeded in maintaining the nineteenth century image of a brave patriot, Neill was not stupid. He recognized that if he was going to be successful he needed more men and more arms. Therefore, he immediately sent a request for reinforcements and provisions to Gen. Sam Houston, who at the time was at Goliad trying to resolve the problems Captain Dimmitt was having with Dr. James Grant, specifically over Grant's insistence that he take all the supplies stored there for his Matamoros campaign.

General Houston, however, had other ideas. He did not consider Neill's manpower sufficient to hold the Alamo and could not spare the number of men the colonel would need to hold it. Consequently, Houston ordered Bowie, who was also in Goliad at the time with Dr. Grant, to take 30 men with him to the Alamo, remove all the artillery and then blow the place up. These were orders Bowie refused to carry out. Instead, on January 19, 1836, when Bowie arrived at the Alamo with the 30 men, Neill and Bowie discussed Houston's order and decided the Alamo was much too important to destroy. Furthermore, when Bowie saw how impressively Neill and the others had modified the Alamo into resembling a well-fortified fort, he pitched in to help mount the remaining cannons atop the Alamo walls. (Actually, Mexican colonel Ugartechea's men did much of the fortification effort.)

Also arriving at the mission around this time was David "Davy" Crockett and about a dozen friends of his from Tennessee. Crockett was quite popular in those days, having gained a glowing reputation as a frontiersman, Indian fighter, explorer, humorist, and bear hunter extraordinaire. Somewhat puzzled over his fame, he once wrote in the narrative of his life, "Obscure as I am my name is making a considerable deal of fuss in the world. I can't tell why it is, nor in what it is to end. Go where I will everybody seems anxious to get a peep at me."[1] Taking advantage of his notoriety, he was elected to the U.S. House of Representatives as a Tennessee congressman in 1827 and 1833. Despite his celebrity status, he failed to secure his bid for another term. Crockett then traveled to Texas and enlisted for a six-month stint in the Texas fight for independence. And since uniforms did not exist for the volunteers, they appeared at the Alamo like all volunteers did, in street attire, which in his case consisted of a so-called hunting suit and coonskin cap. Adding to their frontier image were the long rifles each carried and Bowie knives sheathed on their belts. Also arriving that month was Capt. Philip Dimmitt with about 30 men, having come from La Bahia in Goliad after he resigned his command over the problems with Dr. James Grant.

Within days of their decision to defend the Alamo, Colonel Neill was notified that his family was extremely ill and he had to leave to tend to their needs. In his place, the men elected a redheaded colonel named William B. Travis, Neill's 26-year-old second in command, and Jim Bowie as co-commander. Colonel Travis, being in the Regular Army, would command the army soldiers while Bowie, a civilian, would lead the volunteers. For Travis, having to defend the Alamo was a bittersweet proposition. Although he was eager to perform his patriotic duty, at the same time he considered the Alamo doomed if he wasn't reinforced. For Bowie, it was an honor just to be associated with Neill, a man he greatly admired.

The old mission was originally called the Mission of San Antonio de Valero. Over the years it became known as the Alamo, the name a group of Spanish soldiers gave it as a tribute to their hometown of Alamo de Parras, Coahuila. The Alamo was actually a home for missionaries and converts. Located on the outskirts of Béxar, before it was modified into a fort with artillery batteries the mission consisted of a plaza that covered three acres, a chapel, a sacristy, a baptistery, and a convent. There were also sleeping quarters, a kitchen, an area used as a stockade for cattle and horses, two aqueducts providing water, and various other small buildings. The entire property was surrounded by a massive adobe wall nearly 3 feet thick and from 9 to 12 feet high. As for offensive firing power, the Texians were armed with 19 mounted pieces of artillery, most strung along the rooftops around the perimeter of the compound, a supply of cannonballs and small arms, and a wooden catwalk built so the men could fire from the top of the wall. Nevertheless, as impregnable as it appeared, the designers never intended it to withstand an assault such as Santa Anna would soon inflict. It was intended to stop the arrows of hostile Indians who were not fortunate enough to possess 18-pounders in their arsenal.

However, what really mattered was the things they lacked the most, such as an ample supply of ammunition, weapons, food, and, most important, manpower.

In the final analysis the fight at the Alamo was an epic battle in the history of Texas and an epic disaster just waiting to happen.

In early February of 1836, two weeks before Neill left the Alamo, Bowie penned a letter to the Texas governor. In the letter Bowie explained the circumstances that were motivating him and the others to stand up to the power of Santa Anna and the reason he did not follow Houston's instructions to destroy the fort. "The salvation of Texas depends in great measure on keeping Béxar out of the hands of the enemy. It serves as the frontier piquet guard, and if it were in the possession of Santa Anna, there is no stronghold from which to repel him in his march toward the Sabine. Colonel Neill and myself have come to the solemn resolution that we will rather die in these ditches than give it up to the enemy."[2]

On February 23, the Mexicans were sighted off in the distance by the lookout positioned in the bell tower of the San Fernando church. The first troops to appear were the cavalry belonging to General Sesma. They could be seen approaching from about two miles away with their bloodred flag fluttering in the cool morning breeze, an indication that no prisoners would be taken alive. To make that point even clearer, in a matter of a few weeks Santa Anna had this same flag positioned atop the dome of the church to ensure the Texians received the ominous notice.

To locate the exact position of the main army, during the afternoon of Sesma's arrival Travis ordered Captain Dimmitt and Lt. Ben Nobel to scout the surrounding area for any sign of Santa Anna's forces. That night, recognizing the ill-fated predicament his men were in, with a sense of urgency Travis writes to the alcalde in Gonzales, "The enemy in large force is in sight. We want men and provisions. Send them to us. We have 150 men and are determined to defend the garrison to the last. Give us assistance."[3]

The following day when Dimmitt tried to return to the Alamo with his scouting report, he was shocked to find his approach blocked by a number of Mexican troops as they prepared to place the Alamo under siege. Dimmitt wisely left the area and traveled to Victoria.

During all this time, inside the Alamo Bowie came down with pleura-pneumonia that forced him to spend his remaining days bedridden in the officers quarters now used as an improvised hospital. It was now up to Colonel Travis alone to plea for the help they so desperately needed and to direct the defense of their untenable position.

In the Alamo, the men silently lined the top of the walls watching intently as Santa Anna rode into Béxar, less than a mile away. Sitting proudly upright on his mount, the general had regained the prize he so desperately wanted without firing a shot.

As some fifteen hundred Mexican troops settled in after their long march, Santa Anna dispatched an emissary to offer a deal to Travis. From the kindness of the Mexican people Santa Anna offered to spare anyone who surrendered and accepted the terms of a parole. To his great displeasure, however, Colonel Travis responded to the inquiry with a cannonball that smashed into their camp. It was, as Santa Anna later remarked, a decision that sealed their fate. A short time later between five and six hundred Mexican reinforcements began to arrive and the siege was on.

Voicing his distress in another letter he wrote the following day, Travis pleaded:

> I am besieged by a thousand or more of the Mexicans under Santa Anna. I have sustained a continual Bombardment and cannonade for 24 hours and have not lost a man. The enemy has demanded surrender at discretion; otherwise the garrison is to be put to the sword if the fort is taken. I have answered the demand with a canon shot, and our flag still waves proudly from the walls. I shall never surrender or retreat. Then, I call on you in the name of Liberty, of patriotism, and everything dear to the American character, to come to our aid with all dispatch. The enemy is receiving reinforcements daily and will no doubt increase to three or four thousand in four or five days. If this call is neglected, I am determined to sustain myself as long as possible and die like a soldier who never forgets what is due to his own honor & that of his country. Victory or Death.[4]

Over the next several days the Mexican troops brought up their howitzers and light artillery and during the night fired well over one hundred rounds into the Alamo walls and plaza only to have many of the same cannonballs fired back by the Texians. Undeterred, each night Santa Anna's artillery was moved closer and closer to the Alamo.

Becoming more and more concerned over the desperate situation he was in, Travis sent out couriers to solicit reinforcements. Col. James B. Bonham, one of the two messengers, broke through the Mexican lines to reach Fort Defiance in nearby Goliad, approximately 85 miles away. Responding to the plea for help, on February 26, 1836, Col. James W. Fannin, Jr., the 32-year-old commander at the fort, marched his men away from Fort Defiance to reinforce the besieged mission but, due to a number of problems of his own, was forced to return to the fort.

Except for 32 members of the Gonzales Company of Mounted Volunteers who came to help, the Travis pleas fell mostly on deaf ears. Not even the men living in Béxar came out to help as Travis expected they would. Growing increasingly frustrated that no one was coming to their assistance, on March 3 he dispatched one final statement that illustrated the depth of his commitment to their cause. "The power of Santa Anna is to be met here," he said, "or in the colonies; we had better meet them here than to suffer a war of devastation to rage in our settlements. A blood red banner waves from the church of Béjar and in the camp above us, in token that the war is one of vengeance against rebels: they have declared us as such, and demanded that we should surrender at discretion, or that this garrison should be put to the sword."

"Their threats," Travis continued, "have had no influence on me, or my men, but to make all fight with desperation, and that high souled courage which characterizes the patriot, who is willing to die in defense of his country's liberty and his own honor."[5]

Meanwhile, as the siege of the Alamo was playing out, on March 1 a delegation of 41 men who represented most of the settlements in Texas at the time met in Washington-on-the-Brazos for the Convention of 1836. This was an enormous moment for the delegation. Besides being the third such meeting, having first assembled in October of 1832 and then in April of the following year, this meeting had as its purpose to settle once and for all the real purpose of their fight. During the past conventions, and especially the meetings held by the Consultation, the delegates were generally indecisive in voicing their true convictions. There was always the lingering question of whether the fight against the Mexican regime was to uphold the Constitution of 1824 or for the Texians' independence from the state of Coahuila. But this delegation was different. The delegates at this convention were younger and many had fought in at least one of the battles of the Texas Revolution. And so this time the die was cast—they would do neither. Instead, they were prepared to declare their independence from Mexico herself.

A committee of five took one day to submit its draft of the declaration of Independence. It was immediately approved by the signatories proclaiming that Mexico "ceased to protect the lives, liberty, and property of the people, from whom its legitimate powers are derived" and concluded that "the people of Texas ... do hereby resolve and declare, that our political connections with the Mexican nation has forever ended, and that the people of Texas do constitute a free, Sovereign, and independent republic."

Following the writing of the declaration of independence, the Texas Constitution was prepared with wording that in most cases resembled that of the U.S. Constitution, with the exception of the treatment of Africans. Under the Texas Constitution, free blacks were forbidden from entering Texas and citizenship could not be granted to any African, their descendants, or Indians. In addition, any future Texas Congress was prohibited from emancipating slaves and slave owners could not emancipate a slave without the consent of the Texas Congress. Following the approval of the constitution, a vote was taken to elect the interim government leaders. Evidently, although he was only a visitor at the convention and not a delegate, David G. Burnet's persuasive opinions influenced enough of the delegates to elect him as the president. He was selected from a list of such notable candidates as empresario Stephen F. Austin, Sam Houston, and William H. Wharton, a delegate representing Victoria. Among the other appointees selected that day was Sam Houston, who was reaffirmed as commander of the Texas military forces. Before the meeting was adjourned for the day, however, Burnet told the delegates that he was transferring the capital from Washington-on-the-Brazos to Harrisburg, a town near Galveston Island. The capital's being closer to the U.S. border, Burnet reasoned, would make it much easier to communicate with American authorities. In reality, it was also farther away from Santa Anna's army.

During the sixth day of their deliberations the convention received a letter from Colonel Travis dated March 3 that described the dire conditions at the Alamo and asked for supplies and reinforcements. Responding to the colonel's plight, General Houston promptly called for more volunteers and militias to rendezvous with him in Gonzales. His intent was to organize a new army there and reinforce the Texians in the Alamo at this most critical time. Before the day was over, Houston left the convention for Gonzales.

Unknown to Houston was the fact that 32 members from the Gonzales Company of Mounted Volunteers had been patiently waiting for his orders for them to march to the Alamo, which, regrettably, Santa Anna attacked that very day.

Following a 12-day siege, at 5:30 on the chilly morning of March 6, 1836, Santa Anna's army commenced their attack on the Alamo. With a perimeter of over a quarter of a mile, Santa Anna knew the small number of Texians inside could never defend such a large area. The men defending the fort would have certainly agreed. Each man knew full well by this time that once the Mexicans gained access to the grounds they were all doomed, as Santa Anna's no-quarter declaration promised. Nevertheless, even though they still had a fighting chance to shoot their way out and escape if they moved quickly, when asked by Travis to choose they accepted their ultimate fate by choosing to stay and fight to the death. Without the slightest hesitation and with a rousing cheer they all agreed to stay and die together.

Santa Anna, the master strategist, organized his attacking forces into four columns. Each column was ordered to scale a wall, gain access to the numerous buildings, and mercilessly attack the Texians defenders. On hand was General Cos, whose army had joined that of General Sesma in Laredo and who was back to redeem himself. Leading the other three columns were Cols. Francisco Duqué, José María Romero, and Juan Morales.

The initial attack was to silently reach the dozing sentinels and with either bayonets or knives eliminate any chance of being detected by the sleeping defenders. At that point, Cos's responsibility was to lead the first column of three hundred men. With ladders for scaling the wall, once inside the mission they would use axes and crowbars to break down the doors of the various buildings. Meanwhile, the cavalry was strategically positioned on the perimeter to prevent the Texians from escaping.

Aroused from his sleep by an inadvertent shout from the approaching Mexicans outside the walls, Colonel Travis quickly sprang into action. Seizing his weapon in one sweeping motion, he shouted to his men that the enemy had arrived and to be prepared to give them hell.

As they tried to maneuver and climb their scaling ladders, each of the attacking columns was massed in large groups at the base of their respective walls. They provided easy targets for the Texian artillerists firing their cannons now loaded with assorted scrap metal. With the cannons acting as giant shotguns, the blast tore through the crowd of soldiers like a huge sieve, sending blood and body parts scattered on the ground below. This was followed up by firing nine-pound lead cannonballs into the groups of Mexicans trying desperately to breach the walls.

As the fighting continued, Travis quickly realized that despite having 19 guns mounted, it was impossible to utilize all of them with the small number of men available. Also, the riflemen on the homemade wooden catwalk discovered they had to expose themselves from the waist up in order to fire their weapons over the wall, a factor that severely limited this form of defensive capability.

Although it took three attempts, when the walls were finally breached the Texians were overwhelmed as the Mexicans swarmed across the mission's grounds. As the Mexicans fanned out from all four sides, most of the Texian artillery was quickly taken over and used to blast down the walls and doors of the nearest rooms. As the soldiers stormed into the buildings they were instantly cut down by Texians inside, but with no time to reload after firing their first shots most of the men were bayoneted where they stood. The scene turned into a cacophony of terrifying sounds as the continuous reports of small-arms fire and booms of cannon blasts intermingled with the sickening sounds of screams, moans, and shouting. This terrifying and bloody butchering continued from one building to another for nearly two hours.

A Mexican soldier who had survived the battle described the scene some time later:

> The Texans fought like tigers. The proportion was one to thirty, yet no quarter was asked and each sold his life as dearly as possible. The last moments of the conflict were terrible. The darkness of the rooms, the smoke of the battle and the shrieks of the wounded and dying all added to the terror of the scene. Unable to distinguish friend from foe, the Mexicans actually brained each other in their mad fury. After the battle was over and all were dead, the scene beggared description. The floor of the main building was nearly shoe deep in blood, and weltering there were hundreds of dead men, many still clenched together with one hand while the other hand held the sword, pistol, or knife which told how they had died in that last terrible struggle.[6]

When it was over nearly all of the defenders were killed and the few who did survive were immediately lined up and executed. In fact, it was reported that Mexican soldiers examined each of the bodies one by one and bayoneted those that still moved. Santa Anna's no-quarter rule was successfully carried out.

Following the battle the bodies were collected, stacked, and burned, William Travis, Jim Bowie and Davy Crockett among them. The only survivors were two women, one child, and a slave who had belonged to Colonel Travis. In his diary for the date of May 25, 1836, Dr. J. H. Bernard wrote "that we went to visit the ashes of those brave defenders of our country, a hundred rods from the fort or church to where they were burnt. The bodies had been reduced to cinders; occasionally a bone of a leg or arm almost entire. Peace to your ashes!"[7]

On February 25, 1837, a memorial service was held to honor the fallen heroes. The ashes from two small piles were collected and placed in a black-draped coffin. On the underside of the lid the names of Travis, Crockett, and Bowie were engraved. The coffin was then brought to a church in San Antonio for blessings, followed by a solemn procession back to the spot where the ashes were collected for burial.

Many years later, Santa Anna explained why the men in the Alamo had to be killed. He blamed the matter entirely on Travis for insulting Santa Anna on receiving his offer to allow the Texians to surrender and adamantly refusing to capitulate. Under that scenario, Santa Anna had no alternative but to attack the fort and to give the enemy no quarter, as the red flag indicated.

Santa Anna remained in Béxar until the rest of the army arrived, namely, Gen. Antonio Gaona, who finally appeared on March 8. At the end of March, once the various commands were dispatched to other locations, Gen. Juan José Andrade was left in command. At that point, on March 29, Santa Anna left for Gonzales to begin his pursuit of General Houston. General Andrade remained in the Alamo until May 24, 1836. Before leaving, however, he made sure the Alamo was "completely dismantled, all the single walls were leveled, the fosse (moat) filled up, and the pickets torn up and burnt. All the artillery and ammunition that could be carried off has been thrown in the river."[8]

The Goliad Massacre

Contemplating the current state of affairs, Santa Anna was pleased that the war was progressing so nicely. He also felt fortunate that the Texian leaders had blundered by dividing their forces into small groups and then scattering them to various locations. But he also knew this thing was far from being over. After all, he pondered, there were still two pockets of rebels who had yet to be dealt with. For one, General Houston was still active in Gonzales raising troops for a new army. In that regard, there was little doubt in El Presidente's mind that he had to deal with Houston himself. And the only other organized fighters left of any real threat were the 450 or so volunteer soldiers commanded by Col. James W. Fannin, Jr., at Goliad whom General Urrea would soon be confronting.

General Urrea, as you recall, was dispatched by Santa Anna to Matamoros back in January to operate northward along the Gulf Coast before heading to Goliad. Since then, on February 27 Urrea's forces had discovered Col. Frank Johnson and 34 men from Colonel Fannin's command at San Patricio collecting wild horses for the Matamoros campaign. In that battle, a number of Texians were either killed or taken prisoner, but Johnson was one of the lucky ones to escape. Several days later, on March 2, Urrea's forces came upon more of Fannin's men also rounding up wild horses at Aqua Dulce Creek, just south of San Patricio. Urrea easily won that battle as well, with Grant being one of the Texians killed. Then Urrea went on to win the Battle of Refugio about two weeks later. It was a one-sided affair with over fourteen hundred Mexican troops having an easy time of it against about 150 Americans. With three wins under his belt, General Urrea was now approaching Goliad to make it four.

While General Urrea was taking care of business just south of Goliad, on February 26, 1836, Colonel Fannin departed Fort Defiance with about three hundred troops, artillery, a number of wagons, and oxen teams. He was heading to the Alamo in response to an urgent message delivered by an emissary from Travis that called for reinforcements to help him fight the overwhelming forces of Santa Anna. However, a short distance from Goliad some of the wagons broke down, which forced the men to stop for repairs. Later that day, as the waning light interrupted their journey, they unhitched the oxen teams and set up camp in a driving rain. The next morning they discovered a number of oxen had wandered off and that the men had neglected to bring along food, rations they would need to sustain themselves on the move to the Alamo. It took most of the day to round up the oxen and by then the decision was made to abort the mission and return to the fort. No sooner had they arrived, on March 1, than the emissary under orders from Travis returned but this time failed to persuade Fannin to make another attempt at reinforcing the Alamo. However, ten days later Fannin received word from General Houston that General Urrea was quickly approaching Goliad on a mission to attack his forces. As a result, he was ordered to abandon Fort Defiance immediately and to march his troops to Victoria.

Despite this order, Colonel Fannin decided to wait until he received information on approximately 150 troops he had dispatched earlier to collect horses and to help defend the folks in Refugio against the Urrea forces. In addition, Fannin insisted on waiting for the much-needed wagons and yokes of oxen he was expecting to replace those that had broken down earlier. By the time he learned his troops would not be returning anytime soon, the wagons and oxen had arrived and more time was taken up loading and hitching up the wagons. Finally, on the morning of March 19, 1836, Fannin's troops marched out of the fort once again and began a leisurely move across the open prairie with their artillery, wagons, and oxen trailing behind. At one point they incurred another delay when Fannin was told the animals had not been fed. Consequently he ordered the movement stopped to allow the animals to graze on a patch of fresh green grass. Once they were fed, more time was taken up hitching the oxen teams before the men could resume their trek, all the time hoping to get to the Coleto River before nightfall.

That very afternoon, as the procession approached the Coleto River, Fannin was surprised that General Urrea's troops not only had arrived but also had them completely surrounded. Astonished by the speed and cunning of the enemy troops, Fannin ordered his men into a defensive hollow square formation. The Mexicans made three attempts to penetrate the defensive works and were repulsed each time in what became known as the Battle of Coleto. The next day, however, after General Urrea began receiving reinforcements of men and artillery, Fannin drafted the terms he hoped to get for their surrender, which included being held as prisoners of war with their eventual parole upon their promise not to bear arms against the Mexican government. Obviously General Urrea could not accept these terms, but instead he told the colonel that he would forward his proposed terms to Santa Anna for review.

With that said, over the span of two days all the captured Texians were taken back to Fort Defiance and incarcerated. During this time General Urrea had gone to Victoria and while he was there he wrote a letter to Santa Anna asking that the prisoners be spared. This was not something unusual for the general to do. In fact, when he captured Texians at San Patricio and Agua Dulce Creek he sent them to Matamoros rather than carry out Santa Anna's no-quarter order. This time, however, Santa Anna became extremely furious when he learned that the "foreigners" were not killed on the spot. Also annoying was that Santa Anna was forced to remind his commanders of the no-quarter policy that classified all foreigners fighting against Mexico as pirates and under this new law it was forbidden to take pirates as prisoners of war. Therefore, to be in compliance with this new law Santa Anna ordered the prisoners at Goliad killed immediately.

Consequently, on the damp and foggy morning of March 27 the roughly three hundred Texians were marched out of the fort in three columns of one hundred flanked by a column of Spanish soldiers on each side of them. When all was ready they marched out in three different directions. At a prearranged and desolate spot outside the fort, the Spanish soldiers on one side of the prisoners joined the column on the other side. The bewildered prisoners were then told to sit on the ground with their backs facing the Mexican guards. Upon a given signal, the men were shot at close range. Those who were only wounded and still alive or were trying to escape were either shot, bayoneted, or clubbed to death. The sick and the wounded men who could not walk at all were either executed inside the chapel where they lay or dragged outside and shot. The few who could walk were executed just outside the door of the chapel.

As for Colonel Fannin, he was saved for last. From the goodness of his heart the squad commander allowed Fannin to make three requests before the firing squad did its duty. Fannin asked that his personal belongings be delivered to his family, that he not be shot in the face, and that he be given a Christian burial, each agreed to by his executioner. When Fannin was tied to a chair in the courtyard of the fort, the soldiers shot him in the face, kept his personal belongings, and burned his body with the bodies of the rest of his men.

From the studies done on various records since, the most reliable figures indicated that 342 men were executed, 28 managed to escape, and 20 were spared because of their valued professions. The bodies of those killed were stripped of their clothing, burned and left for the animals to feed on for three months before the ashes were buried with military honors by Gen. Thomas J. Rusk, who was passing through Goliad and found the remains.

When urged by empresario Stephen F. Austin to get involved militarily, President Jackson responded, "Our neutrality must be faithfully maintained."[9] For the Texian volunteer army, however, their attitude was somewhat different. To avenge the carnage perpetrated at Goliad, the Texians would soon get their revenge.

6

The Battle of San Jacinto and the Pastry War

With the funeral pyre at the Alamo still smoldering, Santa Anna was quite pleased that he was finally able to set up his headquarters in San Antonio de Béxar and that his supply line was back in business. Although he had won back his prized city, the victory had been achieved at an extremely high price in Mexican lives, a loss of many veteran troops that disturbed him very deeply. With the Texian volunteers at the Alamo defeated, as well as those at Goliad, Santa Anna now felt the momentum was turning in his favor. To complete his mission, he set his sights on stamping out any further residual Texian opposition to his centralist agenda. And that meant Gen. Sam Houston and his gang of undisciplined adventurers.

As you recall, in March, during the Convention of 1836, General Houston learned of the dire conditions at the Alamo. Evidently touched by the plight of Colonel Travis, Houston put out a call for more volunteers to assemble in Gonzales, the staging area for the new Provisional Army of Texas. He then excused himself from the meeting to take command of the army and to assist Travis in the Alamo.

Colonel Neill, who had left the Alamo to assist his family shortly before Santa Anna's attack, was already in Gonzales, as was Colonel Burleson. Both men and their companies were in Gonzales waiting for the general to arrive. In addition, a number of young volunteers had straggled into the town as well. Unable to control their excitement, they were highly energized and eager to fill in the ranks with the more seasoned soldiers. Unfortunately, when Houston arrived on March 11, 1836, he was informed by two Mexicans that the Alamo had already fallen. Then two days later it was confirmed by two Alamo survivors, Susanna Dickinson and Colonel Travis's slave Joe, that the Alamo was captured by Santa Anna and all were killed, including the 32 Gonzales volunteers who were now listed among the dead.

Human nature being what it is, some time later folks who saw Houston during his trip to Gonzales began to talk. They wondered about his lack of urgency at the time and why it took him five days for a journey that should have taken only two. "Genl. Houston shew'd no disposition of being in a hurry to the Army,"[1] recalled one man

Houston had met. Another man said Houston "swore that he believed it to be a damn lie, & that all those reports from Travis and Fannin were lies, for there were no Mexican forces there and that he believed that it was only electioneering schemes on [the part of] Travis & Fannin to sustain their own popularity."[2] In response to all the criticism he received, Houston never made a statement in his own defense.

Soon the unsettling news of the Alamo slaughter caused many of the recruits to abandon Houston so they could rejoin their families, who were terrified and fleeing from the divisions of Santa Anna's advancing army. As this ominous news spread throughout the town, Houston began to witness anxious Gonzales citizens packing up whatever they could carry. And when he heard the same stories from fleeing families passing through Gonzales he thought it prudent to retreat as well.

In what was called the "runaway scrape," Gonzales was only one of many locations in eastern Mexico where entire populations, fearful and panic-stricken over the steady advance of Santa Anna's three divisions, engaged in a mass exodus to relative safety. In fact, at the Convention of 1836 it was this panic that forced President Burnet to relocate the provisional capital from Washington-on-the-Brazos to the more distant town of Harrisburg.

After most of the inhabitants had fled the town, on March 13 General Houston ordered his rear guard to burn Gonzales to the ground so nothing remained that could benefit the Mexican army. He then ordered his troops to retreat as well.

Before leaving Gonzales Houston sent a message to Captain Dimmitt, who was in Victoria at the time, to rendezvous with his new army in Gonzales. Dimmitt, as you recall, went to Victoria when the presence of Mexican soldiers prevented him from returning to the Alamo following a scouting expedition. Receiving the message on March 12, Dimmitt and about a dozen men arrived at Gonzales, but it was too late; Houston had already left. At this point, Dimmitt returned to Victoria in time to flee in the so-called runaway scrape as General Urrea was about to enter the town. Dimmitt finally regrouped with Houston on April 22 but again arrived too late and was unable to participate in the Battle of San Jacinto.

Incredulous over the general's decision to evacuate Gonzales, the young recruits urged Houston to stay and confront the enemy as any army was expected to do. Although the commander listened to their pleas and understood their frustration, he thought he knew best. Accordingly, without explanation Houston renewed his order to retreat eastward from Gonzales to the Colorado River.

Although his young recruits may not have thought so, Sam Houston was arguably the right man at the right time. When he was a mere 16-year-old he ran away from home and lived with the Cherokee Indians in Tennessee, and while serving in the War of 1812 he became a close friend of Andrew Jackson. After the war Houston tried his hand in politics, winning a seat in the House of Representatives, and was elected governor of Tennessee when he was 34. Following the breakup of his marriage he resigned from politics and returned to the Cherokees in Arkansas and Oklahoma. During that time he was adopted as a Cherokee citizen, and in 1832 Houston traveled to Washington, where he represented the Cherokee Nation during Jackson's Indian relocation discussions. Soon afterward Houston moved to Texas, and at the meeting of the Consultation in November 1835 he received his military commission to lead the provisional army, which was reconfirmed at the Convention of 1836.

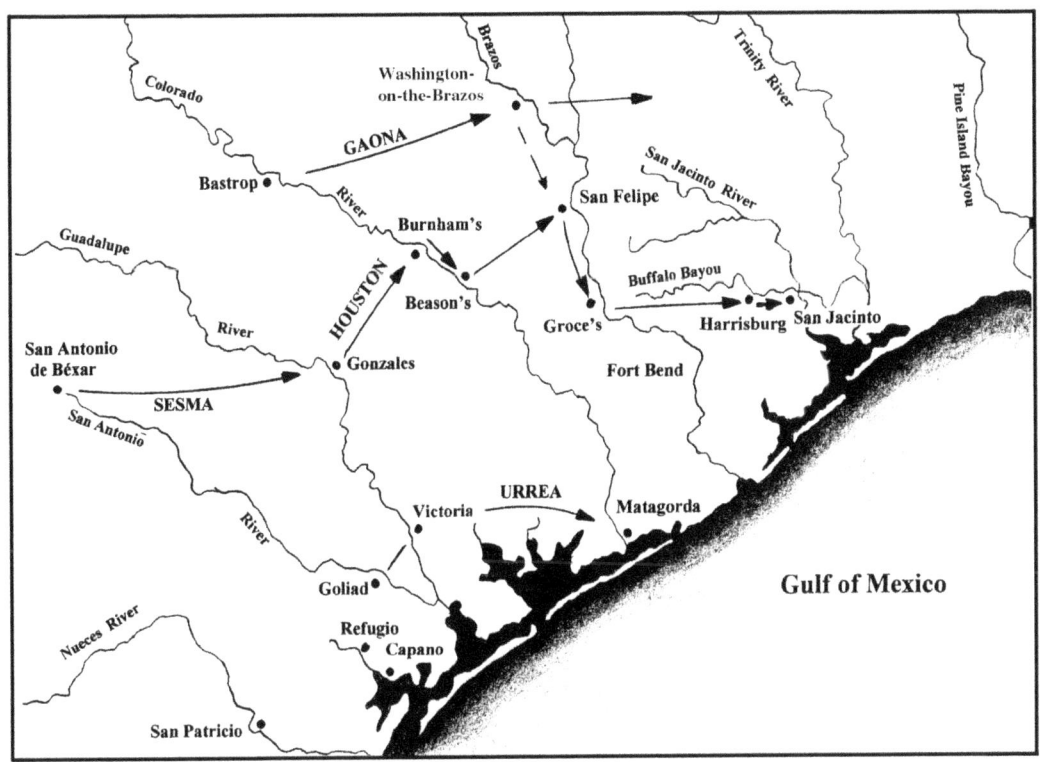

The Drive to San Jacinto

On March 17, General Houston's army crossed the Colorado at a place called Burnham's Crossing, a ferry service established about 1824 by Jesse Burnham near present-day Weimar, Texas. Suspecting that the Mexican army was close behind, Houston destroyed the ferry to prevent its use by Santa Anna's army and moved about 20 miles farther downriver to a settlement called Beason's Crossing, arriving two days later. Named after Benjamin Beason, one of Stephen F. Austin's original colonists, the settlement consisted of his home, gristmill, sawmill, gin, and ferry operation. On this site, Houston's nearly four hundred men settled in for the duration, many still grumbling over Houston's retreat from Gonzales and now his refusal to fight the enemy at Burnham's. During this short hiatus the spring rains came in with all their misery and soaking glory. But despite the mud and the dismal state of morale, there was a bright side. With the Colorado now overflowing its banks, the Mexican forces would be stymied in their efforts to follow. They would be effectively held prisoner on the southern side of the river for some time. Now feeling quite secure, soon Houston's army would more than double in its size, which also provided a boost in his confidence that in due time his army would be better prepared to confront his pursuing enemy. This was especially true when more sobering news arrived from a captured Mexican officer who confirmed that Santa Anna's deployment of troops still relied on a strategy of a divided army.

Santa Anna was not one to confide in his generals over strategy and for that reason was always opposed to councils of war. In fact, on one occasion in 1836 General Filisola remarked, "Because of his maxim of not subjecting military operations to discussions and confiding in his own aspiration which on other occasions had given him such happy results, His Excellency could not suffer an adverse criticism with patience."[3]

Indeed, as related by the Mexican prisoner, once again Santa Anna split his army into three divisions. One division was under the command of Gen. Antonio Gaona, presently holding Bastrop. He was ordered to act as the left flank in a drive along the Old San Antonio Road as far as Nacogdoces, a small town about two hundred miles to the northeast. It was hoped that Gaona, in his wide sweep, would eventually close in on Houston and catch him as he made his eastward retreat. A second division, led by General Sesma, was directly behind the American army and was advancing toward Beason's Crossing along the same route traveled by Houston. The remnants of the main army still remained with Santa Anna at his headquarters in Béxar. In addition, the detachment under General Urrea was ordered to withdraw from Goliad and to continue their advance along the coast from Matagorda.

Ever since leaving Gonzales, the commander was consistently burdened by the unrelenting pressure from the young recruits to stand and fight. They came to engage the enemy, they said, not to continuously run away from them. There was even some talk of replacing the old man. But Houston, better than anyone, knew his small army would never succeed against the size and power of Sesma's forces. Houston always listened to his men's complaints but never explained his real motives to them, evidently assuming they were just venting their frustrations. As the grumbling continued, however, many of the volunteers became more and more fed up not only with the constant retreats but also with the deplorable conditions they had to live under. As a result, they decided to simply quit and return home, which reduced the ranks even more than the rains did.

Living in the soaking rain for weeks on end was certainly taking its toll on the men on both sides. The small makeshift tents used for shelter and sleeping were on ground that had turned into a quagmire. Living in rain-soaked clothes each and every day, eating spoiled food, and drinking contaminated water had reduced the size of Houston's army considerably. Not to mention the sickness and deaths from the appalling unsanitary practices that the soldiers of that time considered normal hygiene.

On March 21, General Sesma and eight hundred troops arrived at the southern bank of the Colorado opposite Beason's Crossing. Also arriving on the following day were reinforcement troops led by Gen. Eugene Tolsa. As predicted, with the river swollen from the continuing downpours Houston knew Sesma would be unable to make a crossing anytime soon. So for six days both armies did nothing but wait and watch the other side through the raindrops. Again Houston's troops wanted to attack. And again General Houston refused. Even the veterans were becoming frustrated that their commander was avoiding a fight, something they did not want to believe themselves.

During their stay at Beason's Crossing, Houston was told of the defeat and capture of Fannin's army. In a very rare display of depression Houston took the news of this defeat quite badly, and after a short period of saddened reflection on March 26 Houston ordered another retreat, this time to San Felipe de Austin. As he had done to Gonzales and the ferry at Burnham's Crossing, Houston ordered his rear guard to reduce Beason's settlement to ashes just before they began moving toward San Felipe. Moving through San Felipe on the twenty-eighth, three days later they reached Groce's plantation, where they pitched their camp for three solid weeks of rest and some additional training. During this time the army received the so-called Twin Sisters, a pair of cannons they would find quite handy in the days ahead.

While at Groce's, Houston held a meeting with his officers to discuss the options available for moving his small army of around five to eight hundred in the weeks ahead. Despite becoming more sensitive to the growing dissatisfaction with his retreats, Houston disclosed that he was still reluctant to engage the enemy and that he preferred to continue toward Nacogdoches and Louisiana, where he could recruit more volunteers. Then, he hoped, with some five thousand troops he could return much stronger to confront the Mexican army. However, the officers were adamantly opposed to any further retreat or even the appearance of one. So was the interim government at Harrisburg. In fact, President Burnet's frustration was quite evident in a letter written to Secretary of War Rusk that remarked, "Sir, the enemy are laughing you to scorn. You must fight them. You must retreat no further. The country expects you to fight. The salvation of the country depends on your doing so."[4]

Despite the objections, on April 12 the army crossed the Brazos and the retreat was on once again. Lacking any specific orders from General Houston, no one knew exactly where the army was going. And to many historians this is where the turning point of the campaign occurred. On April 16 the army literally reached a crossroad. The road going straight ahead was to the north and led away from the enemy to Nacogdoches and was Houston's previously stated objective. The road to the east, on the right, would take them directly into Harrisburg, the recently selected capital of the Texian provisional government, and to Santa Anna. Without orders to the contrary, the three musicians at the head of the column, evidently on their own volition, turned right at the crossroads and with the rousing cheers from the men behind them the army followed and headed toward the fight instead of away from it. General Houston, during this time, simply tagged along with the army.

Meanwhile, in March, Santa Anna and his remaining troops had departed from Béxar and joined up with Sesma's army on April 4 while General Gaona, who had been stuck in the mud in Bastrop, was ordered to disregard his prior orders and to reinforce Santa Anna in San Felipe de Austin. By this time, the rains had diminished to a point where the Colorado could be easily forded. Consequently, once the Mexican army made their crossing they wasted little time and headed directly for San Felipe de Austin. Arriving on April 7, Santa Anna learned that General Gaona had not arrived as ordered, and would find out much later that Gaona had become lost. Santa Anna was also shocked to find the settlement reduced to ashes. San Felipe de Austin was the centerpiece and capital of Stephen Austin's Texian settlements. According to many of the people in these parts, it was one of the most important places in Texas, and here it was now burned to the ground. The question of who ordered the conflagration remained unclear. Supposedly, when Houston left the town was still intact. When Santa Anna arrived it was nothing but blackened ruins. Some people put the blame on Houston because as they saw it, this practice had developed into a custom of his, while others put the blame squarely on the locals themselves. Nevertheless, for several more weeks this cat-and-mouse game continued. Houston's army would always manage to stay one step ahead, and as Santa Anna followed Houston retreated ahead of him.

This scenario continued until April 18, when Houston stopped about eight miles from Harrisburg, which is today a part of the city of Houston. At this point, Houston received intelligence from a captured courier that changed the whole complexion of the chase. During the interrogation of the prisoner Houston discovered that not only did Santa Anna split his forces, but he also had now separated from the main body entirely and with a smaller number of troops. In addition, Houston learned that General Filisola was ordered to dispatch General Cos from Fort Bend to arrive at the Mexican camp with additional reinforcements. According to the Texians' prisoner, after crossing the Brazos Santa Anna veered away from the main army with about seven hundred men in an attempt to intercept and capture the Burnet government on its way to its new capital in Harrisburg. Although they failed to capture Burnet, Harrisburg was set ablaze. At the present time, the courier continued, Santa Anna was marching downstream along the Buffalo Bayou. From there, he intended to establish his campsite at the junction of the Buffalo Bayou and the San Jacinto River.

This was tremendous news to Houston. Santa Anna had made the unforgiving mistake of completely separating from the main army with a much smaller force and without the means to receive help if he needed it. Like a calf separated from the rest of the herd, El Presidente was now isolated from his army and a prime target for an attack.

Later that day Houston called his men together and emphatically told them in no uncertain terms that what they have been waiting for was about to take place. They would be crossing the Buffalo Bayou soon to meet the enemy and in the process many would die. And, Houston said, when they charged into Santa Anna's camp they must remember what happened at the Alamo. This was just the message the men wanted to hear. Unable to restrain themselves, they let out a loud burst of approval and yelled, "Remember the Alamo! Remember Goliad!"

First, they had to get to the banks of the Buffalo Bayou. It took them two grueling days of travel to come within sight of the Buffalo Bayou and the San Jacinto River. Once again, to the enormous disappointment of the men, no attack was made. Instead, on the morning of April 21, 1836, General Houston, worn-out from the exhausting march, remained in his quarters and slept until noon. And as planned, while Houston enjoyed his long nap General Cos arrived at the Mexican camp with about five hundred recruits as reinforcements. (Note: Houston's retreat from Gonzales to Buffalo Bayou roughly follows that of present-day Route 10.)

In the Texian bivouac, only about three-quarters of a mile from the Mexican encampment, much of the morning was spent building breastworks out of anything they could spare, from trunks and saddles to assorted baggage and miscellaneous equipment. To keep themselves amused at the same time the men also complained about the general's lack of motivation and the excuses he was going to use for retreating this time around. However, about three o'clock in the afternoon General Houston, well rested and reinvigorated, surprised and delighted everyone when he gave the order for battle.

In the meantime, even in the Mexican camp, Santa Anna expected Houston to attack. But, when Houston failed to appear, in the late afternoon Santa Anna decided to take a siesta, as did his fourteen hundred tired soldiers who had spent the night constructing breastworks in anticipation of Houston's assault.

Hidden by trees and rising ground, that afternoon some nine hundred Texians quietly crept closer to Santa Anna's encampment. Also on hand were the two newly received six-pounders they called the "Twin Sisters." Fortunately for Houston, Santa Anna committed another error in judgment. So convinced that Houston had retreated again, Santa Anna failed to post sentries on the camp's perimeter.

Suddenly, at the command to advance, Houston's unforgiving men overran the camp in waves surprising the sleeping army. Shouting, "Remember the Alamo! Remember Goliad!" the crazed Texians killed every Mexican within reach and pursued the hundreds trying to escape. But the Texians were still not satisfied. Even when the battle was won, they continued the unrelenting slaughter, still crying out the remembrances of the two bloody tragedies just passed. In less than a half hour, on the one hand, over six hundred Spanish soldiers were killed and most of the rest were either wounded or taken prisoner. On the other hand, the Texians lost only nine men, with Houston himself wounded by a gunshot to his ankle, a glaring example of how one-sided the Battle of San Jacinto was. The formal Mexican surrender was carried out by Col. Juan N. Almonte, whose sword was accepted by Colonel Burleson.

Kate Terrell was in a refugee camp along the Sabine River when news of Houston's victory reached the folks. She later remarked how the people embraced when they heard the report and that everyone laughed, wept, and prayed together, all at the same time.

The following day Santa Anna, wearing the uniform of a common soldier, was found in the nearby marshes and taken prisoner. Unable to speak English, when he was first brought into the camp he tried to identify himself by pointing to his name on a letter he carried. Soon other nearby Mexican prisoners recognized him and in amazement called out, "El Presidente! El Presidente!" With the Texians shocked over what they just had heard, amid the angry demands for the general to be shot, the visibly shaken prisoner was brought to General Houston for questioning. Since he was still unsure of their prisoner's identity, an interpreter was immediately summoned, and he verified that the prisoner was indeed Santa Anna. Still not fully convinced, Houston was finally persuaded when another captive, Col. Juan N. Almonte, Santa Anna's secretary and confidential adviser, also made a positive identification.

The two leaders, finally meeting face-to-face, were in stark contrast with each other, the victor lying on a blanket nursing an agonizing gunshot wound to his foot, the vanquished standing erect before him displaying the demeanor of a proud, loyal, and unrepentant military officer. At one point, for instance, Santa Anna, in an assertive tone, was unable to resist reminding Houston that although he had won the battle, he still had Generals Filisola, Urrea, Sesma, and Gaona and their four thousand troops to contend with, in effect boasting to Houston that although he might have won the battle, the war would certainly continue, and in Santa Anna's favor. However, when Houston reminded Santa Anna that his freedom depended on his willingness to cooperate his whole demeanor suddenly changed. After several hours of discussions Santa Anna was persuaded to write an order to General Filisola telling him to commence the retreat of all Mexican forces from Texas.

Later, after the terms of the surrender were agreed upon, Santa Anna, along with his aides, Colonels Almonte and Gabriel Nuñez, was escorted by President Burnet to the small town of Velasco, Texas, which was at the time the new Texian capital. There, on May 14, Santa Anna signed the Treaty of Velasco along with President Burnet. Meanwhile, General Houston sailed to New Orleans for medical treatment on his foot, leaving the command of the army to Secretary of War Rusk. At the hospital, the doctors supposedly removed 20 pieces of bone from Houston's wound.

In reality there were two treaties, a public treaty and a private treaty. The terms of the public treaty read as follows:

1. Personal undertaking by Santa Anna not to take up arms, or encourage arms to be taken up, against the people of Texas in this war of independence.
2. Cessation of hostilities, on the sea and land, between Texas and Mexico
3. Mexican troops to evacuate the territory of Texas, relocating south of the Rio Grande (Rio Bravo del Norte).
4. Mexican troops to refrain from taking property without due compensation, etc., during their retreat.
5. All property (including horses, cattle etc.) captured by Mexico during the war and negro slaves freed by the Mexican army to be returned.
6. The two armies to avoid contact, keeping a distance of five leagues.
7. The Mexican army to retreat without tarrying.
8. Dispatches to be sent to the commanders of the two armies, informing them of the treaty's content.
9. Mexico to release all Texan prisoners, with Texas releasing the same number of Mexican prisoners of the same rank; all other Mexican prisoners to be retained by Texas.
10. Santa Anna to be conveyed to Veracruz as soon as deemed proper.

The seven terms of the private treaty would not take effect until the ten provisions of the public treaty were fully carried out. The private treaty read:

1. Personal undertaking by Santa Anna not to take up arms, or encourage arms to be taken up, against the people of Texas in this war of independence.
2. Santa Anna to give orders for all Mexican troops to withdraw from Texas as soon as possible.
3. Santa Anna to make arrangements in Mexico City so that a mission of Texans would be well received, all differences settled, and independence recognized.
4. A treaty of commerce, friendship, and limits to be established between Mexico and Texas, whereunder the territory of Texas would not extend beyond the Rio Grande.
5. Government of Texas to provide for Santa Anna's immediate embarkation for Veracruz.
6. Both copies of the document to be kept folded and sealed until conclusion of the negotiations, when they should both be given to Santa Anna; no use to be made of it before that, unless either party failed to abide by its terms.
7. Texas was to have had a trade agreement with Mexico.

When the signing of the treaties became known, however, Burnet was severely criticized for showing too much leniency toward Santa Anna instead of having him executed on the spot as he had always done to his prisoners. Even when Santa Anna was about to board the *Invincible*, the ship returning him to Mexico from New Orleans, mobs of protesters prevented the vessel from sailing, demanding Burnet be tried for treason and Santa Anna shot. To prevent further complications, at that point President Burnet had little choice but to cancel the return voyage and to incarcerate Santa Anna in a small house in Columbia.

With the intercession of General Houston, Santa Anna and his aide Juan Almonte were escorted by three army officers from Columbia to Orazimba. Now enduring conditions unfit for such men of high rank, on August 17 they were secured to a heavy lead ball and chain until arrangements could be made to move them to another location. Approximately a month and a half later, both men, still under heavy guard, were escorted aboard a steamer to Louisville, Kentucky, where they landed on Christmas Day.

After supposedly meeting with Gen. Winfield Scott in Frederick, Maryland, on January 17 Santa Anna reached Washington, where he personally met with President Jackson and later enjoyed a cordial dinner with Jackson and other guests. No factual record exists of their conversations, except for one or two hearsay statements from people who attended the dinner and said some questions were made to Santa Anna about his opinion of Texas independence.

To further injure his enormous ego, when the arrangements were finalized for his return to Mexico he was unable to gain official diplomatic status. As a result, he was put on the USS *Pioneer* and returned in February of 1837 to his hacienda Manga de Clavo in Veracruz, Mexico, where he resided in quiet obscurity. But, yet again, his absence from political and military power would only be temporary.

At the time, General Filisola was in the vicinity of Fort Bend, an area on the Brazos consisting of land grants in Austin Colony. When he received Santa Anna's order to withdraw all Mexican forces from Texas he dispatched instructions to the other commanders widely scattered in the surrounding area to meet for a council of war. As a result, several thousand troops under the commands of Generals Filisola and Urrea assembled on the grounds of a boardinghouse and saloon belonging to Texian colonist Elizabeth Powell, which was adjacent to the Fort Bend area. Also camped about the property were scores of teamsters and women camp followers. Although the building was fairly remote, it was well known to travelers as a suitable place to stop for a night or two.

Soon after their arrival, the council of war was attended by Urrea, Sesma, Gaona, and Cos to discuss Santa Anna's capture and his written orders to retreat. Despite knowing that Filisola was under no obligation to take orders from a captured superior, the generals appeared to accede to Filisola's demands, except for General Urrea. Adamantly opposed to the retreat, he had successfully won all of his battles and wanted desperately to confront Houston and the Texas army on the field of battle. Urrea forcefully argued that duty demanded maintaining the war and that he was very much in favor of a counteroffensive. In the end, with him casting the only dissenting vote, the withdrawal would begin. On April 26, the Mexican army broke camp, but not before the rear guard set fire to Mrs. Powell's boardinghouse, tavern, and other outbuildings as a parting gift for being a Texian hostess.

In his instructions, Santa Anna directed Filisola to retreat as far as Béxar, where he should wait for additional instructions. Further in the order, however, were coded directions that, if read between the lines, urged Filisola to reorganize the army and told how he could finance a counteroffensive. Despite the instructions, Filisola thought otherwise. He was going to continue the retreat all the way to Matamoros. It was a decision that would ruin his career and his fine reputation.

If the retreating troops were not feeling depressed enough, the miserable weather they encountered made them feel even more dispirited. The torrential rains continued for days, turning everything into seas of thick mud. It was nearly impossible for the men to walk, let alone to move the heavy artillery mired in the unforgiving muck. Food had run out, the men were sick and without medical care, their clothing had been reduced to rags, and many were without shoes.

During the trek back to Matamoros General Filisola was unmercifully castigated by the Mexican public and the press for disrespecting the orders of General Santa Anna. Filisola was accused of being a coward, turning his back on the motherland, and refusing to salvage the honor of the Mexican people. In addition, the people demanded the army return to Texas to erase the shame they all deeply felt. Refusing to abandon the retreat, Filisola soon learned that he was being replaced by General Urrea as overall commander. As a result, Filisola resigned his command to Gen. Juan José Andrade, who had joined the retreat in Goliad.

When the army reached Matamoros on June 18, General Filisola declared in his defense that he withdrew all the Mexican troops from Texas because he thought by doing so, first he was saving the life of his illustrious leader. Second, once the inclement weather had passed, his priority was to deliver his wretched men back home safely.

Despite his plea for understanding, which was not forthcoming, General Filisola, now held in disgrace, retired to Saltillo. General Urrea, however, in overall command, continued to bluster about his eventual return to Texas for the good of the Mexican people. But, it was all bluster. With the customary turmoil still brewing in Mexico City, Urrea decided he was needed more in Mexico City and, under that rationale, marched his army southward.

Santa Anna's defeat at the Battle of San Jacinto ended the battlefield phase of the Texas war for independence. As they were a proud people, the devastating loss was an enormous embarrassment to the Mexican population, which only encouraged a larger demoralizing effect on the Mexican soldiers.

Following three years of a bloody war and numerous lives lost, the Texans could now declare the birth of a new nation, the Republic of Texas. While the Texans rejoiced over gaining their independence, Mexican president José Justo Corro refused to accept all agreements entered into by Santa Anna while he was held captive. Santa Anna had no authority under the Mexican Constitution, Corro declared, or legal standing in the Mexican government to negotiate a treaty. And furthermore, he added, even if Santa Anna did, the treaty was never ratified by the Mexican government.

Santa Anna agreed and insisted he signed the treaty under coercion as a prisoner, not as a surrendering general. "I offered nothing in the name of the nation. In my own name I pledged myself to acts that our government could nullify."[5]

Although true peace and an accepted independence still evaded them, the Texas army had to be quite pleased over their successes. Not only did they capture Santa Anna and topple him from power, but they also finally removed all the Mexican troops from Texas.

A year later, at his hacienda, Manga de Clavo, Santa Anna was still extremely disappointed over his loss at San Jacinto. But, as luck would have it, he was given another chance to redeem himself after French forces arrived off the Mexican coast and began to bombard Veracruz. The fracas was over a sensitive and lingering financial dispute between France and Mexico that became known as the French Pastry War.

Apparently, it all started when Mexico refused to compensate French citizens living in Mexico for damages done to a number of French shops that were burned and looted by Mexican soldiers during an 1828 riot. As the name of the battle implies, one of the damaged businesses was a French pastry shop. In addition, Mexico consistently reneged on millions of dollars in loan payments owed to France. To settle the debt once and for all, the French government demanded a payment of some 600,000 pesos, which the Mexican government didn't have and would refuse to pay anyway. Considering the state of the Mexican economy, the French demand was believed to be unrealistic and totally unjustified. Consequently, as retribution for Mexico's refusal to pay, the French blockaded the ports of Veracruz and Tampico for over a year and even captured nearly the entire Mexican navy. If that weren't enough, on November 27, 1838, the French forces began to bombard the Fortress of San Juan de Ulúa, a stone fort on a small island guarding the approach to Veracruz.

At his hacienda Santa Anna couldn't help but hear the echoing reports of the bombardment of his beloved city. Consequently, unable to resist the calling, the following day Santa Anna voluntarily came out of retirement and without authorization offered his services to the Veracruz officials. After years of battlefield experience, it seemed like he was addicted to the sounds and smell of battle and when the opportunity presented itself he was mysteriously drawn back to the front lines once again.

While the shelling of the fortress continued, Santa Anna was asked to inspect the extent of the damage and to report back with his recommendation. Following his inspection, Santa Anna advised the governor to surrender the fortress since, in his opinion, the extensive damage made it unworthy to save. The governor, acting on Santa Anna's advice, promptly surrendered the fortress. With no further instructions forthcoming, a disappointed Santa Anna returned to his hacienda.

When news of the governor's capitulation of the fortress reached Mexico City, Pres. Anastasio Bustamente, who had recently returned to power, was so outraged he removed the governor from office. Ironically, the president replaced the seemingly wayward governor with the very person who had suggested the surrender of the fortress in the first place, their hero, Santa Anna.

Thrilled to find himself back in the fight, as were the authorities in Mexico City who seemed to have forgotten the Battle of San Jacinto, Santa Anna sent out an order for reinforcements. He also dispatched a message to the French admiral disavowing the surrender of the fortress and informing him that they were now at war. The French admiral sarcastically replied on December 4 that since they were at war Veracruz would be razed to the ground.

Around dawn the following day, Santa Anna was suddenly awakened by the sounds of gunfire. According to his account, some three thousand French troops had entered the city and were rushing through the streets aimlessly firing their weapons. His first instinct was to order a counterattack, which managed to drive the French forces back onto their ships in the harbor. In the process, however, Santa Anna was the victim of a canister blast that tore into his left leg, which was later amputated below the knee.[6] Unfortunately, the surgery did not go well. Failing to leave enough skin to cover the protruding end of the leg bone, the surgeons were forced to overstretch the skin to seal the wound. Over the remaining years of his life, Santa Anna had to endure the continuous pain resulting from this medical negligence.

With Santa Anna out of action, President Bustamante had little choice but to negotiate a truce with the French. When a diplomatic agreement was reached that required Mexico to pay the entire 600,000 pesos, the French and their fleet promptly departed Mexico in March of 1839. Curiously enough, because of the gallant sacrifice he made for his country once again Santa Anna used his extraordinary power of persuasion and his famous Latin charm to regain acceptance in the Mexican political arena. Of course, the exploitation of his injury didn't hurt his cause either.

Although Santa Anna was praised and applauded once again for his performance against the French, President Bustamente was not so fortunate. After witnessing over two years of bitter complaints, in August of 1841 Gen. Mariano Paredes and Santa Anna, smelling victory, commanded a reactionary revolt against the regime of Bustamente, whom they then accused of not fighting hard enough for the return of Texas and for yielding to France in the French Pastry War. In October, when Bustamente agreed to resign, Santa Anna, the on-again, off-again favorite son, occupied the presidential office once again.

Three years later, Santa Anna's wife of 19 years, Inés de la Paz García, died. As she was adored by the people of Jalapa, their affection for her was demonstrated by the scope of their mourning, the tolling of church bells, solemn possessions, and daylong prayer vigils in her honor. Although everyone knew of Santa Anna's adulterous reputation, which was the norm in Mexico, it still came as a surprise that only a month later he married Maria Dolores de Tosta, a 15-year-old who would spend the rest of her life living in Mexico City without Santa Anna but financially cared for by her absentee husband.

However, as had happened so many times before, after three years of Santa Anna's rule the people revolted over his blatant corruption and maintaining a dictatorial administration. So outraged were the citizens of Mexico City that a mob broke into the Santa Anna Theater and threatened to burn it down unless the name was changed. Also, a large bronze statue of Santa Anna was destroyed and, as a final insult to the fallen hero, his amputated leg, once enshrined in a sacred crypt atop a stone column, was dragged through the streets while the mob screamed, "Death to the cripple, long live Congress!"[7]

On the run, Santa Anna was apprehended with five servants on January 15, 1845, on the outskirts of Xico, a village near Jalapa, where he spent the night in the local jail. In the morning he was taken to his hometown of Jalapa, where he would be incarcerated in the town council building for four days without any of the amenities he was so used to. From there Santa Anna was moved to the Fortress of San Carlos in Perote. Furthermore, all of his money, properties and assets was confiscated, including his 17-year-old wife's clothing and his son's assets. At that moment, he and his family were left with nothing. Santa Anna spent five months at the fortress before the government decided to release him provided he leave the country forever.

Strangely enough, in a complete turnabout, he was allowed to retain all of his property, his savings, and their possessions besides receiving half pay as general.

Saddened over the whole sordid episode, Santa Anna issued a statement that read:

> Companions in arms! With pride I sustained the loss of an important member of my body, lost gloriously in the service our Native Land, as some of you bore witness; but that pride has turned to grief, sadness, and desperation. You should know that these mortal remains have been violently torn from the funeral urn, which was broken, and dragged through

the public streets to make sport of them.... I know your astonishment and that you will be ashamed; you are right, such excesses were unknown among us. My friends! I am going to leave, obeying destiny. There in foreign lands I shall remember you. May you always be the support and ornament of our nation.... God be with you!"[8]

That being said, Santa Anna, the Savior of the Motherland, and his family were exiled once again. They departed for Havana, Cuba, with 37 pieces of luggage on June 2, 1845.

7

The Republic of Texas and Its Quest for Statehood

Once the Treaty of Velasco was signed it was very difficult for many people in Texas to believe the revolt was really over. The months of fighting, the killing of some seven hundred Americans, and the ruined homes and lives gave the news a somewhat surreal tone. Although the Texans rejoiced in the independence of a new republic, it was celebrated with a sense of apprehension and caution. Knowing that Mexico refused to accept their newfound freedom instilled a veiled fear that their euphoria might only be temporary. How, they wondered, was the Mexican government going to respond?

Now faced with new responsibilities, the provisional government found itself confronting new problems as well. It was just a matter of time before Burnet, the interim president, Secretary of War Rusk, empresario Stephen W. Austin, and several military officers began to bicker over who should lead the new government. When the squabbling finally settled down everyone agreed that the people would be best served by letting them decide the answer to that question at the ballot box.

With his varied political background, particularly in dealing with the Mexican authorities, Austin seemed to be the most logical choice for managing the affairs of the new republic. Consequently, confident over his chances, Austin was the first to agree to submit his candidacy. Two weeks later, Gen. Sam Houston, still recuperating from his surgery, threw his hat into the ring as well. The third candidate was the underdog, Henry Smith, the governor of the provisional government.

Despite his tireless efforts to make Austin Colony a viable and responsible community, his numerous civic appointments on behalf of Texas, and his service as the commanding officer of the volunteer army, the ailing Austin failed to overcome the popularity of the military hero. General Houston won the election overwhelmingly on September 5, 1836.

As expected, the votes for the well-liked general came largely from the military and the eastern part of Texas. The final tally recorded 5,119 votes for Houston, 743 for Smith, and only 587 for Austin. Rounding out the ticket was Mirabeau B. Lamar, who was elected vice president. Lamar had served as a colonel under Houston and distinguished himself as the commander of the cavalry at San Jacinto. The voters also elected 14 senators and 29 representatives to the Texas Congress and set a term of two years for the first president and three years for all the others.

Interestingly enough, also included on the ballot was a referendum for one of the republic's first government initiatives, annexation to the United States. The referendum was also overwhelmingly approved.

The new Republic of Texas claimed land comprising all of present-day Texas, as well as parts of Oklahoma, Kansas, Colorado, Wyoming, and New Mexico. Its southern and western borders, however, were still in dispute. In 1837 the capital of Texas was moved from Columbia to the newly named city of Houston in honor of the general, and two years later, to commemorate the legacy of the "Father of Texas," the capital was relocated for the last time, on this occasion to the city named after him, Austin, Texas.

Following the election, one of President Houston's first appointments was Austin as the first Texas secretary of state, a position he held for only two months. On December 27, 1836, Austin died of pneumonia at the age of 43. The *Texas Telegraph*, the only Texas newspaper at that time, declared in bold print, "**The Patriarch Has Left Us.**"[1] From the War Department, the following General Order was issued:

> The Father of Texas is no more! The first pioneer of the wilderness has departed! ... As a testimony of respect to his high standing, undeviating moral rectitude, and as a mark of the nation's gratitude for his untiring zeal and invaluable services, all officers, civil and military, are requested to wear crape on their right arm for the space of thirty days. All officers commanding posts, garrisons or detachments will ... cause twenty-three guns—the number of counties in the Republic—to be fired, with an interval of five minutes between each, and also have the garrison and regimental colors hung with black during the space of mourning for the illustrious dead.[2]

From the very beginning of Houston's administration, the political ideology was divided between factions that supported Houston and those backing Vice President Lamar. For instance, Houston was an avid spokesman for Texas annexation to the United States, while Lamar favored keeping Texas a republic. The president, a citizen of the Cherokee tribe, wanted to establish a peaceful partnership with the Indian tribes, while Lamar demanded the expulsion of all the Indians. This infighting was resolved in 1838 when Houston lost the presidency to Lamar, but he regained the office once again three years later.

While the new Republic of Texas wrestled with the formalities of pursuing recognition from the United States, at the same time overtures were being made for her annexation into the Union as a slave state. It was a highly sensitive subject that only compounded the difficulties for Congress to agree on statehood. As this movement gathered momentum the opponents of slavery expansion reacted in sheer horror once again at the thought of slavery being extended into the newly acquired western territories, just as they had done in 1818 when Missouri applied for statehood and again in 1829 when President Jackson was attempting to purchase land in northern Mexico.

In the U.S. Congress the annexation issue was one that divided the learned body into two opposing groups that were themselves divided. On one hand, the proponents of annexation preferred to have Texas admitted as a slave state, while others favored a territory. Some insisted annexation ought to be accomplished through a treaty, while a joint resolution was the right way to go for others. On the other hand, opponents of annexation rejected the idea of any further acquisition of territory or stated that annexation of a sovereign nation was unconstitutional, while yet other opponents refused to support annexation if it resulted in the spread of slavery.

For years debating the issue of slavery was taboo in Congress. It was too controversial, too sensitive, and too partisan to discuss in a constructive manner. It was avoided at all times and at all costs. Now, however, our lawmakers discovered that discussions on annexation were not exclusively about statehood. Annexing a new state in the western territories also meant the possible spread of slavery into the western territories. And, as Congress discovered, they could not debate one without debating the other. This left Democratic president Andrew Jackson and Congress in a most terrible bind. Jackson recognized that the clamor for Texas statehood was coming primarily from the South. In that regard, the president thought supporting immediate recognition and annexation by an outgoing southern president would be an unwise policy for the party to take. Even Austin had an opinion on the annexation issue. "Threats and denunciations, he said, will goad the North into a determined opposition and if Texas is annexed at all it will not be until the question has convulsed this nation for several sessions of Congress."[3]

Northern opposition to slavery and the spread of forced servitude had become so intense and so controversial a political issue that by the end of the congressional session further debate on annexation of Texas was postponed indefinitely. Instead, to avoid provoking a war with Mexico, as well as an unwanted congressional debate over annexation and slavery, Congress thought it prudent to simply do what it does best, compromise. Using some parliamentary procedure, they would simply put off the unwanted debate for another day.

In the final days of the Jackson administration, therefore, both houses approved resolutions that merely recognized the Republic of Texas as a sovereign nation and two days later, on March 3, 1837, his last day in office, Pres. Andrew Jackson dispatched a U.S. chargé d'affaires to Texas, one of his final acts as president.

Although President Jackson granted full recognition to Texas as a sovereign nation, Martin Van Buren, his successor and fellow Democrat, refused to go any further during the term of his presidency. Van Buren always opposed Texas annexation because he refused to have any role in spreading slavery to other parts of the country. Slavery, he once said, was an evil of the first magnitude. In fact, he refused to interfere at all with the issue of slavery and made this quite clear in his inauguration address: "I must go into the Presidential chair the inflexible and uncompromising opponent of every attempt on the part of Congress to abolish slavery in the District of Columbia against the wishes of the slaveholding States, and also with a determination equally decided to resist the slightest interference with it in the States where it exists." Furthermore, he opined, since the Mexican government believed Texas was still under its jurisdiction, granting statehood would be seen as a belligerent act against Mexico. Under these circumstances, he said, annexation could provoke Mexico into a war with the United States, something he wanted to avoid. With this kind of support it was obvious that any discussion on the annexation of Texas would have to remain on hold until 1841, when a different administration moved into the White House.

The new administration was that of John Tyler. At 51 years old, Tyler became the first vice president to gain the presidency after the death of the incumbent. In this case it was William H. Harrison, who died from pneumonia on April 4, 1841. Evidently, Harrison chose to deliver the longest inauguration speech on record, nearly two hours. Unfortunately, March 4 was an extremely cold and wet day in Washington, which Harrison completely ignored. Wearing no hat or coat and riding to and from the ceremony on horseback instead of in the traditional closed carriage, the 68-year-old president caught cold, which in three weeks turned to pneumonia. Despite all their valiant efforts, the doctors were unable to save him.

When Tyler stepped into his White House office for the first time his critics mockingly referred to him as an acting president. And his severest detractors saw fit to call him "His Accidency," a clever insult over the question of his legitimacy for assuming the presidency without being elected. Tyler's credentials included terms in both Houses of Congress, where he gained a somewhat unfavorable reputation as a maverick Democrat because of his proclivity to vote according to his conscience rather than adhering to the party line. Unwilling to bend his principles for the sake of party loyalty, Tyler bolted from the party in protest and joined the Whig Party, becoming their vice-presidential candidate on the Harrison ticket.

Now, nearly four years later, Tyler was still faced with the divisive issue of annexation for Texas. Ever since gaining their independence, the Texans had expressed a willingness to join the Union in order to gain a degree of protection against the continuing border raids from Mexico. However, with Congress unable to reach a meeting of the minds, the goal of annexation never quite materialized. The Texas question had now become so pervasive and so disruptive that it threatened to be a major issue in his upcoming presidential campaign.

Tyler was a steadfast advocate of western expansion and was particularly in favor of Texas statehood, but for self-serving reasons. To enhance his image to the voters he firmly believed that annexing Texas would accomplish something of significance in an otherwise mediocre term and would reinvigorate a new constituent loyalty toward his bid for a second term.

Consequently, Tyler began to formulate his strategy for influencing Congress on Texas statehood before the presidential campaigning got under way.

Mexico, however, had other ideas.

Since Mexico never recognized the independence of Texas, they warned Tyler in no uncertain terms that the annexation of Texas was certain to lead to war. But Tyler, looking ahead to the upcoming nominating convention and acting on his own political motives, ignored their warnings and instructed Congress to disregard the Mexican threat.

In the South, statehood for Texas was already a major political issue. Once Texas was brought into the federation, many southerners agreed, they could extend slavery into the West, perhaps create and populate new slave states, and gain more congressional representation and with it the resultant power to determine not only the destiny of the country but also the fate of the South. Over the years ahead, this drive for southern expansion and domination would be perceived in the North as the "slave-power conspiracy."

To confuse the issue even more, there were some southern lawmakers who questioned the much-heralded economic benefits Texas would provide to the South. In their opinion, the soil was unsuitable for profitable cultivation and therefore unsuitable for slavery. One such dissenter was Sen. John C. Calhoun. Although an ardent expansionist for the territorial and political benefits, he questioned the social aspects of such a move. Like many other southerners, Calhoun was very concerned about the introduction of mixed breeds into the South, namely, the inevitable blend of Indians and Mexicans. With the free blacks and southern slaves also added into the equation, the white citizenry was in an enormous quandary.

Addressing Congress, Calhoun made this point quite clear in his so-called Conquest of Mexico speech:

> Ours, sir, is the Government of a white race. The greatest misfortunes of Spanish America are to be traced to the fatal error of placing these colored races on an equality with the white race. That error destroyed the social arrangement which formed the basis of society.... Are they fit for self-government and for governing you? Are you, any of you, willing that your States should be governed by these twenty-odd Mexican States, with a population of about only one million of your blood, and two or three million of mixed blood better informed—all the rest pure Indians, a mixed blood equally ignorant and unfit for liberty, impure races, not as good as the Cherokees or Choctaws?

Even Sen. Waddy Thompson, also from South Carolina, lamented that the country "will add a large population, alien to us in feeling, education, race, and religion—a people unaccustomed to work, and accustomed to insubordination and resistance to law, the expense of governing whom will be ten times as great as the revenues derived from them."[4]

Although the mixing of races, the spread of slavery, and the potential for war with Mexico were critical issues that clouded the congressional debates, there was also a fourth consideration. Ever since the country gained its independence, admission to the Union was usually granted so that political parity in the U.S. Senate was maintained, among other factors of course. If a northern state was admitted, the following state annexed would invariably be a southern state, and vice versa. With the northern state of Michigan being the last to join the Union, the United States consisted of 26 states. To maintain this component of the selection process, the southerners knew the next state to gain admittance had to be a southern state. And they were right. Waiting in the wings for statehood was Florida. With Texas now being the only other potential candidate, the southerners were more fanatical than ever to get a two-state advantage.

Needless to say, the more the South persisted in calling for Texas statehood, the more the North bristled in combative protestations against it.

Then, in 1842, three relatively small Mexican raids on San Antonio, although quickly put down, served to underscore the need Texas had for U.S. military protection, protection that could be provided only after Texas was annexed. The first occurred on March 5 when an army of some seven hundred Mexican troops under Gen. Ráfael Vásquez crossed the Rio Grande and invaded the republic. Following their occupation of Goliad, Refugio, and Victoria, the Mexican army rode into San Antonio en masse and overwhelmed the surprised Texans. Although Vásquez quickly occupied San Antonio and wasted little time in raising the Mexican flag above the town, his occupation was a brief one. Two days later Vásquez and his troops were driven back to Mexico by the Texas militia. Then, in June, another much smaller raid was also repulsed. And three months later, on September 11, sixteen hundred troops commanded by Gen. Adrian Woll, a French mercenary, made a successful attempt to take back San Antonio against fewer than one hundred local Tejanos. Responding to the outrageously one-sided attack was Col. Matthew Caldwell, a veteran of the Texas fight for independence who managed to raise some two hundred volunteers for the counterattack. Caldwell held the distinction of being one of the original Texas Rangers, a signer of the Texas Declaration of Independence as well as the Texas Constitution.

However, with only some 38 horses fit enough to take part in the attack, Caldwell was forced to use only that number of men, 14 of whom were Texas Rangers. Six days later, the Texans arrived and the battle was engaged. Garrisoned in the Alamo, Woll quickly dispatched several hundred troops. But the Texan sharpshooters were so strategically positioned with accurate long-range weapons that they were able to easily pick off the Mexicans one by one without suffering any losses themselves. With their casualties mounting, the Mexicans were forced to retreat. Soon Mexican artillery fire proved ineffective and a second advance by Woll's troops also failed. That night, with campfires burning brightly as a ruse, the Mexicans retreated back across the border. In what was called the Battle of Salado the Mexicans' casualties were reported to be approximately 60. The Texans lost one trooper and had nine men wounded.

Momentum for statehood was further increased when northern abolitionists heard unsubstantiated reports that Great Britain was showing an unusual amount of interest in the new republic. The rumors were that the British government was growing increasingly concerned over disappointing production figures from its widely scattered sugar and cotton plantations. Furthermore, the rumors blamed the production shortfalls on the inability of their free-labor colonies' products to compete with the same products produced by slave-labor enterprises. Therefore, as a defensive measure to protect their interests Britain was seeking methods to simply eliminate the competition by drawing Texas into its fold.

Actually, Britain was growing exceedingly anxious over the prospects that the United States might fulfill its goals of Manifest Destiny. In their view, the larger the United States became, the more powerful it became as well, a sure detriment to the balance of world power. Instead, England wanted Texas to grow into a prosperous and independent cotton-producing nation from whom they could import abundant supplies of inexpensive raw materials. In short, they wanted Texas to establish herself as a reliable trading partner.

When the United States learned of this supposed plot, on four different occasions the British secretary of foreign affairs, Lord Aberdeen, vehemently denied that Britain had any interest in Texas or "to acquire any dominant influence in Texas, or to have any kind of connection with her except the fair and open trade and commerce which she has with all other nations."[5]

Nevertheless, the fear of British takeover of Texas persisted. In Washington, most of this fear was advanced by those who considered our national security at risk if a British colony was only a border away.

Despite the British disavowals, many influential southerners in and around Washington remained absorbed in this developing drama and immediately recognized the consequence of losing Texas, a vital component in any plan that might arise for their economic growth and social expansion.

To circumvent the British, pro-annexation southerners called for the Tyler administration to resume the stalled discussions with Texas on this most critical issue. Whether the southern demands played any role remains unclear, but secret negotiations resumed in September of 1843 between Secretary of State Abel P. Upshur and Sam Houston, who was approaching the end of his second term. However, in February 1844 Upshur was tragically killed when a new gun exploded during a demonstration aboard the USS *Princeton*, a vessel commanded by Cdre. Robert F. Stockton. Upshur's successor, Sen. John C. Calhoun of South Carolina, completed the final negotiations with the Texas envoys and delivered the annexation agreement to the White House in April. Following his review, President Tyler forwarded the signed agreement and its supporting rationale to Congress, where it was finally brought to the floor of the Senate for ratification. It would require a two-thirds majority to pass.

As the debate raged on it became clear that the president, in a desperate attempt to salvage his presidential credentials, was using the unproven British interest in Texas as a justification for annexation. Tyler argued that under British control Texas would be a major competitor to the United States and a danger to American prosperity and security.

Tyler insisted it was in the best interest of the nation to take hold of Texas now while it had the opportunity rather than to let her fall into British hands. Sen. Thomas H. Benton of Missouri wasn't buying it. It was all a "pretext," he said, "a cry of wolf where there was no wolf,"[6] but rather a cover for the self-serving purposes of Tyler and Calhoun.

Other opponents of the treaty were just as insistent that annexation of Texas would, in all likelihood, lead to an unwanted war with Mexico. When the final vote was tallied, the treaty for Texas statehood was rejected 35 to 16.

In the House the treaty received even more scrutiny than it received in the Senate. As the debate raged on it became clear that the same old problems still plagued the passage of the treaty. A major sticking point was the unresolved dispute between Texas and Mexico over the two-thousand-mile southern border. Evidently, in 1819, when the United States formally renounced its claims to Texas by signing the Adams-Otís Treaty, the boundary between the United States and Mexico was neither agreed upon nor clearly marked. An attempt was made to correct the problem in 1827 when a five-member Boundary Commission was dispatched to survey and mark the boundary as identified in the treaty. Headed by Gen. Manuel de Mier y Terán, the commission issued its report, but Mexican politics was focused on more urgent matters. Since then, on the one hand Texas authorities had vehemently insisted that the Rio Grande was the southernmost line separating the two adversaries. On the other hand, Mexico was just as adamant in its insistence that the border with the United States extended along the Nueces River northward, which effectively cut Texas in two. For that reason, the 150-mile-wide land area in between these two claims was appropriately called the "Disputed Territory." The treaty, however, conveniently avoided the border dispute by including a provision for the United States to negotiate the issue with Mexico, but only after the treaty was ratified.

To counter the southern support for statehood, the northern legislators were just as unyielding in their opposition, such as Ohio Whig congressman Joshua R. Giddings, whose opinion pretty much summed up the attitudes of all the opponents. "Texas annexation," he said, "involved the great question of slavery or liberty. Will we extend slavery or will we promote Liberty & Freedom? To give the south the preponderance of political power would be itself a surrender of our Tariff, our internal improvements, our distribution of the proceeds of the public lands. In short it would be a transfer of our political power to the slaveholders. And a base and degrading surrender of ourselves to the power & protection of slavery. It is the most abominable proposition with which a free people were ever insulted."[7] The question of whether Texas would be admitted as a slave state or a free state remained unanswered. Evidently the northerners had a plausible reason to be troubled about this critical question. There waiting in the wings, also primed and ready to accept statehood, was Florida, another Deep South slave state. Also a point of concern was the fact that the United States had never before offered statehood to a sovereign country. There simply was no precedent for this kind of congressional action. Once again, on June 8, 1844, the treaty for Texas statehood went down in defeat.

Even Texas president Sam Houston was frustrated over the inaction of the United States. At one point he considered the idea of signing treaties with Britain and France as protectors against a Mexican invasion. Outraged at such a suggestion, from his estate, the Hermitage, former president Andrew Jackson wrote a scathing letter to Houston warning the president against establishing any alliances with European governments.

In the new session of Congress the issue over Texas statehood was again the principal subject of debate. In early December 1844, after the Twenty-Eighth Congress convened for its second congressional session, the lame-duck Tyler reintroduced a Texas annexation measure in the House that still maintained his support for immediate statehood. During the debate, however, a second resolution was introduced by Tennessee congressman Milton H. Brown that admitted Texas as a single slave state but allowed Texans the right to divide the state into four addition states with one caveat: the states had to be below the 36°30′ line of the Missouri Compromise of 1820. With immediate admission as a slave state and the potential for ten additional senators to improve its political power, this resolution was sure to win over the southern vote, which it did. The Brown bill easily passed the House in January 1845 and was sent to the Senate.

In the Senate, however, the debate over the Brown bill took on a more argumentative tone. Besides the old concerns over the unresolved border between Texas and Mexico, and the slave or free state issue, there was a new one—the potential disproportion in congressional parity should Texas transform into five additional southern states.

When a preliminary vote count showed the Brown proposal would fail, a second proposal was introduced that would postpone all debate on the Brown bill until there were additional treaty negotiations between Texas and the United States that would answer all the questions once and for all.

Following additional hours of heated debate on the two proposals it became apparent to both sides that an agreement could not be reached. At that point, a compromise amendment was introduced whereby both the measure submitted by Brown for immediate annexation and the proposal for more treaty negotiations would be submitted as a Joint Resolution for the president to decide—but which president? The Senate vote on the Joint Resolution was a 26 to 26 tie. However, Sen. Henry Johnson of Louisiana was persuaded to change his vote, enabling the bill to pass 27 to 25.

At the White House Tyler reviewed the Joint Resolution, and to no one's surprise on March 1, 1845, he signed the bill that offered immediate statehood for Texas. And for good measure two days later, on his last full day in office, he signed the bill that granted statehood to Florida, now the twenty-seventh state in the Union and the fourteenth supporting slavery.

8

Prelude to War

In a torrential rainstorm, Democrat James K. Polk was sworn in on March 4, 1845, as the eleventh president of the United States. A North Carolinian by birth, he represented Tennessee in the U.S. House of Representatives from 1825 to 1839, then as House Speaker for three and a half years, followed by three years in the governor's chair. His original intent in 1844 was to be nominated for the vice presidency, but when Martin Van Buren, the leading candidate for president, failed to gain the necessary votes for nomination Polk was presented as the so-called dark horse candidate. After eight ballots the Democrats selected Polk to carry the party's banner in the upcoming campaign. His opponent was the highly distinguished Whig Henry Clay, a Kentuckian whose credentials included stints as congressman, senator, House Speaker, and secretary of state. For the voters, the primary difference between the two candidates was quite clear. It was statehood for Texas, the most popular and the most divisive issue of the campaign.

In a letter published by the *National Intelligencer* Clay said that "annexation and war with Mexico are identical.... I consider the annexation of Texas at the present time as a measure compromising the national character, involving us certainly in a war with Mexico, probably with other foreign powers, dangerous to the integrity of the Union, inexpedient in the present financial condition of the country, and not called for by any general expression of public expression."[1] With this precise declaration, Clay made his position quite clear. Although a southern slaveholder, he did not support statehood for Texas, a position that ultimately cost him the presidency.

However, Polk did. In fact, it was the centerpiece of his campaign and the issue that enabled him to win the election. In his inauguration speech, he said:

> The Republic of Texas has made known her desire to come into the Union, to form a part of our Confederacy and enjoy with us the blessings of liberty secured and guaranteed by our Constitution. Texas was once a part of our country—was unwisely ceded away to a foreign power—is now independent, and possesses an undoubted right to dispose of a part or the whole of her territory and to merge her sovereignty as a separate and independent state in ours. I congratulate my country that by an act of the late Congress of the United States the assent of this Government has been given to the reunion, and it only remains for the two countries to agree upon the terms to consummate an object so important to both.

To Texas the reunion is important, because the strong protecting arm of our Government would be extended over her, and the vast resources of her fertile soil and genial climate would be speedily developed, ... as well as the interests of the whole Union, would be promoted by it.

The Mexican minister, former general and aide to Santa Anna, Juan N. Almonte, wasted little time to show his displeasure with the offer of statehood. Two days after Polk's inauguration Almonte asked the State Department for his passport and in a fit of anger resigned and returned to Mexico.

Polk not only supported the annexation of Texas but was also a committed proponent of Manifest Destiny, a new ideology that was in vogue among the Washington Democrats. Principally sponsored by John L. O'Sullivan, the co-founder of the *Democratic Review* and the *New York Morning News*, its concept carried expansionism to yet another level by emphasizing the notion that the United States was divinely ordained to extend her borders and her ideals of freedom and prosperity from coast to coast and even to the far reaches of the continent. As Polk was a fanatical advocate of Manifest Destiny, Texas was only one of the territories he wanted to add to the Union. The Oregon Territory was also on the table if he could only negotiate her away from Great Britain, as were the Mexican territories of California and New Mexico. Within the next four years, Polk would more than live up to his western expansionist principles.

On his first day in office, the new president was somewhat annoyed that Tyler, a lame-duck president, had made this critical decision to offer statehood to Texas. Polk was convinced that the final determination on such a controversial issue should have been his and his alone. Therefore, to resolve this matter, at least in his mind, he decided to place the annexation offer on hold until he and his cabinet could review Tyler's decision. Final approval by Polk would then be based on the recommendations from that meeting.

He met with his cabinet on March 10 to discuss the issue and to seek their opinions and advice. At the end of the day, pleased with their wisdom and expert counsel, Polk decided to renew the offer.

On the one hand, in Texas, of course, the news of Polk's decision was received with great excitement. In most southern cities, the display of approval by the people was quite evident as cheering crowds soon filled the streets and town squares with music and dancing. They celebrated with parades, bonfires, the firing of cannons, and speeches throughout the day.

On the other hand, the response was somewhat different below the Rio Grande. When word reached Mexico that statehood had been offered to Texas the reaction was both swift and vengeful. The ever-changing governments in Mexico City had always considered the Treaty of Velasco an illegal sham. In fact, the Mexican authorities consistently claimed that Santa Anna, while being held captive in chains, was coerced into signing the pact as a stipulation for his release. In their opinion, Texas was stolen by the United States, but in reality, they opined, she still belonged to Mexico and they would most certainly fight to get her back.

In this setting, diplomatic relations between the two governments were effectively severed and the prospect for war was growing stronger each day.

Not helping the situation was the fact that thousands of Mexican troops were now assembling close to the Mexican town of Matamoros, where artillery batteries were being set up along the southern side of the Rio Grande.

In response to this aggressive posturing and fearful for the safety of her citizens, Texas officials urgently pleaded to Washington for military protection. This plea was made even though they knew full well that Washington was under no obligation to provide military support until the Texas government officially accepted Polk's annexation order.

At the White House, the situation at the Rio Grande was taken very seriously. Although there was nothing Polk could do at the moment without making matters worse, he did have information that the vote in Texas to accept statehood would occur within a few months or so. Until then, as a precaution, Polk ordered the army dispatched to the vicinity of the Rio Grande to counter any aggressive actions by Mexico if that became necessary.

As a result, Secretary of War William L. Marcy forwarded a message to Gen. Zachary Taylor on May 28, 1845. In the message Taylor was forewarned that military action might be imminent against Mexico over the Texas annexation issue. In this regard, he was instructed to assemble several thousand troops at Fort Jesup, Louisiana, and to place them on a standby status. Once the Texans accepted annexation, Marcy wrote, she would be entitled to the defense and protection from foreign invasion. Until such time, his troops should be "placed and kept in readiness to perform this duty."[2]

As expected, in June the Texas Congress unanimously accepted the terms for annexation and on July 4, 1845, the Texas Convention followed up with their endorsement with a vote of 55 to 1. And finally, to put the matter to rest, a popular referendum agreed overwhelmingly. All that remained was the ratification by the next congress scheduled to convene on December 1.

However, not everyone in Texas was pleased, especially Anson Jones, the former Texas secretary of state who wanted Texas to remain an independent republic. Jones, now the new president following his election over Houston in 1844, was trying to delay the vote in hopes of making a deal with Mexico. He was willing to pledge that Texas would "not annex herself or become subject to any country whatsoever"[3] in exchange for Mexican recognition of her independence. Failing to reach an agreement in time, Jones had no choice but to declare, "The great measure of annexation, so earnestly desired by the people of Texas, is happily consummated.... [T]he final act in this great drama is now performed; the Republic of Texas is no more."[4]

Within days of the approval by the Texas Congress, Taylor was ordered by the White House to begin his departure from Fort Jesup. He was told to transfer his army, called the Army of Occupation, to a location most convenient to carry out a future expedition if conditions there warranted such a move.

Taylor immediately began to review the logistics involved for transporting three regiments of several thousand men, hundreds of wagons, and all their equipment and supplies from Fort Jesup to Texas. Following a consultation with the U.S. chargé d'affaires, Taylor decided to deploy his two infantry regiments down the Sabine River to New Orleans and from there the army would set up their camp near a small settlement along the Nueces River on the Gulf Coast called Kinney's Trading Post, soon to be named Corpus Christi. A third regiment consisting of three hundred dragoons (mounted infantrymen formed as a cavalry) would travel overland via San Antonio.

By the end of August Taylor's entire army, now grown to around thirty-five hundred strong, was bivouacked on the side of the Nueces River, the northern border of the so-called disputed territory. At that point Taylor couldn't help contemplate what political ramifications his provocative movement of troops and artillery was having in Mexico City and the risk he was taking militarily.

At the age of 60, "Old Zack," or "Old Rough and Ready" as he was called by his admirers, had spent nearly 40 of those years in the army. He was a Virginian by birth, whose weathered and heavily creased features were a badge of honor and a testament to his many years of enduring the hardships of frontier life and fighting Indians for the military. And like his ordinary soldiers, he could bed down on the cold, wet ground and dine on rancid hardtack and stale coffee. He shared in their risks and grieved with them in their losses. It was no wonder that Old Zack was so admired by his troops. As described by one of his officers, "he was short and very heavy, with pronounced face lines and gray hair, wears an old oil cloth cap, a dusty green coat, a frightful pair of trousers and on horseback looks like a toad."[5] However, as a general his commands during battle were at times based on impulse rather than calculated strategy. Without considering the inherent risks in dealing with the enemy forces on the battlefield, he could easily send his troops to certain death without hesitation.

Living primarily on a diet of pork and beans, Taylor and his army somehow endured their stay in Corpus Christi, a haven for shysters, gamblers, and thieves. The settlement itself consisted mostly of brothels, sutlers, prostitutes, smugglers, and a couple dozen nondescript shacks, which after the arrival of the army were turned into rotgut saloons almost overnight. It wasn't long before the troops were restricted to their camp, having to make do with the limited choices of entertainment. To relieve the incredible boredom, the troops wiled away their time playing cards, running horse races, staging theater shows, and going through the soldiers' time-honored pastime of practicing drill formations. The unforgiving heat from a scorching tropic sun didn't help much either.

If war developed, Taylor was under no illusions, knowing that manpower-wise he was severely outnumbered and at an enormous disadvantage. At the same time, he felt reassured that he could count on his battle-seasoned regulars and his junior officers when the going got tough. Many of his fine officers, men destined to fight against one another in another and even larger conflict 15 years from then, were the likes of infantry captains Ulysses S. Grant, Edmund Kirby Smith, and George Sedgwick. Taylor could also count on his young artillerists, such as Lt. Braxton Bragg, and George W. Meade, one of his ablest engineers.

While Taylor's army settled into their new home and waited for further instructions, in November 1845 Polk learned from one of his agents that Mexican president José Joaquín de Herrera wanted to settle the disputes between the two countries. Herrera, a moderate, recognized the fact that Mexico was in no condition to risk another war. He was more inclined to settle the whole affair by recognizing the independence of Texas and even received authorization from the Mexican congress to open negotiations for an honorable treaty to replace the one signed in Velasco.

Polk welcomed this news since it provided him with another opportunity to exercise his expansionist inclinations. Western expansion of the United States from ocean to ocean was one of his presidential goals and would certainly be a tremendous achievement in carrying out his Manifest Destiny philosophy. For some time the purchase of California and New Mexico had been on his to-do list, and now was the time to do it. He wanted this territory very badly and to purchase this territory before it fell into British hands was far more acceptable than going to war for it. In that regard, he was willing to spend up to $25 million to get it. Therefore, Polk recommended that Congress appropriate a cash payment, as high as $40 million, for the purchase of California and New Mexico. In addition to selling the land, the Mexican government would also have to agree to the Rio Grande border, which, under this agreement, would extend westward straight to the Pacific. Polk was now exercising his expansionist agenda with fervor, pushing the Mexican government to hand over a considerable amount of southwestern territory. With little debate, Congress dutifully agreed.

To carry out the negotiations Polk dispatched a highly praised Louisiana politician named John Slidell to Mexico City. Being bilingual, he was recently named the minister extraordinary and plenipotentiary. Slidell was a man of limitless ambition surpassed perhaps by his enormous ego, a craving he seemingly never quite satisfied. In the years ahead he would become an adopted southerner and take on strong Confederate allegiances. In fact, as the Confederate commissioner to France he would gain a bit of notoriety for his role in the Trent Affair scandal in November of 1861.

Slidell was well aware that in 1840 Mexico had been ordered by a commission to pay millions of dollars to American citizens to settle damage claims from years of revolution. He also knew the government was unable to pay this debt because the Mexican treasury went bankrupt four years later. Using this knowledge as a bargaining chip, Slidell was instructed to pick up the tab for these damage claims, approximately $3 million, if Mexico agreed to recognize the Rio Grande border. Employing a second ploy, Slidell also planned to offer an additional $5 million if Mexico agreed to relinquish New Mexico. And to sweeten the pot even more, if Mexico agreed to extend the boundary to include San Francisco Bay an additional $20 million would be provided, or even $25 million for all of California.

Slidell's mission, however, could not have come at a worse time. In Mexico City, the power brokers were somewhat divided over the possible annexation of Texas. As a result, the government was going through a crisis not only with powerful political interest groups but also with a maverick portion of the Mexican army. Gen. Mariano Paredes y Arrillaga, a rabid anti–American, and a large body of loyal troops were creating a great deal of unrest over the government's handling of the Texas debacle and saw this incident as an excellent opportunity to challenge the power of the Herrera government. Extremely influential and fanatical, Paredes refused to accept the fact that Texas had won its independence from Mexico and adamantly opposed the U.S. annexation of Texas and, for that matter, any government dialogue with the United States. He angrily denounced the Herrera government and protested any further dealings with the United States over what they perceived as their property. Radical politicians and journalists as well were relentless in their slanderous demagoguery. Herrera was a coward and weak, they declared. As president he was expected to defend Mexico's honor, not give in to American thieves who had stolen a piece of her sovereignty.

The Mexican citizens listening to this political rhetoric were also told that the Americans had nothing but disdain for them, believing that the Mexican people were lazy, stupid, insolent, uncivilized, and an inferior race, in the same class as black slaves and Indian savages. This hateful discourse only humiliated and angered the people even more, not only for their army's retreat from Texas after the loss at San Jacinto but also for the vile language emanating from the United States. By the same token, the Mexican people firmly believed the Americans were nothing but a bunch of illiterate farmers and frontiersmen, not much better than peasants. Even the American soldiers could not compare to the Mexican troops, they said. The Americans were undisciplined ruffians while the Mexican soldiers were professionals, well trained, and attired in magnificent uniforms. Speaking from the heart, the Mexican people were fed up with the arrogant, land-hungry thieves from across the border and demanded the army return to Texas. They demanded a war to take back what was rightfully theirs.

In this context, when Slidell arrived in Mexico City on the sixth of December representing the United States, he was roundly harassed by the Mexican officials who challenged his credentials and refused to recognize his authority. It seems under Mexican law the government was forbidden to negotiate with a minister plenipotentiary. To do so Mexico would be, in effect, renewing diplomatic relations with the United States, something they were not prepared to do. Unable to carry out his mission, Slidell was ordered to leave Mexico City and to wait in Jalapa for further instructions.

Under intense demand to resign, President Herrera was unable to gather enough support to sustain his presidency. His government quickly collapsed under the pressure exerted by revolutionary forces commanded by Paredes, who marched into Mexico City at the head of the army on January 2, 1846.

To force the new Mexican government, now under Paredes, to make a decision on the land deal, Slidell decided to send an ultimatum to the foreign minister that gave Paredes two weeks to decide between peace and war. Obviously, the tone of the message was outrageously insulting to Mexican sensibilities. Slidell should have known that the Mexicans by their very nature would not respond positively to intimidation and threats. Instead they would do just the reverse and deepen their perceived tenacity.

Two weeks later Polk received a report from Slidell that described the shabby treatment he had received from the authorities in Mexico City and the difficulties he had just trying to discuss the land deal. The president was extremely disappointed, of course, but what was most troubling to him was the lack of civility afforded to Slidell, which Polk considered a national insult not only to the U.S. government but also to its people.

As the anti–American rhetoric continued to worsen, Slidell was promptly recalled to Washington.

That December of 1845, as the new session of Congress was gaveled into order, the Texas question was still a hot issue in both houses. As you recall, in July Texas had accepted the terms for annexation. On the docket for this session was a review of the Texas state constitution and a final ratification for statehood.

The reality was that Texas statehood was a solid Democratic Party initiative. However, the issue divided the Whigs between a northern and southern faction. Although not opposed to Manifest Destiny and its basic concept of extending American democracy to others, the northern Whigs were adamantly against expansion in any form if it was to be accomplished by force. The coercion of others to satisfy one's self-interest alarmed them immensely. Southerners, the northern Whigs pointed out, were in fact quite reluctant to live among the people of mixed races, as they had always been. Except for extending slavery into Texas and to the country farther west, the northern Whigs opined, southerners were rather lukewarm to the notion of expansion. In Texas, the northern Whigs suggested, the southerners, Whigs included, merely wanted the land but not the people. Southern Whigs were extremely livid over these insensitive accusations and responded rather bluntly that they "could never unite with the northern Whigs and do any good. The northern Whigs are the most cold-hearted–bigoted-selfish & incorrigible people upon earth.... They are the abolition party of the U. States. They have no common feeling with us whatever."[6]

Despite the potential repercussions from the Mexicans and certainly from the northern abolitionists as well, Texas annexation was approved by Congress and signed by the president on December 29, 1845. After ten years as an independent republic, Texas was now the twenty-eighth state as well as the fifteenth and, as future events would dictate, the last slave state to join the Union.

The day after Polk read Slidell's report, an infuriated president directed Secretary Marcy to forward a letter to General Taylor that demonstrated the sincerity of the government's resolve. Taylor was directed to remove his army from Corpus Christi without delay and to advance southward to the Rio Grande. Specifically, Marcy told Taylor, "I am requested by the President to instruct you to advance and occupy, with the troops under your command, positions on or near the east bank of the Rio de Norte.... It is not designed, in our present relation with Mexico, that you should treat her as an enemy; should she assume that character by a declaration of war, or any open act of hostility toward us, you will not act merely on the defensive, if your relative means enable you to act otherwise."[7]

Being told they had to leave Corpus Christi was great news for Taylor's men, news they wanted to hear after many months of sheer boredom.

Reinforced to six regiments, Taylor's army consisted mostly of regulars, the kind of men who were tough and had gained a discipline derived from years of fighting hostile Plains Indians. The veterans were in stark contrast to the young recruits who had served anywhere from three months to one year. The raw newcomers were seemingly impervious to military discipline. Very few of them paid much attention to their officers and, as with all new soldiers, complaining became second nature. In most instances the regulars kept to themselves, wanting as little as possible to do with these brash and unruly volunteers.

While the army traveled overland, the artillery and other materials would travel via the Gulf of Mexico to Taylor's supply base at Point Isabel, just over a hundred miles north of the Rio Grande. That is, if he could get his hands on several ships. What made this problem even more frustrating was that no matter how often Taylor pleaded for transports, he was always either denied or offered unseaworthy vessels. Learning of Taylor's plight, Cdre. David E. Conner stepped in to offer Taylor some help. As commander of the Home Squadron, a fleet of nine ships patrolling the Gulf coastline, Conner offered Taylor the use of several small vessels, which he gladly accepted.

Once the logistic problems were resolved, the army marched out of Corpus Christi, two months after receiving their orders. Leading the way was General Taylor on his horse, Old Whitey, followed by the dragoons, nearly four hundred of them in a long column of four abreast. Bringing up the rear were over three hundred rickety wagons creaking along on iron-rimmed wheels, carrying food, supplies, ammunition, and other materials to ensure a self-sufficient fighting force. And in between were the six infantry regiments and three light-artillery batteries called "flying batteries." It was an impressive sight indeed.

Tough as they were, the two-hundred-mile trek southward to the Rio Grande was a punishing test of stamina and fortitude for both men and beast alike. The blistering heat on the sun baked barren landscape was brutal, and for those few wearing woolen uniforms the march was even more unbearable. Despite being without water, at times for over 36 hours, somehow, someway, the troops endured.

Finally, on March 24 the dehydrated and scorched army arrived in the vicinity of the Rio Grande. From that point the army shuffled eastward for another ten miles to their supply base at Point Isabel, a site selected primarily for its ample anchorage and direct access to the depots in New Orleans. Several days later, reassured that his three supply ships had already arrived safely, Taylor doubled back to a spot opposite the town of Matamoros. There, for the first time, they gazed upon the threatening guns and soldiers of the Mexican army just one hundred yards across the river. After seeing nothing but hot sand for days on end, the troops were enraptured by the sight of the white stucco houses and the abundance of green foliage. Especially catching their eye were the young women who frequently came down to the water's edge, disrobed and began to bathe as the men cheered them on.

In due course, over a dozen pieces of artillery were put in place and a makeshift earthen fortification was built, which the troops initially referred to as Fort Taylor but shortly after called Fort Texas. In the shape of a star, it was designed by Capt. Joseph K. F. Mansfield with walls 9 feet high and 15 feet wide at the base, and at each corner stood a piece of artillery primed and ready to fire. The massive walls, securing a 30-foot flagpole, covered a perimeter of about eight hundred yards, which was also surrounded by a ditch 8 feet deep. Here, with the Rio Grande separating them, both armies postured in a show of force.

The Mexican army at Matamoros was commanded by Gen. Pedro de Ampudia. Consisting of eight thousand troops, not including the sixteen hundred lancers under Gen. Anastasio Torrejón, it was ill equipped and, like the American army, noticeably lacking in military discipline. Their only advantage over the American forces was their overwhelming numbers and, to some degree perhaps, the battlefield experience gained from the numerous revolutions Mexico was notorious for.

Although there was a false sense of relative peace, just the presence of American forces at the Rio Grande was deeply insulting to Mexico, as was the American flag seen fluttering over Mexican territory. It represented a blatant demonstration of the American arrogance that, in their eyes, belittled the modest power of a smaller and poorer nation. In this regard, their pride, their honor, and their esteem were profoundly offended. Under this scenario, the American invaders had to be repulsed no matter the cost in lives and treasure. It would be just the thing Polk knew would happen, some people would later preach.

As a result, General Ampudia could not resist the urge to attack, and the sooner the better. Beforehand, however, he sent Taylor a message that demanded the withdrawal of the American army to the northern side of the Nueces River. Furthermore, if Taylor did not comply within 24 hours Ampudia would declare war and attack. But, although Taylor quickly rejected Ampudia's threat, the attack never occurred. Instead, the Mexican general was replaced by Gen. Mariano Arista, the 43-year-old commander of the so-called Army of the North.

Despite the change in Mexican leadership, Taylor anticipated an increase in aggressive behavior from the Mexican side following General Ampudia's threat. To counter that prospect, Taylor thought it best to inhibit the flow of food and military supplies destined for the Mexican troops at Matamoras. In this regard, on April 15 he ordered his ships at Point Isabel to blockade the mouth of the Rio Grande and requested his old friend Commodore Conner to intercept and remove all such supplies from ships coming into Brazos Santiago.

And so it was that the month went by with both sides glaring at each other across the river, each side waiting for the other to blink first.

And then it finally happened.

On April 23, 1846, a Mexican cavalry force of about two thousand riders led by General Torrejón was ordered by General Arista to cross the Rio Grande several miles upstream from Fort Texas. Learning of the Mexican incursion, Taylor dispatched Capt. Seth Thornton and a reconnaissance force of over 60 dragoons to scout the immediate area for signs of the intruders. With information gathered from a local, around 8:00 a.m. on the morning of April 25, while riding through the dense chaparral along a narrow road they spotted an abandoned adobe house. Thornton and his men had dismounted to search the house and other outbuildings when suddenly they came under fire from the field of chaparral. It was all a trap. A large number of Mexican troops, knowing the Americans were looking for them, were waiting in ambush for the unsuspecting dragoons to arrive. Quickly returning to their mounts, the dragoons attempted to escape only to find the only road out was blocked by General Torrejón's troopers. Outnumbered and surrounded, the Americans had no choice but to surrender. While 11 of his men were killed, Thornton and the other men were taken prisoner and brought to Matamoros the following day.

At Fort Texas, General Taylor immediately understood the gravity of this incident when he reported to Washington, "Hostilities may now be considered as commenced, and I have this day deemed it necessary to call upon the governor of Texas for four regiments of volunteers, two to be mounted and two to serve as foot."[8]

It should be noted that this one relatively minor attack on Thornton's troops, in itself, was not the sole cause of the war but was merely another of the aggressive Mexican encroachments that helped set it off. Also to be considered was the fact that many Americans, particularly those living in the southern states, harbored an extreme hatred toward Mexico. This was particularly true for those who remembered the Alamo and the merciless slaughter of its entire garrison by General Santa Anna's troops and the senseless massacre of over three hundred Texans at Goliad only weeks later. By the same token, many Mexicans were hostile to America and its citizens, a resentment created by the death and destruction from America's aggressive and unrelenting quest for Mexican land.

In any event, the combination of several factors, including mutual animosity, political instability, unending border clashes, the annexation of Texas, and the goals of Manifest Destiny, had all contributed to this bad blood. Finally, Polk's order for Taylor to occupy land in the disputed territory at the Rio Grande, a move the administration must have known would be perceived as an invasion of Mexican territory and challenged, brought the simmering resentment to a head. And with each move by one side followed by a countermove by the other side, conflict was sure to follow.

On May 9, during the evening dinner at the White House, Taylor's report arrived. That night the president conferred with his cabinet in the White House over the Thornton affair and its impact on U.S.–Mexican relations. The debate among Polk's most trusted advisers lasted for several hours as they discussed the ramifications that might arise from declaring war with Mexico. Would it bring on problems with the British? How was Congress going to react to the president's recommendation? And, Polk realized, it would be the first time the United States would be engaged in a major conflict on foreign soil. Whatever the argument was against war, Polk felt he could not stand by any longer. The status quo was over. The cabinet, which previously displayed some hesitation over declaring war, was now in favor of announcing a state of hostilities. Furthermore, with the murder of the American dragoons in cold blood and on American soil, if the president was looking for an excuse for Congress to declare war with Mexico, this was it.

Standing before Congress two days later, Polk declared:

> Mexico has passed the boundary of the United States, has invaded our territory and shed American blood upon the American soil. She has proclaimed that hostilities have commenced, and that the two nations are now at war.... As war exists, and, notwithstanding all our efforts to avoid it, exists by the act of Mexico herself, we are called upon by every consideration of duty and patriotism to vindicate with decision the honor, the rights, and the interest of our country.... In further vindication of our rights, and defense of our territory, I invoke the prompt action of Congress to recognize the existence of war, and to place at the disposition of the Executive the means of prosecuting the war with vigor, and thus hastening the restoration of peace.

Congress responded to the president's recommendation on May 13, 1846, when it voted overwhelmingly to declare war on Mexico, and with the full consent of Congress $10 million was appropriated and authorization given to recruit a new army of up to fifty thousand volunteers for a term of one year. Called the War Bill, it was signed into law by Polk that very same day.

At first blush the congressional vote was somewhat misleading. There were many questions still unanswered about Polk's motives for going to war. On the one hand, most Whigs in the North and South opposed the war. Instead, the Whigs were more inclined to focus on the economy and to strengthen it through increased industrialization. That, they believed, would better serve the United States than forcefully taking land from a weaker and smaller country just to expand her own. But they were in a terrible bind. If they voted for the war, they would be doing so against their principles. If they refused to agree to the war, they would be voting against the support of American troops who were in harm's way on the border.

On the other hand, most Democrats supported the war. Southern Democrats especially, and for self-serving reasons, were motivated by the current and popular belief in the principles of Manifest Destiny. They supported the so-called land grab because it would provide the South not only with more territory to expand slavery but also fresh fertile soil on which to grow their cash crops, both of which would help boost the sagging southern economy.

And even countering that rationale were the northern antislavery elements. They feared acquiring more land by the South would only provide more strength to the "slave-power conspiracy" and the deleterious effects that would have on the country. They were convinced that Polk's motive for going to war was only to acquire the Mexican territories regardless of the cost in blood and treasure. Once that was achieved the new land would be opened up to accommodate the South and to further the expansion of slavery. After all, they asked, wasn't he the owner of a large number of slaves himself, slaves who worked on his Mississippi cotton plantation? To others, the motive for the war was quite different for both countries. On the one hand, Mexico never recognized the Treaty of Valasco or, for that matter, Texas statehood. In that regard she was fighting for the return to the homeland of Texas, territory Mexico believed was stolen. On the other hand, the United States was fighting to acquire all the Mexican territory west of the Mississippi.

But despite one's objections for going to war or the bitterness over the suspicious manner in which the war was invoked, Congress knew this was a time for solidarity and support for the fighting men in the American army.

Following the signing of the War Bill, Polk called Gen. Winfield Scott to the White House and reluctantly offered the new command to the 60-year-old general who was serving as his general-in-chief and military adviser. With his military experience highly applauded as second to none, Scott was the epitome of a military hero. Known as "Old Fuss and Feathers" for his insistence on precise military appearance and strict discipline, he had commanded troops in the Battle of Lundy's Lane and the Battle of Chippewa during the War of 1812; the Black Hawk War; the Seminole and Creek Wars in Florida; and the Aroostook War along the Canadian border, as well as during the Cherokee removal in 1838. Three years later, as senior army commander, he was appointed general-in-chief upon the death of his predecessor, Gen. Alexander Macomb. At a height of six-five, Scott's imposing figure in full dress uniform not only captivated the ladies but also intimidated everyone else. In short, the general was an impressive sight and his military presence was undeniable. But there was one problem. The president was not very fond of General Scott. He was egotistical and quite overbearing, personality traits completely contradictory to Polk's. "I have strong objections to Gen'l Scott," wrote Polk in his diary, "and nothing but stern necessity and a sense of public duty could induce me to place him at the head of so important an expedition."

During the days ahead, as the president contemplated the enormity of the war effort he began to have serious doubts about Scott's capacity for undertaking such a leadership position. Furthermore, since Scott outranked General Taylor, he would be the overall military commander of the war effort, a scenario Polk was a bit hesitant to endorse. Growing uneasy over offering the command to Scott, the president had to find a diplomatic way to withdraw his offer and at the same time appear to maintain his full confidence in his military adviser.

It was hardly surprising that even though Congress had already accepted Texas into the Union, Polk was still obsessed with acquiring even more Mexican territory, such as the land comprising present-day California and New Mexico. In fact, he was so obsessed with this notion that on the very day he signed the bill that declared war with Mexico he was planning to hold a secret meeting with the exiled Santa Anna about a scheme they would undertake if he should return to power

In July of 1846 the president received a report to inform him about this meeting, from the undercover emissary who had held a secret meeting with Santa Anna, who, as you recall, was exiled to Havana only a year ago. He was Cdr. Alexander Slidell Mackenzie, John Slidell's brother. The agent's mission was to arrange a meeting and to inform Santa Anna that Polk, wanting to avoid further hostilities, was urging him to return to Mexico at the first opportunity, regain power, and arrange a peace settlement satisfactory to both sides. Furthermore, the president was prepared to offer Santa Anna a considerable amount of cash in return for the territory Polk hoped he would cede to the United States in the settlement, namely, California and New Mexico. As Mackenzie and Santa Anna relaxed in the cool shade of his guarded estate sipping their drinks, he listened to Polk's proposition with keen interest. Then, in Santa Anna's customary hospitable manner whenever cash was mentioned, he must have smiled broadly and raised a toast when he agreed to participate in this generous proposition.

With the endorsement of Polk's cabinet and several loyal senators, the following month he asked the Senate for $2 million "for the purposes of satisfying any unforeseen expenses which might arise in the settlement of differences with Mexico."[9] Everyone, of course, knew what the money was really for, even the British press, which said that "most probably, the price of his restoration to power will be a treaty of peace, advantageous to the United States."[10]

Evidently Polk must have anticipated this plot was going to work, because, as discovered later, on May 13, the very day President Polk signed the War Bill, he also instructed Secretary of the Navy George Bancroft to forward a one-line message to Commodore Conner in the Gulf that simply stated, "If Santa Anna endeavors to enter the Mexican ports, you will allow him to pass freely."[11]

However, Polk's naïveté would eventually backfire on him.

By some strange coincidence, in the meantime a movement had been ongoing in Mexico City for the return of Santa Anna to the presidency. Revolutionary groups were unhappy with the latest government and its failure to provide adequate protection to the northern provinces against Taylor and the American invasion. Therefore, as was the custom in Mexican politics, this latest group of protestors was seeking to oust the current undesirable president and replace him with Santa Anna, their beloved Savior of the Motherland. Finally, unable to silence the personal attacks from his opponents or the condemnation of his presidency, Mariano Paredes chose to resign from office.

Despite being in exile, Santa Anna had always paid very close attention to the political and military turmoil that was tearing his country apart. The information he received came from the ongoing reports provided by his most loyal supporters. In all probability, Santa Anna must have interpreted the latest instability in Mexico as yet another opportunity for him to satisfy his instinctive urges to rescue his homeland militarily and at the same time fulfill his ego politically. In this regard, Santa Anna wrote a carefully worded letter to the government in Mexico City that declared he no longer had aspirations for the presidency but would eagerly use his military experience to fight off the foreign invasion of General Taylor's army as he had done to other invaders many times before. The new interim president, Gen. Mariano Salas, was desperate enough to accept the offer and agreed to return Santa Anna as the leader of the Mexican army.

As a consequence, on August 16, 1846, former president and general Santa Anna was allowed to pass through the American naval blockade as agreed to by Polk and disembark in the port of Veracruz. It was the end of Santa Anna's yearlong exile in Cuba. Not only were the revolutionary factions in Mexico overjoyed but also President Polk, who was beginning to see his prearranged scheme with Santa Anna starting to materialize. The following month Santa Anna returned to Mexico City and won the hearts of his people with his special brand of bravado and political manipulation. Standing before a wild and admiring throng, he ended his speech with the words, "Mexicans! There was once a day, and my heart dilates with the remembrance, when leading on the popular masses and the army, to demand the rights of the nation, you saluted me with enviable title of soldier of the people. Allow me to again take it, never more to be given up, and to devote myself, until death, to the defense of the liberty and independence of the republic."[12] As one adoring Mexican later expressed, "The most illustrious of its children is home again; he who has saved us always during the great conflicts.... The courageous and great Santa Anna is in Veracruz. God has saved Mexico."[13]

Back in favor with the masses and praised as the savior of Mexico once again, Santa Anna journeyed on to San Luis Potosí, where he would assemble an expeditionary army to fight the American invaders.

9

The Battles of Palo Alto, Resaca de la Palma and Monterrey

At Fort Texas, the sudden display of aggression against Captain Thornton and his dragoons forced General Taylor to seriously contemplate the strength of the Mexican army. In turn, he became increasingly concerned about his ability to sustain his troops against such an army with the meager rations, ammunition, and other supplies he had on hand. Therefore, after leaving behind two weeks of supplies and a sufficient number of troops to defend the fort, on May 1, 1846, Taylor marched the majority of his army, along with three hundred empty wagons, to his supply base at Point Isabel. He had two tasks to complete; loading all three hundred wagons with supplies and improving the defenses of Fort Polk, a small fortification Taylor established at Point Isabel. (The Port Isabel lighthouse now stands on the site of the fort.) Two days later, while still loading the wagons, the men were startled by the unmistakable sounds of artillery fire resonating from the direction of Fort Texas. Reacting quickly, Taylor ordered a detachment back to Fort Texas to make contact with the commander, Maj. Jacob Brown, and to report back to Point Isabel with their findings.

The report back confirmed Taylor's suspicions. Since most of the Fort Texas garrison was in Point Isabel, Ampudia's artillerists in Matamoros had seized this opportunity to lob artillery shells into the fort to harass the remaining small number of defenders. Confident that Major Brown had the situation under control, the army remained at Point Isabel for two more days to finish loading supplies into the hundreds of wagons. Meanwhile, as the cannonading continued, General Arista also took advantage of Taylor's absence by crossing the Rio Grande to a position he thought would entrap Taylor's enormous wagon train as they returned from Point Isabel.

Once the wagons were fully loaded, returning to Fort Texas was a slow and tedious piece of work for Taylor's men. Transporting two 18-pounders by teams of oxen and pulling hundreds of overloaded and rickety wagons was no easy task. While Taylor's troops were retracing their way back to Fort Texas, in the afternoon of May 8, they were surprised to encounter the Mexican forces that had been patiently waiting for them and their enticing train.

Taylor Crosses the Rio Grande

According to Taylor's official report, the opposing army was occupying the road before them in a double line nearly a mile long at a place called Palo Alto, artillery interspersed sporadically among them. "Their left," Taylor continued, "was composed of a heavy force of cavalry ... while masses of infantry were discovered in succession on the right greatly outnumbering our own force." Spoiling for a fight since their arrival, Taylor ordered an entire dragoon regiment to protect his all-important supply train while the remaining regiments were assembled into their battle lines and his artillery dispersed intermittently across the field. "At two o'clock we took up the march by heads of columns, in the direction of the enemy, the 18-pounder following the road," he reported. "The first fires of the enemy did little execution, while our 18-pounders and the [light] artillery ... soon dispersed the cavalry which formed his left."[1]

For the rest of the afternoon both sides continued to exchange cannon fire without any apparent success. Gen. Ulysses S. Grant, who was a captain at the time, would later write in his memoirs, "As we got nearer, the cannon balls commenced going through the ranks. They hurt no one, however, during this advance, because they would strike the ground long before they reached our line, and ricocheted through the tall grass so slowly that the men would see them and open ranks and let them pass."[2] Around the same time, General Arista ordered Torrejón and his lancers, about eight hundred riders, to charge into the American army. By forming a hollow square, the textbook procedure for fighting a cavalry charge, Taylor's men were able to repulse the assault with relatively little damage.

Elsewhere, when clouds of heavy black smoke from a grass fire obscured the field, fires accidentally ignited by the burning wadding of the artillery, Taylor seized the advantage and sent his dragoons rushing through the smoke screen toward the enemy artillery. As the smoke quickly lifted, however, Arista's artillery opened up with fervor and sent the dragoons reeling back to safety. Following their withdrawal from the field, a counterattack by the light artillery was ordered and when firing begun within point-blank range proved to be too much for the Mexican artillerists to handle they were finally persuaded to retreat.

By that time approaching nightfall called an end to the Battle of Palo Alto, the first major battle of the American–Mexican war. According to Taylor's own report, "The actual number engaged with the enemy did not exceed one thousand and seven hundred. Our loss was three officers killed and twelve wounded; thirty-six men killed and seventy-one wounded."[3]

Early the following morning, the ninth, General Arista abandoned the battlefield in search of a more secure and stronger position. Just before noon he located a dry lake bed called Resaca de la Palma, where the natural fortifications made it an excellent spot to form his lines and to shore up his defenses. When Taylor discovered his opponent had evacuated the field a reconnaissance team was dispatched to locate his whereabouts. In the meantime, Taylor conducted a council of war with his staff to determine the best strategy for dealing with his Mexican foe. Following a loud and somewhat animated exchange of opinions, they were left with two options, stay where they were and wait for reinforcements or, despite being vastly outnumbered, pursue the enemy and attack. Seven of the ten officers preferred to wait for reinforcements, but Taylor wanted to attack now—so that's what they did.

Since he suspected that his wagon train was the focus of his enemy's attack, that afternoon, while the Mexican army was preparing their columns for the fight, the first priority for Taylor was to secure the train with four pieces of artillery, the two 18-pounders used the day before and two 12-pounders. At that point, the army suddenly came under withering artillery fire so intense that a light-artillery battery was ordered to continue up the road to confront the trigger-happy Mexicans. At the same time, a detachment of infantry troops was dispatched into the dense chaparral to locate their exact position. As the infantry forces struggled to get through the thick, thorny brush on both sides of the road, artillery rounds shrieked over their heads, forcing them to advance in a crouching position.

Receiving word from the troops that the Mexican guns on the left side of the road were firing from a position directly in front of them, around 3:00 p.m. Taylor ordered his dragoons to charge into the enemy's position. The American horsemen created an enormous amount of damage on their first pass and in so doing cleared the way for the infantry to finish the assault. In fact, this phase of the Battle of Resaca de la Palma was so intense there was little time for either side to reload their muskets. As a result, the fight escalated into a bloody bayonet duel. In time, the Mexicans had had enough and abandoned the field, leaving several of their big guns behind in their haste to retreat.

According to Taylor, "The Mexicans contested every inch of ground with a bravery and determination that only the valor of American soldiers could have overcome. But the deadly discharge of artillery and musketry, and the repeated charge of our troops, was too much for flesh and blood long to endure, and they now began to waver, and at last to give way."[4] Despite the ferocity of the American troops, the Mexican cannonading continued; as recalled by Taylor, "The action now became general; and although the enemy's infantry gave way ... his artillery was still in position to check our advance, several pieces occupying the pass across the ravine."[5] The contest in the ravine was long and bloody. And again the dragoons were called into action, and again in quick fashion the annoying guns were silenced. Meanwhile, on the right side of the road, several of Taylor's infantry regiments easily captured the remaining batteries as the Mexican troops fled to the rear. To the delight of Taylor's young fighters, just before dusk the dispirited Mexicans finally broke and in a massive rout a large portion of General Arista's army was sent fleeing back across the Rio Grande to Matamoros. In fact, the attack on the Mexican position was so overwhelming that in the army's haste to retreat General Arista left all of his belongings behind in his quarters. Consequently, as an extra bonus, along with the armaments of war, Taylor's troops confiscated all of General Arista's official correspondence, along with his personal items as souvenirs.

For the American army, the day's action resulted in 39 men killed and 71 wounded. Beside the immense loss to his self-esteem, General Arista suffered an estimated loss of nearly 1,200 casualties.

In his report, General Taylor also recounted the extraordinary courage of one of his officers, an example of the terrible carnage experienced by both sides that day:

> In the excitement, Lieutenant-Colonel McIntosh dashed on a wall of chaparral, although it was lined with infantry and cavalry. Under a galling fire he broke it down by repeated blows of his sword, and the weight of his horse. The instant he got through, his horse fell dead from under him; Colonel McIntosh sprang to his feet; a crowd of Mexicans, armed with muskets and lancers, rushed upon him; still he gallantly defended himself. A bayonet passed through his mouth and came out below his ear; seizing the weapon, he raised his sword to cut the fiend down who held it, when another bayonet passed through and terribly shattered his arm, and another still, through his hip; borne down by a superiority of force, he fell, and was literally pinned to the earth.[6]

Rejoicing over their accomplishment the following day, the American fighters had every reason to celebrate. Taylor's men had beaten an army more than double their number and in their first engagement with the enemy. The Americans had clearly demonstrated their ability to fight and whip a larger army, and their self-confidence and morale soared.

When the first news of Taylor's victories at Palo Alto and Resaca de la Palma reached the White House Polk was thoroughly ecstatic. The battlefield victories gave him the opportunity he had been looking for. It seems Congress had recently authorized the addition of one major general and two brigadier generals for the new army. With the news of Taylor's accomplishments Polk decided to keep Taylor in his position on the

Rio Grande as the new major general and the two brigadier ranks went to Col. Stephen W. Kearny in New Mexico and Col. David E. Twiggs, one of Taylor's commanders. Scott, however, was politely told that the country would be better served if he remained in Washington to devote his efforts to making arrangements and preparations.

Before the Army of Occupation resumed their march southward toward Fort Texas, Taylor traveled back to Point Isabel to discuss new procedures for processing incoming goods, materials, supplies, and troops with Commodore Conner. Having already secured the waters around the mouth of the Rio Grande, they made arrangements whereby cargo and troops would bypass Point Isabel entirely. Instead, all incoming men and supplies would be delivered to Brazos Island. From that point they could easily be transported to bases along the Rio Grande and then to Matamoros or other interior campsites.

When the headlines announced that war was declared against Mexico, American men of all ages felt morally and politically obligated to offer their services in support of their country. It was a form of mid-nineteenth-century political correctness. At that time, defending one's country in time of need was not something one merely thought of doing or letting someone else do; it was from a sense of deep pride and patriotism that the men were expected to risk their lives to uphold the honor of their family name and for the good of their state and their country. Volunteers by the thousands rushed to enlist. In fact, within the first several months about eight thousand recruits were added to the crush of personnel already waiting on Brazos Island for processing, men whom General Taylor could not accommodate immediately to fight in the northern provinces. They would have to wait until the new army just authorized by Congress was formed.

For the thousands of volunteers waiting for processing the conditions on the island were atrocious. The first test of their stamina was being exposed to the terrible heat each day. Without much available shade, which was mostly reserved for the sick volunteers (the sick and wounded regulars enjoyed the shade inside the hospital), the men had to find ways to avoid being grilled between the hot glaring sun from above and the incessant heat radiating from the burning sand they stood on. Furthermore, during the process of becoming impervious to the searing temperature the volunteers had to endure the swarm of annoying insects of all kinds that were a constant source of sickness. Of course, the hardships the men had to endure on Brazos Island were, in a way, part of the indoctrination process, part of boot camp. Whether they liked it or not, the men were being forced to acclimate to these horrid conditions, since once they were assigned to the field they would more than likely face the same conditions or even worse, not to mention being under fire at the same time. About the only encouraging aspect of their stay on Brazos Island was that volunteer soldiers could, on average, be processed into units and shipped out to an inland base in about five days. For the officers, however, it took less than 24 hours.

When Taylor returned back to Fort Texas he was deeply saddened when he learned his old friend Maj. Jacob Brown had died during the Mexican attack. An army veteran of thirty years, Brown was killed instantly by the blast of an incoming artillery shell as he was inspecting his defenses. As a tribute to the fallen patriot, General Taylor issued an order that changed the name of the fort to Fort Brown. Over the years since then, a city grew around the fort that is today called Brownsville, Texas.

Emboldened by their battlefield victory and supremely confident in their fighting spirit, the brash and cocky Americans proudly marched out of Fort Brown on May 17 and with the use of several boats crossed the Rio Grande the following day. Fully prepared to engage Arista's entrenched forces, to their surprise the following day Taylor was told that the Mexican army had split up and was moving southward. General Arista and a portion of his army were marching to Linares, Mexico, about 60 to 70 miles to the southwest, and General Ampudia and the other troops were on their way to reinforce Monterrey. (At Linares Arista was severely reprimanded for failing to defend the honor of his country, and as a result he was tried by court-martial and dismissed from the army two months later.) At the White House, however, the fact that Taylor allowed Arista to evacuate Matamoros unchallenged did not go unnoticed.

Taylor's forces occupied Matamoros completely unchallenged, and once settled in their new surroundings the young and undisciplined volunteers began to enjoy their stay to the fullest. As in any town where the American troops pitched their tents, the locals saw a great opportunity to drain every last dollar off the rowdy groups of young men looking for a good time. The saloons sprang up overnight serving rotgut drinks and the ever-present houses of ill repute were always ready to accommodate the men for the right price. And of course, with this combination there was always trouble with fights, robberies, and even killings.

While all this merriment was going on, General Taylor, not one known for being overly strict with his troops, began to outline his advance to Monterrey, a trek of some 190 miles to the south. Taylor had two routes he could use to reach Monterrey. One was by way of Linares, the other via Camargo, the town where Taylor preferred to establish his base. Since a reconnaissance team had already ruled out Linares because Arista was still there with around one thousand men, Taylor's Army of Occupation gradually left Matamoros beginning in July using a number of riverboats and traveled upriver to Camargo, a town three miles off the Rio Grande on the San Juan River.

On the one hand, the journey was far from easy. The strong currents of the river forced frequent delays, much frustration, and many angry outbursts from the highly annoyed riverboat pilots. On the other hand, the time onshore were greatly appreciated by Taylor's men, who welcomed the chance to leave the steamers, mingle with the people they met along the way and take part in more of the good life they had enjoyed in Matamoros.

Life in the Camargo campsite, however, was somewhat different and very deadly. In time, the camp developed into a cesspool of filth and unsanitary conditions. The unhygienic lifestyles of thousands of men living together only exacerbated the spread of diseases and deaths. In fact, by the time the Army of Occupation left Camargo for Monterrey well over a thousand troops had died. So many funerals were held that the camp actually ran out of wood to build coffins. Instead the bodies were laid to rest wrapped in blankets or whatever else was available.

It was here in Camargo that Taylor was the recipient of several volunteer generals who had just arrived from the United States. They included Gens. William O. Butler, Gideon J. Pillow, James Shields, and John A. Quitman. Unfortunately, when Taylor decided it was time to leave Camargo not everyone was lucky enough to be with him.

A reserve garrison of some forty-five hundred men remained behind under the command of Gen. Robert Patterson.

Three days after they arrived in Camargo, beginning on August 29, the army of about six thousand troops gladly marched away from the festering town and headed southward toward the town of Cerralvo, some 60 miles away. Half of the troops were untested volunteers getting their first taste of the hardships of army life and a reality check of their training on Brazos Island. Marching with full backpacks in the searing heat proved too much for many of the young recruits. On many occasions some of the men were unable to properly ration their daily supply of drinking water, a deadly lack of judgment under these trying conditions. Obviously, they soon became dehydrated, which only resulted in frequent delays to rest, a complete loss of discipline, intermingling of units, and further delays in arriving at Cerralvo.

In Cerralvo the troops who survived were rewarded with plenty of water, rest, and another opportunity to socialize with the Mexican people. Once the army was reorganized and refreshed, the Army of Occupation resumed their march, this time departing Cerralvo by divisions until they reached the deserted town of Marin. There Taylor halted until his army regrouped, all the while being shadowed from a distance by a contingent of Mexican cavalry led by General Torrejón, remembered for his ambush of Captain Thornton. As the army paused in Marin they could only contemplate the inevitable battle that awaited them in Monterrey, only 25 miles away. "To all ranks," one soldier wrote, "particularly to us raw volunteers, the proximity of our enemy, and the certainty of combat, was strangely exciting. How anxiously did the mind at that hour contemplate the future! How busy, too was memory of the past!"[7]

Since they had left Camargo the only sight of the enemy was of the constant surveillance of the Mexican cavalry "escorting" them some distance away. As they approached Monterrey, however, the sight of the city returned them all to the harsh reality of the moment.

On the morning of September 19, 1846, the American forces arrived at the outskirts of Monterrey and were warmly greeted by artillery fire from the city's defenses. A city of about fifteen thousand people, Monterrey was well defended under the military leadership of Gen. Pedro de Ampudia, a popular officer in Mexico, although not of the good sort. At 41 years old, he was notorious for being a ruthless killer noted for his needless cruelty. In May, when he was the overall commander in Matamoros, the citizens who were wary of his wicked reputation appealed to the authorities in Mexico City to reconsider his assignment. Surprisingly, they listened and he was quickly replaced with General Arista. In 1844, for example, Ampudia had boasted how he allowed a condemned prisoner by the name of Francisco Sentmanat, a former governor of the state of Tabasco and political agitator, the time to make his will and to receive the last rites of the church before he had him executed by a firing squad. Ampudia then ordered the deceased man to be buried in consecrated ground only to be dug up a few minutes later and displayed as a public spectacle. If that weren't gruesome enough, Ampudia then ordered the man's head removed, boiled in oil, and displayed in a cage outside a government building in San Juan Bautista as an example to others.[8] Now commanding Monterrey, General Ampudia was indeed a force to be reckoned with.

Finding no tactical advantage in continuing their advance while under assault, the army set up their bivouac at a location called Bosque de San Domingo. It was a pleasant respite for the weary troops, being strewn with cool gushing springs and a collection of trees to relax under out of the Mexican midday sun. The camp was situated on a road that some distance ahead branched off into a fork. The left-hand road skirted around one edge of the city while the road that branched off to Taylor's right went directly into the center of Monterrey. Taylor's first order of business, therefore, was to dispatch a reconnaissance expedition down the right side toward Monterrey to determine the strength of Ampudia's defenses.

That night the reconnaissance report, submitted by Maj. Joseph Mansfield, head of the Engineers, convinced Taylor that to capture Monterrey his six-thousand-man army was in for the fight of their lives. The city was well defended on three sides by about seven thousand troops while the foothills of the Sierra Madre and the meandering Santa Catarina River protected the city from the rear. One side of Monterrey was defended by two small forts, both accessible from the left side of the fork. One was called Fort Diablo or Devil's Fort, a well-built stronghold possessing three heavy guns. The other was a converted tannery, now fortified and heavily manned; it was believed to be the stronger of the two.

Also part of Ampudia's defenses were several gun emplacements defending the right side of Monterrey. These batteries were located on two distant hills roughly 45 degrees to the right of Taylor's position. One was called Independence Hill, and across the Santa Catarina River was Federation Hill. However, the most ominous defensive structure in Monterrey lay directly ahead of their camp on the right side of the fork and was the culprit showering them with solid cannonballs each day. What towered before them was a massive masonry quadrangle, locally known as the Citadel or the Black Fort, which stood like a giant sentry guarding the entrance into the center of Monterrey. Although the fort had been built to hold some 30 guns, its towering height put nearly the entire city in range of the 8 guns it actually mounted.

Taylor's army was organized into three divisions. Recently promoted Gen. David E. Twiggs commanded the 1st Division; Gen. William J. Worth, the 2d; and Gen. William O. Butler the 3d. (A fourth commander, Gen. Robert Patterson, was still in Camargo.)

Following a council of war, General Taylor's battle plan called for splitting his army into two flanking pincers. A regiment of Texas Rangers and two thousand regulars under General Worth would conduct a wide-flanking movement to the right, which would circle around the far perimeter of the city through the woods to the Saltillo Road. The capture of this road was the most critical stage of the mission. Once it was secured, not only would Ampudia's only escape route be closed, but that would also prevent incoming reinforcements and supplies from reaching the city from Saltillo, only about 75 miles to the southwest. Once the road was secured, the following day Worth had to capture the batteries positioned on the tops of both hills. It was a very demanding mission, but Taylor had the utmost confidence that his general was capable of succeeding. While Worth was carrying out his movement on their right flank, the remaining two divisions under Generals Twiggs and Butler would advance along the left side of the fork. Their orders were to merely create a diversionary attack in order to prevent a shift of Mexican

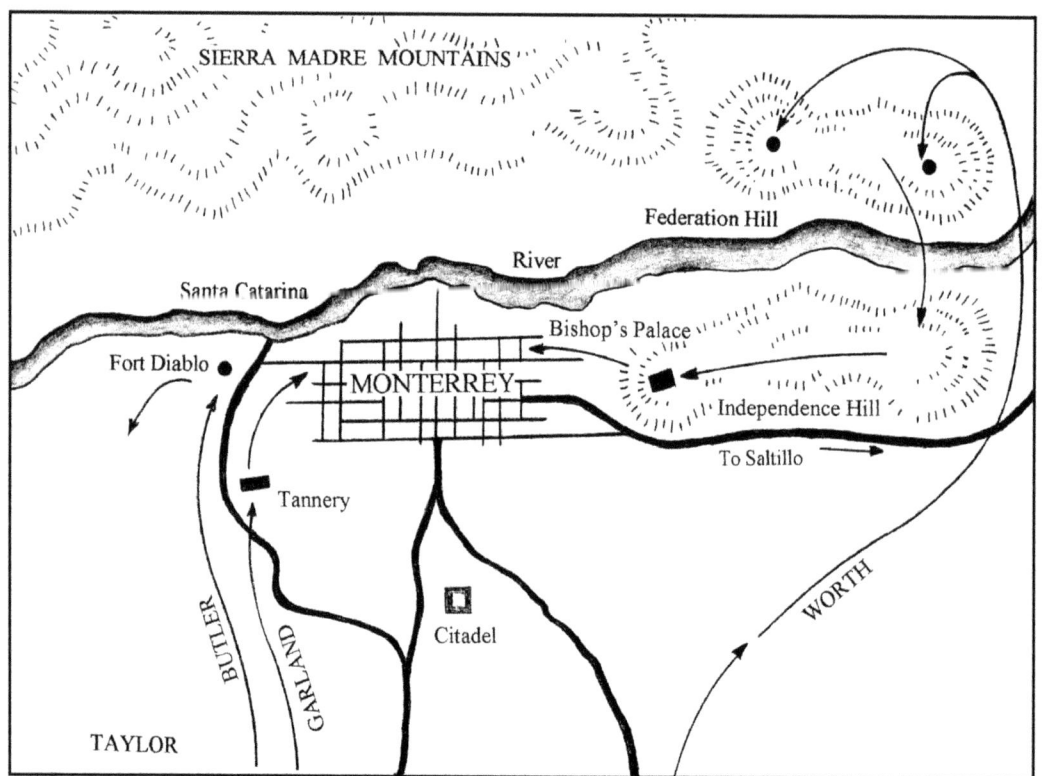

The Battle of Monterrey

troops to challenge General Worth. Taylor's main batteries, meanwhile, would bombard the city from the front. From his years of combat experience Taylor was well aware of the risk he was taking by splitting his army in the face of a superior army. With both halves of his forces separated from each other by a considerable distance, it would be virtually impossible for either one to reinforce the other if attacked.

With the army in high spirits, on the afternoon of the twentieth General Worth began his right-flanking movement while Taylor's artillery opened a steady barrage into Monterrey. Following a march of about seven miles and with dusk approaching, Worth's troops set up a small makeshift camp and settled down for the night.

Taylor knew he was fortunate to have General Worth in his command. He was an officer who had distinguished himself in the War of 1812, where he saw action at the battles of Chippewa, Lundy's Lane, Fort George, and Crysler's Farm. Following the war he became the commandant of cadets at West Point and later served in the Second Seminole War in Florida. In May 1841 he became the commander of the U.S. forces in Florida before joining the Army of Occupation.

The following day Worth's men were nearly at the Saltillo Road when the advance scouts of the Texas Rangers began to receive incoming fire. The shots came from a Mexican contingent of infantry and lancers approaching from the vicinity of the Saltillo Road. Instinctively taking up defensive positions, the American troops returned the deadly fire from behind the relative safety of boulders, stone walls, and trees. Undeterred, the Mexican lancers charged into the fray, many falling victim to the merciless blasts of the two American batteries now unlimbered for action. As quickly as it began it was over. After a 15-minute exchange of gunfire the Mexicans abruptly abandoned the field, leaving nearly one hundred dead soldiers behind. With the Saltillo Road cut off the Mexican army was now trapped within the city. The downside was that once General Ampudia realized his army had no escape route they might be encouraged to fight even more fiercely. Nevertheless, the capture of the Saltillo Road was indeed a very major victory for General Taylor's army.

Maintaining their circuitous route in the pouring rain, General Worth decided to take on the lightly defended Federation Hill first. The first order of business was to locate a point where the army could safely cross the Santa Catarina River. Following a quick reconnaissance, a shallow segment of the river was easily forded and the storming party of about three hundred men continued on to the base of Federation Hill. After climbing the four hundred feet with several pieces of artillery in tow they quickly overwhelmed the Mexicans manning an earthwork. Then, as the Americans moved on toward the enemy battery emplacement an effective display of artillery firepower quickly persuaded the Mexican artillerists to abandon their guns and flee into Monterrey. With Federation Hill and the road to Saltillo secured, Worth's exhausted but victorious troops called off their assault on Independence Hill until the morning. Exhilarated over their conquest, the troops bedded down in the rain without blankets or food but anxious to resume their work in the morning.

Using the early morning darkness, fog and rain for cover, on September 22 a fresh supply of troops easily scampered up the slope of Independence Hill. About four hundred yards away on the opposite side of the hill was a sandbagged ruin called the Bishop's Palace housing a garrison of about two hundred Mexican soldiers. After a quick appraisal of their field position, the rest of the morning was spent hauling a howitzer up the eight-hundred-foot hill. What followed in the afternoon was a relatively ineffective artillery duel.

Toward evening the Mexican soldiers became somewhat desperate and in the growing twilight launched an all-out charge against the American lines. Quickly repulsed, Worth's men then counterattacked, swept the field, and captured the Bishop's Palace, its surviving defenders retreating for their lives into the city below. The sight of the Stars and Stripes fluttering smartly atop Federation and Independence Hills was a great boost for the troops back in camp. With a resounding cheer, the newly inspired men were again ready to fight another day.

In the meantime, while General Worth's men were occupied on the right side of Monterrey on the left side five hundred men from General Twiggs's division, temporarily commanded by Col. John Garland, were tasked with drawing attention away from General Worth. Evidently, General Twiggs had taken a heavy dose of laxatives the night before and was now feeling quite ill. At the same time, General Butler's assignment was to demonstrate before Fort Diablo.

Marching in close order, their bayonets flashing in the bright Mexican sunlight, the troops began their advance. As they approached their objective, the big guns of both the tannery and the Citadel opened up a devastating barrage on Garland's troops. Continuing on with their drive, the Americans began to suffer even heavier casualties, but despite the onslaught, they still maintained their forward movement through the devastating fire. Enraged over the stubborn Mexican resistance at the tannery, Colonel Garland decided to modify Taylor's orders from a diversionary attack to a direct assault. But as Garland's troops edged even closer to their target, they were taking additional fire from Fort Diablo as well. The firing became heavier and more deadly as the Mexican gunners found their marks. Amid the chaos of the smoke, the artillery reports, and the screams of wounded and dying troops, the order to retreat was given and Garland's troops quickly retreated back out of range. When a brigade of reinforcements under Gen. John A. Quitman arrived they were astonished to discover some of Garland's men might not have heard the order to retreat and were still in the thick of the fight. Garland's men, firing from a nearby rooftop, saw several Mexican fighters fleeing from the tannery. At that point they stormed the tannery and captured the works along with a number of prisoners in the process. It was by anyone's standards a dreadful and bloody fight, but in the end the tannery was finally occupied by U.S. forces. The price for this small victory, however, was much too high in dead and wounded.

General Butler's troops, however, were in even worse trouble. The stiff enemy resistance at Fort Diablo forced their offensive to sputter, and with their casualties mounting steadily they were forced to retreat as well. By this time Taylor was totally exasperated. What he had planned as a mere demonstration left him no other choice but to call the troops back to camp with the exception of those occupying the tannery. In their first major encounter with the enemy, Taylor's army suffered nearly four hundred casualties in dead and wounded. And Monterrey itself had yet to be attended to.

As the exhausted men straggled back, the once pleasant campsite was suddenly transformed into a chaotic blend of loud staccato commands amid the moans and sobs of the walking wounded. Soon the bloodied scene was embellished even more as wagons of severely wounded were brought in. As they were attended to by the surgeons wielding their instruments and saws, the screams and heart-wrenching cries reminded everyone of the price they paid for defending their country's honor.

Now that his tannery and hilltop fortifications were occupied by American forces and his line of retreat closed, General Ampudia withdrew his army from the city's perimeter (except for the Citadel) and moved into the relative safety of Monterrey itself. There they could ambush the Americans from the rooftops and hide in the dark corners of the white adobe houses lining the narrow streets.

With little rest for the weary, from their camp the next day Taylor's troops entered the streets of Monterrey, carefully advancing house by house. Hearing the gunfire coming from the city, General Worth also ordered his men to advance into Monterrey via the road from Independence Hill.

The streets were quite narrow and the houses that lined them on both sides were the typical flat-roofed dwellings. Most of them were constructed with adjoining walls and were virtually impregnable fortifications. To avoid being exposed to the hidden snipers among the sandbagged and parapet rooftops, the American troops were forced to enter the dwellings by battering through the walls. This procedure, reminiscent of the battle to take Béxar, was used from house to adjoining house as the Americans flushed out the Mexican soldiers. Recognizing the end was near and fearing his secretly hidden stash of ammunition in the cathedral might be blown up, General Ampudia asked for a halt to hostilities and negotiations for a truce. By this time Taylor's men were totally exhausted, casualties were well over five hundred and further fighting would only add more to an already-spent army. Furthermore, his ammunition was dangerously low and the army's rations had been depleted. Taylor, therefore, agreed to the cease-fire.

At a brief face-to-face meeting between Taylor and Ampudia, the Mexican general offered to surrender Monterrey on condition his army was free to leave. Taylor, however, insisted on an unconditional surrender of Monterrey as well as the Mexican army, a provision Ampudia was not willing to comply with. As a result, over the next several days three commissioners from each side haggled over the terms that would be agreeable to both sides. By this time, however, Taylor had relented and agreed to allow Ampudia and his army to simply leave to fight another day, soon to be a glaring point of condemnation from Polk and Taylor's other critics. Since the surrender of the army was now off the table, the only matter discussed by the commissioners was how much government equipment the army could take with them. In the end, Ampudia was permitted to keep six pieces of artillery and 21 rounds of ammunition and their sidearms and the cavalry retained their horses. U.S. Grant was one observer who wrote in his memoirs, "My pity was aroused by the sight of the Mexican garrison of Monterrey marching out of town as prisoners, and no doubt the same feeling was experienced by most of our army who witnessed it. Many of the prisoners were cavalry, armed with lances, and mounted on miserable little half-starved horses that did not look as if they could carry their riders out of town."[9]

With the army band playing "Yankee Doodle" amid the cheers of the bedraggled and exhausted men and a 28-gun salute fired from Independence Hill, the American banner was hoisted in the town square on September 25, 1846.

The victory at Monterrey was an enormous win not only for General Worth, who was named governor of Monterrey, but also for Taylor. The respect from the men who served under him could not have been greater and his political standing among the folks back home was definitely on the rise.

In Washington, however, Taylor's capture of Monterrey had injected a whole new wrinkle into the political complexion of the war. On the one hand, General Taylor, it seems, was now approaching the level of a national hero. In response to reports of his battlefield victories, he had acquired a soaring popularity at home and was even being mentioned as a possible presidential candidate. On the other hand, President Polk recognized that Taylor supported the Whig Party and with growing concern was keenly following the movement with interest. Consequently, at the White House the news of the truce at Monterrey was not well received. Irate over a perception that Taylor had acquired a truce when he could have captured the whole lot, Polk ordered the pact between Taylor and Ampudia terminated. In his message to Taylor, Secretary Marcy explained, "In relation to the terms of the capitulation of Monterrey, the President instructs me to say that he regrets it was not deemed advisable to insist upon the terms which you had first proposed.... Certain it is, however, the present rulers of that republic have not yet given any evidence that they are favorable to the interest of peace." And finally Taylor was ordered to "give the requisite notice that the armistice is to cease at once, and that each party is at liberty to resume and prosecute hostilities without restrictions....

It is therefore proposed that you should make the necessary arrangements for retaining possession of it during the war."[10]

Taylor felt somewhat rebuked by Polk's action but nevertheless complied with the order by notifying General Santa Anna in November. At the same time, Taylor was extremely troubled over rumors that he was being replaced by General Patterson.

"There is, I hear from high authority," Taylor lamented, "an intrigue going on against me; the object of which is to deprive me of the command; my only sin for this is the want of discretion on the part of certain politicians, in connecting my name as a proper candidate for the next presidential election, which I very much regretted, for even admitting I aspire to that high office for which I have not the most distant intention of doing, this is no time for agitating that question, it will be time enough to do so in 1848."[11]

Once their dead were laid to rest and the wounded tended to, during the last week in September 1846 Ampudia and his men departed Monterrey to join forces with General Santa Anna, who had just returned from Cuba and was beginning to assemble an expeditionary army at San Luis Potosí, nearly three hundred miles to the south of Monterrey.

10

A Shift in Strategy and the Battle of Buena Vista

By the fall of 1846 the war with Mexico had developed into a full-blown conflict as the American army and several naval fleets were mobilized on three different fronts.

On the northern front, General Taylor's mission was to occupy the northern provinces of Mexico. As a result, he had troops stationed in such places as Matamoros, Tampico, Camargo, Victoria, and Saltillo and was presently occupying Monterrey.

On the western front, Gen. Stephen W. Kearny was ordered to challenge Mexican forces in New Mexico and to occupy Santa Fe. And third, in the far west the Pacific Squadron under Cdre. John D. Sloat was to assume a standby status off the coast of Monterey, California, in a show of force.

These wide-ranging movements of U.S. forces reflected Polk's initial strategy in dealing with her southern neighbor. That strategy, simply stated, was to equip a sufficient number of troops to contain the Mexican army, to occupy the northern provinces, and to harass the Mexican government in the western territories. Being exposed to this level of military duress, Polk predicted, would quickly force the weaker and cash-strapped Mexican government to the bargaining table, where they would readily accept a land settlement consistent with American demands. Under this scenario, Polk was sure California and New Mexico would be given up, or even more.

In the meantime, however, public support for the war was beginning to wane. Reports in the press of American brutality against Mexican civilians, desecration of their Catholic churches by American troops, and disease-ridden conditions for the American boys to live in were causing much consternation.

In the White House, it was also becoming apparent to Polk and to his cabinet that the progress of the war was not living up to their expectations. As mentioned, Polk wanted to fight a brief war; a war that would bring Mexico quickly to her knees begging for a negotiated peace. And during these negotiations California and New Mexico would be put on the table. The Mexicans, he now assessed, were a proud and determined people and not about to concede easily. Therefore, a different strategy had to be employed to put this matter to rest, since the Americans' current program of a limited war in the northern provinces wasn't working. The problem, the administration concluded, was that the army was only hitting Mexico's extremities, not her soul. As a consequence, following weeks of deliberations, Polk recommended a concentrated drive on the very heart of Mexico herself—Mexico City. But there was one problem: who would lead the way?

Following numerous discussions with his cabinet and with close advisers from Congress over this very question, only two viable candidates stood out from all the rest, Zachary Taylor and Winfield Scott. And that's where Polk was in a dilemma. It seems both of these generals were members of the opposing political party and both were gaining support for political office, whether they wanted it or not. Other generals were considered, to be sure, but they either were too old, lacked the background and experience for this campaign, had personalities that made them unsuitable to work with, or were needed somewhere else. In the end, Polk rejected them all, including Taylor, whose reputation had dropped a notch in the White House since he signed the truce at Monterrey.

Perhaps closer to the truth was that having committed himself to only one term, the president, a loyal and incorrigible Democrat, on the one hand reckoned that the Whig Party would be significantly strengthened by Taylor's further rise in stature and would therefore be a potential threat in the next presidential election. On the other hand, although Scott was Polk's military adviser and a national hero from his exploits in the War of 1812, Polk's affection for the general was somewhat strained. Polk always felt that Scott was an overbearing egotist. And by virtue of his military stature, the general always tried to impress on Polk that he was the wiser of the two, that he was the one in control of the situation and the person with all the answers. Also, as it was with Taylor, Polk's hesitation was also based to a large degree on his suspicions of Scott's presidential ambitions. General Grant in his memoirs stated the situation quite eloquently. "He [Taylor] could not be relieved from duty in the field where all his battles had been victories; the design would have been too transparent. It was finally decided to send General Scott to Mexico in chief command, and to authorize him to carry out his own original plan; that is, capture Vera Cruz and march upon the capital of the country. It was no doubt supposed that Scott's ambition would lead him to slaughter Taylor or destroy his chances for the Presidency, and yet it was hoped that he would not make sufficient capital himself to secure the prize."[1]

Finally persuaded by Secretary Marcy that his general-in-chief was not a serious political threat to the Democratic Party and was the right man for the job, the decision was made. Accordingly, in November 1846 Polk reluctantly selected Scott as the commander to lead U.S. forces into Mexico City. As a result, an extremely delighted Scott was ordered to immediately prepare for his expedition to Mexico City.

As General Scott began to devise a plan to raise troops for his expedition, he discovered a problem. Most of the currently available manpower was in the pool of young volunteers with little or no military experience and the troops in the various militias. This, he pondered, would never do. Scott thought his army, especially one on such an important mission, should not be dependent on so many raw and inexperienced recruits but should be staffed by more battle-seasoned regulars. After all, he further opined, its commander was nothing less than the general-in-chief, who deserved to field the best troops he could find. Fortunately for Scott, the only place to find these troops was in the army at Monterrey, and Taylor was so notified in a letter Scott wrote from Matamoros the day after Christmas of 1846, a letter Taylor never read. Therefore, failing to receive a response from Taylor, Scott planned on going to the Rio Grande personally to do a bit of recruiting.

General Scott arrived in early January 1847 in Camargo, where he learned that Taylor was in Victoria. Consequently, Scott wrote a letter to General Butler at Monterrey explaining why he was in Camargo and with all the assertiveness he could muster in a letter directed him to send forty-five hundred cavalry and forty-five hundred infantry troops from Taylor's command to the Rio Grande, and Scott insisted, half of each group were to be regulars. Scott then used two couriers to deliver copies of the letter to Taylor, each taking a different route.

In Victoria, General Taylor was handed a copy of Scott's letter and reacted immediately. Outraged over the "kidnapping" of both General Twiggs and General Patterson and their troops along with many more of Taylor's soldiers still garrisoned in Camargo, he protested wildly that his army now had fewer than a thousand regulars and a volunteer force that was expected to fight an enemy of over twenty thousand seasoned combatants.

Arriving back in Monterrey, an embittered and defiant Taylor was still reacting in utter frustration and anger over Scott's seizure of his troops. Although Taylor was tempted to resign, he decided to stay on for the good of the country "however much I may feel personally mortified and outraged by the course pursued, unprecedented, at least in our own history."[2]

All his complaints of injustice were brushed aside by Scott, however, who merely reiterated his instructions that Taylor didn't need the troops since he was to remain in a defensive position at Monterrey. Furthermore, Scott said, "I hope I have left, or shall leave you, including the new volunteers who will soon be up, a competent force to defend the head of your line (Monterrey) and its communications, with the depots in the neighborhood. To enable you to do this more certainly I must ask you to abandon Saltillo, and to make no detachment, except for reconnaissance and immediate defense, much beyond Monterrey."[3] It was an order that infuriated Taylor even more.

By this time, Taylor was convinced that a conspiracy concocted in Washington was being played out against him. Evidently, he thought, his soaring popularity among the potential voters was causing some hard feelings in the capital city. Consequently, despite Scott's orders to the contrary, Taylor decided to keep Worth and his troops at Saltillo while Butler remained at Monterrey.

Ironically, back in the states, the news of this incident created enormous sympathy for Taylor's plight and sent his popularity soaring even higher. "Taylor for President" banners were now being seen everywhere and political rhetoric castigated the villains, Polk and his general-in chief.

While Santa Anna was in San Luis Potosí preparing to lead his new expeditionary army into battle, he received some very startling news. To demonstrate their renewed faith in their resurrected general, in December 1846 the Mexican Senate decided to return him to the presidency once again by electing him to replace the most recent deposed president, Mariano Salas. As usual, instead of going to Mexico City to take over the administrative duties as president, Santa Anna permitted the vice president, Gómez Farías to take charge of the country in his absence.

When President Polk received the news that Santa Anna was back in power he must have been quite thrilled that his covert plan with Santa Anna was progressing as he had hoped it would. As you recall, Santa Anna had secretly collaborated with Polk, pledging that if he was returned to power he would work to acquire a peace settlement that transferred Mexican territory to the United States. Living up to his unsavory reputation, however, Santa Anna denied any knowledge of the meeting or of the money he received.

Preparing his troops for battle against Taylor's invading troops was an enormous undertaking, if not an impossible one. Santa Anna knew his army lacked sufficient quantities of food, arms, ammunition, clothing, and all the other materials and supplies needed to remain self-sufficient over many days. On other occasions Santa Anna pleaded for funds from the government only to be denied. Even the Catholic Church, with its enormous wealth, refused to support the expedition. Becoming increasingly desperate, despite knowing the government treasury was depleted; he sent a letter to the Mexican congress informing them that if they failed to support their army he would not be held responsible for the defeat they were allowing to happen. Finally, Santa Anna was relieved to learn that an executive order by his vice president was passed that authorized the government to confiscate up to 15 million pesos by mortgaging or selling unused church properties.

This new edict, however, caused such an uproar that Santa Anna had to leave San Luis Potosí and return to Mexico City, where he struck a deal with the church. He convinced the clergy that the new law would be repealed and in return he persuaded them to lend the government 1.5 million pesos. And to placate the furor over the vice president's policy to finance the army with church funds, Santa Anna agreed to replace Farías with Gen. Pedro María de Anaya. Paradoxically, the money from the church was never received, which forced Santa Anna to fund part of the expedition out of his own pocket. He raised a half-million pesos when he mortgaged all of his properties as well as the property of his children.

Despite the army's shortfalls, Santa Anna was extremely confident that his larger army would crush the American forces. With that in mind his plan was to attack on his birthday, February 21.

With pressure increasing for Santa Anna to engage, on January 28, 1847, the new president and military commander broke camp and confidently left San Luis Potosí leading his roughly twenty thousand ragged and half-starved troops northward toward Monterrey.

Approximately three months before Santa Anna marched out of San Luis Potosí, around the first week of November 1846, Taylor learned that a U.S. Army unit was in Monclova, a town some 120 miles northwest of Monterrey. This unit was under the command of Gen. John E. Wool, a dapper officer who served as the army's inspector general for twenty years and in 1841 was selected to command the Army of the East. At 77, he held the distinction of being the oldest general on both sides and probably the strictest. Wool had just arrived from San Antonio on a mission to seize the small town of Chihuahua, some distance away to the northwest. Taylor, however, as senior commander in the field considered his present need for reinforcements a higher priority and quickly directed Wool to continue his march but toward Saltillo instead, where he would rendezvous with General Worth and his division.

In February, when General Wool and his three thousand troops arrived to join Taylor's remaining army, the newly formed Army of Occupation headed for a large hacienda called Agua Nueva, only 20 miles south of Saltillo.

Once he was settled at his new camp Taylor's first order of business was to order a reconnaissance of the surrounding area to ascertain the location of Santa Anna's army. Ben McCulloch of the Texas Rangers, the most reliable scout in the camp, was tasked with this duty. Once McCulloch located the Mexican army he slipped by the sentries under the cover of darkness and gained access to a hill overlooking the bivouacked troops. From his hidden vantage point on the hill, the next morning he enjoyed a sweeping view of the enemy's encampment spread out before him. McCulloch reported back on February 21 that General Santa Anna's legions were only about 60 miles away. Falling back on his military instincts from years of fighting Indians, Taylor was prepared to battle it out right there if it were not for the persistence of General Wool against such a risky defensive position. Persuaded that their present field position would not sustain an attack from the larger Mexican force, Taylor agreed to withdraw a short distance to La Angostura, otherwise known as the "Narrows," not far from the Hacienda de Buena Vista. At this point, Taylor left General Wool in charge and headed to Saltillo with a contingent of dragoons as escorts supposedly to check on the safety of his supplies.

General Wool knew Santa Anna and his troops were advancing along the main road from San Luis Potosí. Wool also knew that just before reaching Taylor's current position the road ran through a stretch of land that tapered down to a width of less than a hundred feet. Along that stretch of road one side was bordered by high bluffs and the other side by a small river and deep gullies, hence the name the Narrows. Since Wool expected Santa Anna to launch his initial frontal attack along this approach, a portion of the American army was straddled across the narrow road with artillery and two regiments of infantry to await Santa Anna's arrival. The balance of the troops and artillery were in position along a plateau to the army's left, which Wool determined would be a logical second route for Santa Anna to launch his flanking attack. It was a strong defensive position, thought Wool, the best tactic to neutralize the Mexicans' superior numbers.

The fact that he was significantly outnumbered did not deter Taylor in the slightest. His forces had been in this position many times before at Palo Alto, Resaca de la Palma, and Monterrey, where his men had proven the value of fighting spirit over mere numbers. The U.S. troops consisted mostly of raw volunteers equipped with the standard flintlock muskets and paper cartridges charged with powder, buckshot and ball. In fact, fewer than eight hundred had ever been in combat. Presently reduced to around five thousand men from desertions, deaths, and sickness, the Army of Occupation consisted of infantry units from Illinois and Indiana, two cavalry regiments from Arkansas and Kentucky, 18 pieces of artillery, 60 Texas Rangers, close to 200 dragoons, and the 368 members of the Mississippi Rifles. Now fully entrenched, they anxiously waited and watched the road ahead for the action that was sure to come.

On the morning of February 22, 1847, the day after Santa Anna celebrated his fifty-third birthday, the Mexican cavalry appeared and wisely halted out of gun range. By early afternoon Santa Anna's main force came into sight. They were exhausted, dehydrated, and weakened from the long, hard march from San Luis Potosí, a distance of some two hundred miles. It was a journey that took them across the hot desert and mountains, with the loss of over four thousand soldiers. Their lack of artillery and long-range rifles was also noted by Wool as a definite advantage for the American army. Also spotted on the field were General Pedro de Ampudia, the Mexican general Taylor had allowed to leave Monterrey after his surrender of the city in September, and his army.

Shortly after General Taylor returned from Saltillo, a courier carrying a white flag suddenly appeared on horseback with a message from Santa Anna requesting the surrender of Taylor's army. "You are surrounded by twenty thousand men, and cannot in any human probability avoid suffering a rout and being cut to pieces with your troops.... I wish to save you from a catastrophe, and for that purpose give you this notice, in order that you may surrender at discretion, under the assurance that you will be treated with the consideration belonging to the Mexican character; to which end you will be granted an hour's time to make up your mind, to commence from the moment when my flag of truce arrives in your camp."[4]

The request was declined.

The opening shots of the Battle of Buena Vista came that afternoon. And as predicted, one of Santa Anna's brigades opened fire from the San Luis Potosí road. The battle quickly escalated into a steady exchange of gunfire, although each side accomplished very little except to "feel out" the tenacity of the other. When the day ended and the firing had ceased, the volunteers all felt a sense of pride and a renewed camaraderie, knowing they had all survived an encounter with the enemy.

Taylor, meanwhile, returned to Saltillo for the night bringing along his former son-in-law, Col. Jefferson Davis, and his men of the Mississippi Rifles for company. At the outbreak of the war in 1846, Jefferson had resigned his seat in Congress and raised the volunteer rifle company. Meanwhile, the rest of the men left behind nearly froze to death shivering in the cold rain and sleeping on the wet ground.

Of course the Mexican troops suffered under the same trying conditions, including Santa Anna. It was reported that El Presidente complained a great deal because it seems all the action that day caused the wound on his amputated leg to open once again, a painful problem he had had to endure since the botched surgery was performed in 1838.

On the morning of the twenty-third, the men could hear the sounds of the Mexican reveille as it echoed from camp to camp. As their enemy stirred in the early morning cold and drizzling rain, it only reminded them that despite their eagerness to fight, they were perilously outnumbered by four to one.

Santa Anna's attack came fast and furious from two different directions, the San Luis Potosí road in the Narrows and, as predicted by General Wool, along the plateau on the army's left flank. The charge on the Narrows was opened by the same Mexican brigade that attacked the day before and again they were thrown back, stung by Taylor's artillery support and the keen eye of the American sharpshooters, some of whom were firing the latest Model 1841, .54-caliber muzzle-loaders, arguably the most accurate rifles of them all.

The Mexican offensive on the left flank, however, was quite a different story. Unable to hold back the two Mexican divisions along the plateau, Taylor's men broke and were sent scurrying back in full retreat. This left the American left flank wide open and placed

Taylor's entire army in peril. Furthermore, on the army's far left the Mexican cavalry had swung around the fighting and was seen heading toward Taylor's supply train, the loss of which would be a definite coup de grace for the Army of Occupation. Miraculously, General Taylor and the Mississippi Rifles reappeared on the battlefield and almost immediately Colonel Davis and his men were dispatched to close up the breach. Working together with a renewed and devastating bombardment from Lt. Braxton Bragg's superior artillerymen, Santa Anna's forces were persuaded to retreat.

Santa Anna, however, who was determined to return to Mexico City as a national hero, would not give up the fight. Following a conference with his officers, that afternoon Santa Anna made another attempt to circle around Taylor's army in what became the bloodiest day of the battle. In one display of his callous attitude, Taylor said when told the army was going to be defeated, "I know it, but the volunteers don't know it. Let them alone, we'll see what they can do."[5] With American forces again secure on the plateau, Santa Anna dispatched a fresh division and a contingent of cavalry to circle around Taylor's extreme left in an apparent attempt to encircle the entire American position. This time the Mexican forces were spotted during their advance and Davis was again tasked to thwart the incursion. Rising to the occasion a second time, the Mississippi Riflemen, along with two regiments of recruits and Bragg's artillery, assembled in formation and waited for Santa Anna's army to appear within range. When the Mexican troops came within a hundred yards of the waiting guns the signal was given and with a mighty roar a large swath of Santa Anna's men was cut down. Taken totally by surprise in the withering fire, the invading division broke in full retreat—but only to regroup once again. The Mexican counterattack was intense and brutal on Taylor's troops and many Americans lost their lives, but in the end Santa Anna was driven off.

Surmising that Santa Anna's retreating troops were now extremely vulnerable, late that afternoon Taylor ordered a concentrated charge by three infantry regiments. In the bloody fight that followed, the onrushing Americans were decimated and were forced to retreat, saved only by the murderous onslaught of grape and canister from the Bragg's massed artillery. Exhausted, both sides called it a day. And what a day it was!

By now the light rain had become a deluge. Without tents, blankets, and campfires Taylor's troops were forced to do the best they could to get through another cold, windy and wet night.

On the morning of February 24, 1847, the sun was back in full splendor and to the pleasant surprise of Taylor's soggy troops; Santa Anna's army was gone. He reported later that he was compelled to leave the field since the food and supplies he had would not sustain his army for another day.

Taylor's volunteers had come through despite the enormous disparity in troop strength and battlefield savvy. The young volunteers were ecstatic and the cheers were deafening as the two leaders hugged each other in a congratulatory salute. The Army of Occupation limped back to Agua Nueva, where they mourned their loss of some seven hundred killed. Unfortunately, over a thousand had deserted as well.

Santa Anna and his defeated army staggered back to their camp at San Luis Potosí. By any standard the Mexican army had suffered terribly from the Buena Vista campaign.

Between the combat losses on the battlefield and the casualties from the round-trip march through horrendous conditions, the army was reported to have lost some fifteen thousand men over the three months from January to March. "The army seemed made up of dead men," lamented one observer, "the miserable conditions to which the sick were reduced caused their skin to stick to their bones, and its shrinking exposed their teeth, giving to the countenance the expression of a force laugh, which filled one with horror."[6]

The Battle of Buena Vista was the last fight in Mexico for the Army of Occupation. They would spend the rest of the war in a defensive capacity, holding the lines they had already established. Although the campaigns in the northern provinces failed to end the war as Polk had envisioned, it was due to no fault of the army's very capable commander or its brave troops but due to the failure of the government to strike at the heart of the Mexican nation. And for his exemplary service in saving the army at Buena Vista Col. Jefferson Davis, who was a graduate of West Point and commander of the Mississippi Rifles, was highly praised. He was honored as a hero and spoken of by many as a patriot assuredly destined for even greater things in the years ahead.

As for Old Zack himself, the war and his military career were finally over but would never be forgotten. Commanding an army that proved fighting spirit could and did triumph over enemy troop count, he had defeated much larger forces in Palo Alto, Resaca de la Palma, Monterrey, and Buena Vista and occupied such strategic points as Matamoros, Tampico, Camargo, Saltillo, Victoria, and Monterrey. With his political popularity soaring like never before, he went to Washington, where in two years he would become the twelfth and next president of the United States.

11

The Western Campaigns

In keeping with President Polk's war strategy, while General Taylor and his Army of Occupation continued their successful advance through the northern provinces the American military was also making their presence known in New Mexico and California, albeit with a much smaller mortality rate.

U.S. troop movements in the West involved four separate campaigns. The first was in the Sacramento Valley area of California, the second was in the coastal town of Monterey, and the third was in New Mexico. The principal participants in each of these three movements ultimately joined forces to carry out the fourth and final campaign, the capture of Los Angeles.

Polk's interest in the Mexican territory of California was particularly acute and, to some of his critics, provided the real gleam in his eye. The province was sparsely populated in 1846 with an estimated twenty-five thousand inhabitants. Of that number, less than half were white settlers, the rest being Mexicans, Indians, and native-born Californians, called "Californios," who were in every other respect Mexican.

California was largely a desolate and lawless region much too distant from Mexico City for any real meaningful oversight. Its government was managed superficially by a civil governor residing in its capital, Los Angeles or, in the Spanish vernacular, Ciudad de Los Angeles. As a result of these inherent weaknesses, California was a frequent victim of violent revolutionary forces. But despite these and other detractions, true believers in Manifest Destiny, those in the United States who envisioned a country extending from coast to coast, had long assumed that California would soon join the Union under somewhat diplomatic conditions as Texas had done in 1845. What they failed to understand was that even though California was so remote and difficult to govern, Mexico was just as determined to keep her from falling to outside powers. Except these were volatile times and evolving events were rapidly altering that prospect.

In California, the U.S. strategy was to publicly deny any interest in the region while at the same time seeking ways to encourage the local inhabitants to rise up against Mexico. It was hoped, this tactic would persuade the people to petition the American government for statehood. Also, American warships were tasked to merely maintain a presence in the harbors of the major coastal ports but at the same time be prepared to claim U.S. sovereignty over them if and when the time was right.

According to Polk's initial strategy, the peace negotiations would occur soon after Taylor invaded Mexico. And by occupying both California and New Mexico he would have the upper hand in acquiring this territory in the settlement.

As in the case with Texas, President Polk was particularly concerned over rumors that Britain was preparing to purchase California and, even more suspicious, that the British navy was planning to seize her ports. These unreliable rumors may have been started by misinformation from the U.S. Consul or in 1841 when an English diplomat in Mexico enthusiastically proposed the establishment of an English colony in Upper California, writing, "I believe there is no part of the World offering greater natural advantages for the establishment of an English colony than the Provinces of Upper California; while its commanding position on the Pacific, its fine harbours, its forest of excellent timber for ship-building as well as for every other purposes, appear to me to render it by all means desirable, in a political point of view, that California, once ceasing to belong to Mexico, should not fall into the hands of any power but England ... in fact, there is some reason to believe that daring and adventurous speculators in the United States have already turned their thoughts in that direction."[1]

Upon receiving this communication, the British officials were quite distressed that one of their diplomats was actually discussing the seizure of California from Mexico while at the same time he was being tasked to help them. Consequently, the British Foreign Office made it quite clear to him in their response that the English government no longer had any interest in foreign colonization. The letter said in part, "His Lordship directs me in answer, to acquaint you for the information of the Earl of Aberdeen, that he is not anxious for the formation of new and distant Colonies, all of which involve heavy direct and still heavier indirect expenditures, besides multiplying the liabilities of misunderstanding and collisions with Foreign Powers."[2]

The British position was similar to the position of the United States. Although the English would not publically admit they had a specific interest in acquiring California, at the same time they would not hesitate to prevent the United States or France from taking California before they could. Accordingly, British diplomats and the British navy were also instructed to merely keep their eyes and ears open and to report anything that was suspicious in this regard.

Nevertheless, with each country distrustful of the other, in Washington the rumors persisted, which left the White House with no other choice but to continue their operations in California under the assumption that the British were waiting for their opportunity to make a move for California.

In keeping with his strategy on California, on the night of October 30, 1845, President Polk had a meeting with special agent Marine Corps lieutenant Archibald Gillespie. During their closed-door meeting Gillespie was handed a package of documents, one of which contained secret instructions for the lieutenant to follow. Also included in the package were four additional items. One was a secret message from Secretary of State James Buchanan to be delivered to the U.S. Consul, Thomas O. Larkin in Monterey; a second was orders for Cdre. John D. Sloat, the commander of the U.S. Pacific Squadron presently located off the west coast of Mexico at Mazatlán. The third was a letter of introduction addressed to Capt. John C. Frémont of the U.S. Topographical Agency that was attached to a packet of personal letters from his wife, and the fourth and last was a letter from his father-in-law, the powerful senator from Missouri, Thomas H. Benton. Strangely enough, when the meeting was over Gillespie was left with the impression that besides delivering the packages his real mission was to assist Frémont in a scheme to encourage the residents of California to revolt against the Mexican government.

Since traveling from Washington, D.C., to California via the western plains was so time-consuming and dangerous in those days, Gillespie was ordered to cross Mexico instead. The clandestine travel arrangements for the 33-year-old secret agent were made by the Navy Department included passage down the East Coast to Veracruz. From there he would cross Mexico dressed as a businessman to the West Coast, where he was to report to Commodore Sloat at Mazatlán. Following this meeting a naval vessel would transport Gillespie up the coast to Monterey according to the instructions in the orders Gillespie was to deliver to Sloat.

The journey to Mazatlán was quite uneventful and in February of 1846 Gillespie met Sloat aboard his flagship, the USS *Savannah*. During their meeting Gillespie delivered the orders to Sloat, who promptly arranged Gillespie's transportation to Monterey aboard the sloop of war the USS *Cyane*. With the British watching their every move, however, they feared the British would become so suspicious that before the United States could intercede they would claim Monterey for the Crown. The best way to minimize this eventuality from happening, they concurred, was to travel a roundabout route to Monterey. Instead of traveling directly up the Pacific coast to Monterey, several days later Gillespie boarded the *Cyane* for his journey to Monterey by way of Hawaii.

Consequently, instead of taking a relatively short sixteen-hundred-mile pleasure cruise, after a ninety-seven-hundred-mile voyage he finally disembarked in April 1846 at Monterey, where he promptly paid a visit to the U.S. Consul and delivered his secret message. During their conversation on the current state of affairs, Gillespie was given the general location where Frémont could be located. With all the pleasantries attended to, the undercover agent resumed his clandestine assignment.

A Massachusetts native, Thomas O. Larkin was a wealthy merchant in Monterey who had many friends in high places and carried considerable influence with all of them. Since Polk was scheming behind the scenes to win over the Californios, Larkin was the best man for Polk to wheel and deal with.

With the secret message in the hands of Consul Larkin and the orders successfully delivered to Commodore Sloat, all Gillespie had to do now was locate Captain Frémont, who was tucked away somewhere in the heavily forested area of northern California.

In a matter of days, Gillespie headed north toward the Sacramento Valley area, stopping first at Sutter's Fort, where he borrowed a mule and a guide. Begun in 1839 by John A. Sutter, Sutter's Fort was a walled complex consisting of a frontier-style trading post, stockade, sawmill, and several outbuildings located near the junction of the American and Sacramento Rivers. In three years Sutter's enormous estate would gain worldwide notoriety when it became known that one of Sutter's employees had discovered gold nuggets in the American River. Soon hundreds of thousands of "prospectors" would swarm into the area in the so-called California Gold Rush. From Sutter's Fort, Gillespie continued to move northward, stopping for a short time at Lassen's Ranch, where he picked up four more traveling companions.

As for Captain Frémont, he first stepped foot in Sutter's Fort about four months earlier, in December of 1845. Guided by his close friend Kit Carson, the 32-year-old army captain was popularly known as the "Pathfinder," a moniker that reflected his many accomplishments exploring uncharted territory, mapping trails in the wilderness, and documenting his expeditions. He and his party of some 60 heavily armed frontiersmen had departed Fort Leavenworth, Kansas, the previous June to locate a suitable route that would connect the Oregon Territory to the interior of northern California as a link to a transcontinental railroad line to the West Coast. The fact that a surveying party required such a large group of men, and heavily armed at that, only added fuel to the suspicions surrounding Frémont and his motives for being in California.

Failing to gain approval from U.S. authorities to set up a winter camp at Sutter's Fort, Frémont was ordered to disband his expedition and to leave the area. Highly insulted, an indignant Frémont resigned from the army and went to Monterey to obtain permission to remain in the area for the winter from Gen. José María Castro, the ruling military power in Monterey. Castro hesitantly agreed to Frémont's request but insisted he remain in the Sacramento Valley and not in the coastal areas. Characteristically obstinate, Frémont brazenly left his camp and, ignoring the Mexican general's restriction, moved his men to the outskirts of Monterey. Obviously angered over this transgression, Castro ordered the men to leave California immediately. Frémont bitterly protested Castro's order and defiantly erected a crude defensive fortification complete with the American flag mounted proudly over his works. Common sense finally prevailed and Frémont subsequently stormed off into the Oregon Territory after learning Mexican military troops were about to visit his camp with artillery. It was here near the California–Oregon border that a rather bizarre chain of events began that would significantly affect the future of California.

On May 9, 1846, with the help of several Indians who took them across Klamath Lake, Gillespie and his party were able to locate Frémont's camp on the edge of the lake, just over the California–Oregon Territory border. This was where the delivery of letters from Frémont's wife and father-in-law was made. What transpired next remains unclear to this day, but supposedly mistakenly included with the package of personal letters was a copy of the classified dispatch to Larkin from Buchanan.

The letter, in part, addressed the British interest in California and the president's concerns over the possibility of a British scheme to gain influence in the territory. Again, this message was similar to the British position in that although the United States had no desire to interfere in California, the letter granted the authority to prevent any such takeover by a foreign government. One passage of the dispatch read, "Whilst the President will make no effort ... to induce California to become one of the free and independent States of this Union, yet if the people should desire to unite their destiny with ours, they would be received as brethren, whenever this can be done without affording Mexico just cause of complaint. Their true policy for the present in regard to this question is to let events take their course, unless an attempt should be made to transfer them without their consent either to Great Britain or France. This they ought to resist by all the means in their power, as ruinous to their best interests and destructive of their freedom and independence."³

Convinced the dispatch was meant for him despite being addressed to the U.S. Consul, Frémont interpreted the message as a warning that a British seizure of California was imminent unless Americans took matters into their own hands. As he mulled over the dispatch he sensed an urge to return to California to help his country in her hour of need. In the morning Frémont packed his belongings and headed back to Sutter's Fort to play an active role in creating dissent and to win California for his government.

Meanwhile, an irate Castro, still outraged over the episode with Frémont, was now threatening to oust all American settlers from the Sacramento area. Concerned that they would be Castro's next victims, many of the settlers living there decided to join forces and when an opportune time appeared, to strike back. They didn't have long to wait. Frémont's return to Sutter's Fort in June inspired a group of disgruntled American settlers to join up with Frémont and to stage an uprising of their own and, in general, to create as much chaos in the area as possible. In the course of their melee, however, the rioting settlers not only went on to steal hundreds of horses and artillery from Castro's army in an audacious raid but also captured and occupied the small, mostly abandoned town of Sonoma. Emboldened to the point of being totally out of control, the group then took over Sutter's Fort against the ignored protestations of Sutter himself. Finally, to accentuate their revolt, they also declared Sonoma an independent California republic. This incident became known as the "Bear Flag Revolt" when a homemade flag was raised over the town on July 4, 1846, depicting a grizzly bear and the words "Bear Flag Republic." The first Bear Flag, incidentally, was designed by William L. Todd, a nephew of Mary Todd Lincoln, the wife of Abraham Lincoln.

Following their proclamation, the demonstrators, numbering close to two hundred, were emboldened by their rousing success. By this time Frémont had taken command of the rebellious settlers, now called the "California Battalion," with his best new friend, Lieutenant Gillespie, as its adjutant. Frémont's next move was to somehow obtain a horde of sidearms and rifles to continue his revolt. To accomplish this Frémont simply used his bogus identification as a military officer and requisitioned weapons and ammunition from a U.S. warship in San Francisco Bay.

Leading his new rebel "army" toward Monterey, the brash and cocky frontiersman vowed to capture all of California for the United States. Along the way, however, the California Battalion was attacked by a detachment of troops sent out by General Castro. In the skirmish that followed, the Mexican riders were sent in retreat after one of their men was killed and several more wounded, while Frémont's battalion continued on to Monterey unscathed.

While Frémont and his rowdy supporters were causing problems in the Sacramento area, in early July 1846 Commodore Sloat, the frail 65-year-old commander of the Pacific Squadron, arrived in the waters of Monterey from Mazatlán. Standing on the deck of his flagship, *Savannah*, he escorted his five ships into the harbor after maintaining surveillance of the British fleet for months, as they were also doing to him. Although described as an assembly of adobe huts, Monterey held the distinction of being the only port that traded with the outside world.

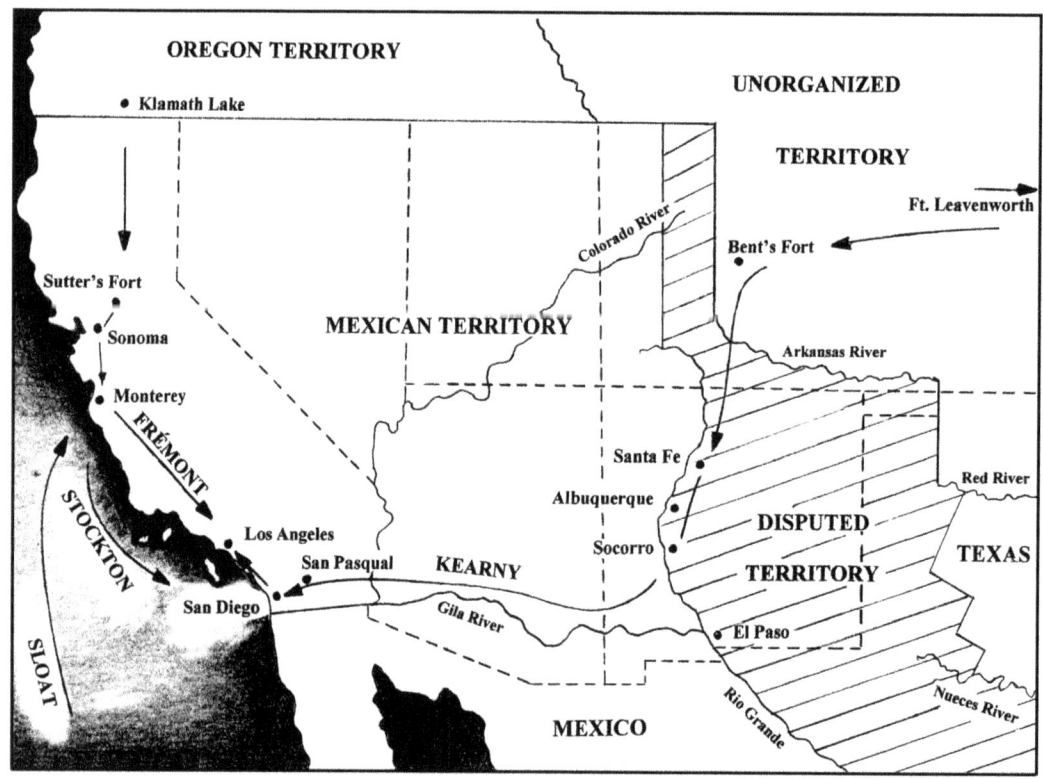

The Western Campaigns

It was a gorgeous summer day in California when Sloat arrived, and as the commodore stood gazing upon the coastline he had was to some extent confused. His thoughts went to a dispatch he received this past October while he was in Honolulu taking on supplies and water. It was from the secretary of the navy, George Bancroft, dated June 24, 1845, and said in part:

> Should Mexico, however, be resolute on hostilities, you will be mindful to protect the persons and interests of citizens of the United States near your station, and should you ascertain beyond a doubt that the Mexican Government has declared war against us, you will at once employ the force under your command to the advantage. The Mexican ports on the Pacific are said to be open and defenseless. If you ascertain with certainty that Mexico has declared war against the United States, you will at once possess yourself of the port of San Francisco, and blockade or occupy such other ports as your force may permit.... The great distance of your squadron, and the difficulty of communicating with you, are the causes for issuing this order. The President hopes most earnestly that the peace of the two countries may not be disturbed. The object of these instructions is to possess you of the views of the government in the event of a declaration of war on the part of Mexico against the United States—an event which you are enjoined to do everything consistent with the national honor, on your part, to avoid.[4]

Sloat's first instinct was to act before the city was taken over by the British, which he feared was a possibility. But this put the flag officer in somewhat of a quandary, because his instructions were to act only if Mexico and the United States were at war and at this point he wasn't quite sure if a state of war actually existed.

As he pondered over the dilemma he was in, Sloat was reminded of a similar episode that had occurred to his predecessor just four years earlier. At that time, Cdre. Thomas ap Catesby Jones landed marines to seize Monterey under the mistaken belief that war had broken out between the United States and Mexico. After Consul Larkin used his diplomatic skills to smooth over the situation, Jones was forced to apologize in writing to the outraged Mexican authorities. Needless to say, Jones was quickly removed from his command.

However, during this time Sloat was getting reports about Frémont's revolt against Castro's forces in the Sacramento Valley. Contemplating the actions of Frémont, the commodore could not help but surmise that Frémont must have had official approval to carry out such aggressive tactics against a person of such authority as General Castro. Considering Bancroft's dispatch, the Jones affair, Frémont's activities, and the suspicious behavior of the British ships, Sloat finally came to a decision. After weighing all these factors together, Sloat finally decided to take the risk.

Suspecting that the British fleet he had been watching was planning to occupy Monterey, Sloat decided to ere on the side of military expediency, that it was better to do something now, before it was too late. In fact, he voiced this uncertainty in a message he sent to Capt. John B. Montgomery, commander of the USS *Portsmouth*, anchored off San Francisco. In his message Sloat explained, "I have determined to hoist the flag of the United States at this place tomorrow, as I would prefer being sacrificed for doing too much than too little. If you consider you have sufficient force, or if Frémont will join you, you will hoist the flag at Yerba Buena [San Francisco], or at any other proper place, and take possession of the fort and that portion of the country."[5]

Confident that a unilateral assault was better than doing nothing at all, Sloat penned a message to General Castro, the ruling power in Monterey and the most corrupt as well, demanding the surrender of the town. Receiving no reply, on July 7, 1846, Sloat entered the following entry into his ship's log:

> We are about to land on the territory of Mexico, with whom the United States is at war. To strike their flag and hoist our own in place of it is our duty. It is not only our duty to take California, but to preserve it afterwards as part of the United States at all hazards. To accomplish this, it is of the first importance to cultivate the good opinions of the inhabitants whom we must reconcile. I scarcely consider it necessary for me to caution American seamen and marines against the detestable crimes of plundering and maltreating unoffending inhabitants.... Finally, let me entrust you one and all not to tarnish our hope of bright success by any act that we shall be ashamed to acknowledge before God and our country.[6]

Shortly thereafter, a contingent of 250 sailors and marines was sent ashore. At Castro's headquarters, however, instead of the expected armed resistance the raiding party was astonished to find the general had fled to Los Angeles to consolidate his forces with Gen. Andréas Pico. In any event, Monterey was occupied without incident and as the American troops cheered the Stars and Stripes whipped briskly high above the customhouse in the plaza. That same day Commodore Sloat issued a proclamation to "The Inhabitants of California," which began, "I declare to the inhabitants of California, that although I come with arms and a powerful force, I do not come among them as an enemy to California; on the contrary, I come as their best friend—as henceforward California will be a portion of the United States."[7]

Three days later Captain Montgomery would occupy San Francisco. With his mission accomplished and with no repercussions from Washington, the aged and ailing sailor retired from sea duty and became the commandant of the Norfolk Naval Yard. To carry on the efforts in California he was replaced by veteran naval officer Cdre. Robert F. Stockton. At 51 years old, Stockton arrived at Monterey on his flagship, the USS *Congress*, leading a fleet of 11 ships. Sailing into Monterey, the fleet was an impressive sight indeed and represented the strongest force at that time in California.

The new squadron commander relished his new assignment and immediately focused on invading Los Angeles, a sparsely populated capital of less than two thousand people. Hot and dirty, Los Angeles consisted mostly of a number of adobe flat-roofed structures but held the most fortified garrison in California.

On July 19, only 12 days after Sloat raised the Stars and Stripes over the customhouse, Frémont and his band of toughs arrived in Monterey and mustered into the army as the California Battalion of the United States. Now taking on the rank of major, Frémont continued to operate as the battalion commander while at his side stood Gillespie, the new army captain and Frémont's second in command. After agreeing to assist Commodore Stockton in the naval operation against Los Angeles, Frémont and the California Battalion boarded a ship and headed to San Diego.

Likewise, eager to plan his attack and launch his campaign on Los Angeles, Stockton boarded his flagship and sailed out of Monterey for San Diego.

Commodore Stockton's plan to win Los Angeles was a simple two-prong attack. Frémont would move directly against Los Angeles from San Diego. At the same time, Stockton and some three hundred marines and sailors would launch their attack from San Pedro, only 18 miles away.

Behind the scenes, however, Generals Castro and Pico were wary of confronting the Americans and had appealed through the American consul for a peaceful solution. But Stockton made it quite clear that he would not negotiate whatsoever with these untrustworthy and corrupt characters. Unable to wait any longer, on August 13, 1846, the U.S. forces launched their campaign and, surprisingly enough, strode into Los Angeles unmolested, pleasantly relieved that Castro and his forces had scattered into the mountains three days earlier. General Pico, however, was caught and held captive but was later paroled.

In a matter of days, Stockton declared California a territory of the United States and appointed Frémont to be the military governor. Captain Gillespie, now the new military commander in that region, was tasked to govern Los Angeles. With everything going rather smoothly in California, the commodore now had his sights on the attack and capture of Mexico City. Since most of his sailors were still in San Pedro, however, he asked Frémont to return to the Sacramento Valley to recruit additional volunteers to take up the slack. With all his immediate assignments being carried out and most of the loose ends attended to, Stockton headed south toward Monterey to organize a military force large enough to overwhelm the troops guarding Mexico City.

Among the Mexican inhabitants of Los Angeles, meanwhile, frustrations lingered, resentment festered, and anger raged. Most of this bitterness was fueled by the policies of Captain Gillespie, policies that the Mexicans thought demonstrated a lack of respect toward them as citizens of Los Angeles. In September a major revolt exploded as approximately three hundred irate citizens, unable to contain their pent-up Latin emotions and led by Capt. José María Flores, stormed the new U.S. government headquarters and forced Gillespie to surrender the city and withdraw its small American garrison.

When the news of the Mexican counterattack reached the commodore, a shocked and frustrated Stockton abandoned his plans for Mexico City and vowed to regain Los Angeles instead. It seems that Stockton failed to realize that the loss of Los Angeles was mostly his and Gillespie's fault. The revolt had little to do with the American flag that was proudly whipping over the American headquarters but was mostly due to the way they treated the people living there. Reacting to the latest crisis, Stockton immediately recalled Frémont and his California Battalion in October. Impatient and anxious to go on the offensive as soon as possible, instead of waiting for the California Battalion Stockton dispatched navy captain William Mervine and a small, makeshift landing party to take on the mission along with Gillespie's garrison. This dismal attempt failed when Mervine found his inept fighters outmanned, outgunned, and outwitted by the forces of Captain Flores. Now thoroughly aggravated, Stockton moved his entire naval contingent back to San Diego, where he would plan and organize another attack on Flores in Los Angeles.

On a third front and also receiving orders to mobilize his troops was army colonel Stephen W. Kearny. In fact, within days of signing the declaration of war against Mexico, President Polk notified Kearny to prepare his regiment of dragoons for an expedition to New Mexico. Along with occupying these far-flung territories, the president also assumed that the folks living there had many needs that were not being fulfilled by the Mexican or the local governments. He believed the citizens would be more than eager to accept an opportunity for a better life. Therefore, to motivate their interest in becoming U.S. citizens Kearny was also instructed to stop at various towns and to hand out leaflets explaining the advantages of living under the U.S. flag. Once Santa Fe was occupied, Kearny was instructed to establish a democratic form of government and, if possible, to move on to California to assist the navy before the winter snows moved in.

The president could not have selected a more capable officer for this mission. Looking much younger than his 52 years, Kearny was a man of small stature and graying hair. Born and raised in New Jersey, he had halfheartedly enrolled in Columbia University and somehow managed to finish the first two years. The excitement and glamour of the military was far more appealing to the young lad, who felt compelled to leave school to fight in the War of 1812. Tough and still effective after some 30 years on the western frontier, he was again called to do what he knew best and to do what he loved the most.

In military circles Colonel Kearny was greatly admired for his unique innovations that ultimately became official policy. Although the use of dragoons in the United States can be traced back to the Revolutionary War, Kearny received recognition for organizing a regiment of dragoons in the 1830s that evolved into the U.S. Cavalry. For this distinction he became known as the "father of the U.S. Cavalry." Also, in the following decade he received additional notoriety for establishing the practice of escorting settlers' wagon trains across the Santa Fe Trail and the western plains to dissuade attacks from marauding

Indians. Eventually, Fort Kearny was built in his honor on 80 acres along the Oregon Trail near present-day Kearny, Nebraska. It was a collection of adobe buildings that served as a way station and supply depot for settlers heading to the Pacific Northwest and for the "Forty-Niners" hoping to find their share of gold nuggets in California. The site was so popular that in time it also became the home station for the Pony Express.

In Fort Leavenworth, a major army post located in the vast stretches of land still unorganized but destined to be the Kansas Territory, Kearny prepared to depart with his 1st Dragoons, a body of several hundred expert horsemen. Also on the expedition were nearly a thousand riders of the 1st Regiment of Missouri Mounted Volunteers under the command of Alexander Doniphan, a Missouri lawyer who was elected to command the group with the rank of colonel. Bringing up the rear were nearly two dozen pieces of artillery and the artillerists and teamsters to manage them, not to mention the hundreds of wagons and the oxen and horses to pull them. Kearny's command was called the Army of the West.

Mostly desolate and dry, New Mexico, like California, was considered for years by the United States too remote, too neglected, and too inhospitable to be taken seriously. Similarly, its relative isolation from Mexico City was also quite significant and did much to explain the quasi-independence of New Mexico, where at times the law was something one interpreted for himself. But times had changed, especially for those with expansionist inclinations who now saw New Mexico in a different light.

Trudging along the Santa Fe Trail in the middle of June 1846 was not easy for Kearny's men, nor was it pleasant for the animals. Even the hard and toughened Missouri frontiersmen in his army found the trek as demanding as any they had experienced before. Tramping through the clouds of dust for seemingly endless miles in the scorching heat, under a blazing sun, and without clean drinking water obviously took its toll on everyone. Many became sick from drinking contaminated water or succumbed to dehydration and disease. Most affected were the horses. With minimal quantities of forage and water, many died along the way.

In due course, the army arrived at Bent's Fort, the first and last western outpost in the local civilized world. Situated among the foothills of Colorado's Rocky Mountains, it was a welcome respite for sure. Pausing at Bent's Fort was a great moment for all the travelers heading west, especially Kearny's worn-out troops. It was a wonderful chance to meet new people, catch up on the news, trade with the enterprising Indians for their skins, or just relax for a spell. It also gave Kearny the time to write a proclamation he would read to the people in the villages and towns along the way.

Understandably, some of the civilians may have been a little annoyed to see the hundreds of men, wagons, and animals pulling into the "parking lot." In fact, one visitor recorded in her diary, "The fort is crowed to overflowing. Col. Kearny has arrived and it seems the world is coming with him."[8]

As the army traveled along the base of the Rockies, they left the trail and took a more circuitous route to Santa Fe, passing through several towns such as Las Vegas, Tecolote, and San Miguel. This side route allowed Kearny the opportunity to read the proclamation he wrote at Bent's Fort and explain to the inhabitants why he was in New Mexico. Also, he wanted to reassure them that they would be treated kindly as long as they continued to carry on with their lives as before. Although it was not mentioned in his proclamation, he also promised them U.S. citizenship. Furthermore, to make sure the people of Santa Fe knew of his proclamation before he arrived Kearny dispatched several Mexican couriers with a large number of copies to post in various locations.

Finally, two months later and after traveling 850 miles from Fort Leavenworth, the Army of the West reached the outskirts of Santa Fe. At a place called Apache Canyon, Kearny, now wearing the insignia of a brigadier general, fully expected a fierce and bloody fight led by Gov. Manuel Armijo and the twelve thousand or so Mexicans and Indians he was forewarned about, the fighters anxiously waiting to oppose him. But, to his surprise, Governor Armijo, in spite of his saber rattling and threats against the approaching Americans, had prudently decided to avoid the confrontation. Instead, he fled to Albuquerque.

Without a shot being fired General Kearny marched into Santa Fe and on August 18 enjoyed a few drinks in the Governors Palace with the alcalde. With all the pomp and ceremony the circumstances would allow, Old Glory was then raised in the plaza amid the reports of a 13-gun salute.

Santa Fe in all respects failed to live up to its status as the territorial seat of government. It was a squalid, dirty, and unkempt town consisting mostly of one-story mud-built houses, which in reality were more like flat-roofed huts. In the days ahead, General Kearny visited nearby towns where he proclaimed New Mexico an American territory and to celebrate such an auspicious occasion he staged an enormous party where five hundred people danced the night away. To further instill the American democratic principles, he called for a constitution and directed the formation of a civil government. A fort, called Fort Marcy, was also built only yards from the Governors Palace to remind the citizens of the American presence. And to further his indoctrination, General Kearny also assured them they had nothing to fear but would receive all the same rights, freedoms, and protections enjoyed in other American territories. As the new government took shape and with other administrative measures proceeding smoothly, Kearny became increasingly impatient to resume his campaign.

Consequently, five weeks after his arrival Kearny decided it was time to move on to California. He also knew that as difficult as the journey to Santa Fe was, the trip through the rugged country ahead to California would be even worse, especially since he was going to leave the Santa Fe Trail. From now on they would follow a less traveled route along worn and narrow Indian trails and then along the Gila River, a route used primarily by trappers. With the administration of the town left in good hands, Kearny moved out of Santa Fe on yet another grueling trek of over a thousand miles along with three hundred dragoons and enough wagons of supplies to sustain them for 65 days. The rest of the army remained behind and later in the year Doniphan and his Missourians were dispatched to reinforce General Wool. (Although Doniphan missed the rendezvous with Wool, he went on to win several battles until March 1847, when the Mounted Volunteers disbanded and returned to Missouri.)

In the early morning hours of October 6, 1846, General Kearny and his men approached the village of Socorro, about 230 miles south of Santa Fe. Here on the outskirts of town he met the frontiersman and scout Kit Carson and a group of other men all heading east to report on the American occupation of California. Stopping to catch up on the latest news, General Kearny learned for the first time that the naval forces there had already occupied Monterey and San Francisco several months earlier. Somewhat disappointed that he was too late for this action, Kearny was also terribly frustrated that his men had come such a long way and suffered under terrible hardships with nothing gained for their sacrifices. Considering this new twist of events, that night Kearny decided to modify his plans. Under the present circumstances he determined it was now unnecessary to continue with such a large force. Consequently, of the three hundred dragoons he had with him only one hundred would stay on while the remainder were ordered to return to Santa Fe. Also replaced were their worn-out horses.

On his command, General Kearny and his downsized army, now all mounted on mules bought from a mule herder, resumed their slow trek toward the California border. This time Carson was persuaded to stay on as a guide until the Army of the West, or whatever was left of it, reached Los Angeles.

The slow and arduous journey was uneventful, at times even pleasant. Although the scenery was extraordinarily beautiful and picturesque, crossing the Gila River at the swift and turbulent junction with the Colorado was described as an absolute nightmare. But, despite the hardships, once the crossing was made, the famished and exhausted troops persevered and pushed on with their expedition riding fresh horses captured several days earlier. On one particular day, as they struggled along a narrow pathway, the advance riders came upon a Mexican courier carrying a packet of letters, who, needless to say, was immediately picked up and held prisoner. Frantically rummaging through the courier's satchel for the latest news, Kearny was shocked to learn that counterrevolutionary forces had driven off the Americans and had regained much of the previous losses, including Los Angeles. Frustrated that the Americans were back at square one but elated that he was now back in the game, Kearny was more eager than ever to get to California.

The next obstacle in the army's adventurous escapade was the Colorado Desert, a stretch of dry and merciless territory where the extremely high temperatures are unforgiving. Part of the much larger Sonoran Desert, which stretches across the North American Southwest, the landscape is home to yucca and cholla cactus, desert saltbush, and red-diamond rattlesnakes. Especially disconcerting were the numerous canyons and sand dunes that made passage with the howitzers and pack mules more than difficult, as was the constant surveillance by wary Apache Indians who kept watching the men from a distance. Although it was a hot and dusty ride, Carson kept their spirits up by reassuring the ragged group that something special awaited them on the other side. And he was right. It was, at least in their eyes, an oasis called Warner's Ranch, a weathered ranch house similar to Sutter's Fort where they soothed their aching bodies in the hot springs, ate relatively decent meals, and had many hours of solid rest. It was built only a couple of years earlier by Juan Jose Warner, a naturalized Mexican citizen who turned his land grant into a successful cattle ranch.

While at the ranch, Kearny changed his itinerary now that he had learned Commodore Stockton was back in San Diego, only 60 miles away. Instead of going to Los Angeles, therefore, Kearny was now going to meet Stockton in San Diego. Consequently, just before the army left the ranch after two days of rest, on December 4, 1846, a courier was dispatched with a message to Stockton telling him where Kearny was, what his plans were, and that he needed reinforcements.

Kearny's Army of the West, feeling quite refreshed from their stay at Warner's Ranch, went back on the road and headed for San Diego. Moving through a drenching rain, on December 5, the soldiers were met by no one other than Captain Gillespie and some 30 or 40 marines and sailors from Stockton's command who had ridden the 60 miles from San Diego to meet them. As the downpour continued, Gillespie informed Kearny that lurking in the nearby Indian village of San Pascual was the cavalry of Gen. Andréas Pico, who, Kearny surmised, was prepared and eager to attack at the first sight of his army. Despite the warning, he and his men continued on with their ride, being careful to reconnoiter the surrounding area for any signs of the enemy. If and when contact with the enemy was made, General Kearny's plan was to catch Pico and his army off guard and attack immediately.

The Battle of San Pascual, the only authentic battle in the fight for California, was fought on December 6 and turned out to be short and decisive. The outnumbered Americans, Kit Carson, Captain Gillespie and his detachment among them, were unable to cope with the overwhelming assault of Pico's 80 or so expert lancers. In less than a half hour, in fact, Kearny lost 22 of his embattled troops to the ensuing rush of Mexican horsemen. When that total was combined with nearly that number wounded, his small army was now reduced by an additional third, and by the end of the day the one-sided battle had turned into a siege. Kearny and Captain Gillespie were two of the wounded. Gillespie suffered a lance puncture just above his heart and was also struck by a lance in the face, which cut his upper lip and broke a front tooth. As for General Kearny, he received a lance wound in the groin, which forced him to temporarily turn his command over to his second in command, Henry S. Turner, a topographical engineer. Miraculously, five days later, just as a desperate Kearny was planning to fight his way out, the Americans were rescued by slightly over two hundred sailors and marines sent by Commodore Stockton from San Diego. Finally, after so many hardships, the Army of the West arrived in San Diego on December 12.

Several weeks after their arrival in San Diego, the combined forces, now assembled as a ragtag fighting team of about five hundred, began their 140-mile advance north to retake Los Angeles. Both commanders were on hand for this mission, Kearny and Stockton, both sharing in the command decisions. Resistance along their march toward Los Angeles was relatively light with the exception of two small skirmishes with nearly five hundred ill-equipped troops under Flores. The first was at San Gabriel on January 8, 1847, and the second on the following day at La Mesa, both of which were easily won by the U.S. combined forces. Meanwhile, Frémont and his men were still riding down from the Sacramento Valley to join them.

In the American camp, as the troops were preparing to advance on Los Angeles, a civilian delegation arrived under a white flag. They had come with news that Flores and his troops would withdraw from Los Angeles if there were no reprisals against them or their property. These were the only conditions, they insisted, for them to surrender the city. Elated over this latest revelation, Stockton readily agreed to their terms and that very day, January 10, 1847, American forces reoccupied Los Angeles with Captain Gillespie doing the honors of raising the Stars and Stripes once again.

Four days later, as the American liberators slept, no one other than John C. Frémont and his California Battalion suddenly came bounding into the American camp on the edge of Los Angeles, rousing the troops from their sleep. As his mesmerized audience listened intently, Frémont handed Stockton a sealed document while he recounted his meeting with General Pico during his ride down from Sacramento. At this January 13 meeting, instigated by Frémont, Pico had offered a peace proposal that Frémont agreed to sign on behalf of the United States. The treaty, or more precisely an informal agreement, called for the Mexican resistance fighters in California to lay down their weapons and resume peaceful activities. In addition, they would be granted all the rights of American citizens without being required to take an oath of allegiance. It was a pact that pleased everyone, except for Stockton. Stunned over what he had just heard, Stockton initially refused to accept the so-called Treaty of Cahuenga as legitimate. The truth is Frémont had unwittingly upstaged Stockton, who wanted all the glory for himself. However, after meeting with General Pico, Stockton relented, saying, "Whilst I do not recognize any authority, or even justification in Frémont, for making to the pledges appearing in his agreement at San Fernando, I, as a Commander-in-Chief, say to you that we do not want to have any ill feeling shown to anyone, much less to the natives of California, who in all probability will be citizens of our common country."[9] His acceptance of the treaty, in effect, closed the military chapter in California. Official recognition of this treaty, however, would not come until the war with Mexico had concluded.

Shortly after Stockton reoccupied Los Angeles, he appointed Frémont as the military governor of California. Following this appointment, Stockton and Kearny became involved in a bitter dispute over conflicting orders on who should have been the governor. (Kearny had a letter from Polk naming him to the position, which Stockton refused to accept.) The strain in their relationship was quite apparent from the letter Kearny sent to Stockton on January 17, 1847, which read in part, "I must for the purpose of preventing a collision between us and possibly a civil war in consequence of it, remain silent for the present, leaving you the great responsibility of doing that for which you have no authority and preventing me from complying with the President's orders."[10] Frémont, for obvious reasons, sided with his benefactor Stockton. Outraged over Frémont's blatant insubordination, General Kearny instituted court-martial proceedings against him, which in the end resulted in Frémont's being found guilty and dismissed from the service. President Polk, in turn, soon got into the fray by overruling the dismissal, but Frémont, resentful and highly offended over the entire matter, chose to resign from the army and to return to exploration assignments for the railroad. As for the dispute between Commodore Stockton and General Kearny, the general was made both governor and the military chief of California. At the same time, Stockton's rank was now reduced to captain.

12

The Battles of Veracruz and Cerro Gordo

With U.S. troops occupying California and New Mexico and General Taylor about to engage in the battle at Buena Vista, in mid–February of 1847 General Scott launched his campaign to invade the very heart of Mexico herself, Mexico City. After considering several invasion routes, he decided the most sensible one was to travel down the Gulf Coast to Veracruz, Mexico's principal seaport. Scott's strategy at that point was to launch an amphibious landing onto the beach and once in position assault the Mexican forces garrisoned there. Once the port was taken, Veracruz would then be used as a supply depot. Finally, before the dreaded yellow fever set in, he planned to advance his troops inland through such towns as Cerro Gordo, Jalapa, and Puebla, before launching his bold assault on the eastern gates of Mexico City herself. It sounded routine enough but in reality it was the most ambitious military operation yet attempted by the U.S. Army. To execute this plan were the twelve thousand handpicked troops Scott gathered at his staging site on Lobos Island, a small coral and sand reef about one hundred miles north of Veracruz. Within that total, some nine thousand veterans alone came from General Taylor's Army of Occupation.

The harbor at Lobos Island was large and could easily accommodate the approximately 40 or so ships in the expedition. The troops had arrived from two different locations. The volunteers who were assembled in the United States came via a staging area on Brazos Island, and those already in Mexico, which included most of Taylor's army, were transferred through Tampico, 60 miles to the north, the port city Commodore Connors had captured in November of 1846. At that time the Regular Army was organized into several branches or corps such as the infantry, cavalry, engineers, and artillery. Generally, infantryman received an average salary of around $7 a month.[1] With such low wages and having to endure such harsh conditions, the military attracted men who were for the most part largely uneducated, unemployed and without much of a future to speak of.

Scott's army consisted of three divisions of infantry and included artillery, regiments of mounted rifles, and dragoons. The cavalry was in reality a contingent of dragoons, or soldiers trained to fight mounted or dismounted. The divisions were mostly composed of regulars and were commanded by Gen. William J. Worth and David E. Twiggs, while the volunteer division was under Gen. Robert Patterson, the most capable generals of them all and each an alumni of General Taylor's hands-on school of warfare.

Also included in Scott's army were men destined to accomplish higher achievements in another war just 14 short years away. They were such men as Ulysses S. Grant, Robert E. Lee, George B. McClellan, George G. Meade, Philip Kearny, Jr., Richard S. Ewell, William S. Harney, Joseph E. Johnston, James Longstreet, George E. Pickett, John B. Magruder, Franklin Pierce, Gideon J. Pillow, Edmund Kirby Smith, and Pierre G. T. Beauregard.

In the days ahead, the harbor was transformed into a chaotic hub of activity as scores of chartered transports dotted the seascape carrying men, animals, artillery, rations, ammunitions and everything else the army required to be reasonably equipped for their campaign in Mexico. Several of these transports held the 65 flat-bottomed surf boats that were custom-made to Scott's specifications, the vessels that would convey the soldiers to the beach. It was a big disappointment for Scott that the original order for 141 boats could not be filled on time. The boats came in three sizes averaging nearly 40 feet long and were capable of carrying up to 40 men plus 8 oarsmen.

At Lobos Island, the biggest problem for Scott was the frequent delays with getting supplies, ordnance, ships, and the bulk of his troops. As a result, the highly aggravated general was forced to periodically modify his scheduled departure date, a date quite critical for the welfare of everyone. With each passing day, a growing sense of urgency began to overwhelm Scott and his staff because the summer season was quickly approaching, the most dreaded time of the year for outsiders to be in Veracruz. Yellow fever would soon plague the city like it does most every year in late April or early May making it imperative for the army to do its business at Veracruz before then. Spread by mosquitoes, the disease could be deadly to nearly half of the people infected. Eager to launch his campaign, Scott continuously complained of the delays and the possible onset of the disease that could compromise his expedition.

On March 2, 1847, Scott could wait no longer. Amid the cheers of the eager and jubilant troops, the long procession of ships filed into the horizon. Standing proudly on the deck of the lead ship, the USS *Massachusetts*, General Scott responded with a wave to the batteries firing gun salutes as he passed by.

The journey to Veracruz was not pleasant for the men, as described by Grant, who was on board one of the ships: "The passage was a tedious one, and many of the troops were on shipboard over thirty days from the embarkation at the mouth of the Rio Grande to the time of debarkation south of Vera Cruz. The trip was a comfortless one for officers and men. The transports used were built for carrying freight and possessed but limited accommodations for passengers, and the climate added to the discomfort of all."[2] Three days later the skyline of their target appeared before them as well as the blockading ships of Commodore Conner's Home Squadron.

Veracruz was a rather unique city of about roughly fifteen thousand people, a picturesque city situated beautifully some 50 miles below the majestic peak of Orizaba, the highest mountain in Mexico. Considered the most fortified city in the Americas, the crescent-shaped seaport was completely surrounded by a 15-foot stone wall, connected intermittently by four old Spanish forts. Each fort posted several pieces of heavy artillery behind walls 3 feet thick and on a little island in the harbor a fifth fort, called Fort San Juan de Ulúa, loomed 60 feet high, which provided additional protection from the seaside approach to the city. This was the same fort bombarded by the French in 1838 during the so-called Pastry War. Capable of mounting up to 135 pieces of artillery, the fort was definitely an embattlement Scott was hesitant to challenge.

The navy would play a pivotal role at Veracruz, one that demonstrated the integrity and selflessness of its commander. Over the next two days, in fact, amid sporadic fire from the defenders, Scott and his staff were personally escorted by the navy commander to peruse potential landing sites. Even Scott's final selection of the beach the troops would land on was greatly influenced by the advice from Commodore Conner. The commodore's fleet off Veracruz consisted of two frigates, the *Raritan* and the *Potomac*; three sloops of war, the *Princeton*, *Albany*, and *St. Mary's*; one large steamer, the *Edith*; a brig, *Porpoise*; three gunboats, the *Petrita*, *Massachusetts*, and *Eudora*; and five schooner gunboats, the *Reefer*, *Petrel*, *Bonita*, *Tampico*, and *Falcon*.

The eventual plan agreed to by Scott was for the troops to transfer from the transports to several larger naval vessels. Under this scenario a minimal number of ships would be used for the actual landing. At this point, Conner's vessels would move into the harbor and Scott's army would be transferred a second time to the waiting surfboats hidden out of view of the forts. Once the boats were filled, naval oarsmen would ferry the troops toward the beach well out of range of the enemy guns.

On the morning of March 9, anticipation ran high as the historic invasion plan was put into action. To the astonishment of everyone, the joint operation was carried out with no significant problems and by dusk Scott's entire army had waded ashore at Collado Beach about three miles southeast of the city. The first to make the historic landing were a group of men from General Worth's division. To everyone's surprise, it was reported that as their landing craft approached the water's edge General Worth jumped into the shoulder-high water and with much effort managed to wade through the surf to the shoreline. Whether Worth's actions were merely to be the first man on the beach or a symbolic gesture to demonstrate his leadership remained unclear. Nevertheless, thanks to an omission in judgment by Mexican general Juan Morales in not opposing the landing, the rest of Scott's troops were safely ferried in. Once on land the men immediately scampered up the sand dunes and without delay secured the beachhead. The empty surfboats were then towed by a steamer to Sacrificios, a small island off the coast of Veracruz. To Scott's credit, the amphibious landing was the largest ever carried out up to that time and a textbook example of a successful joint army-navy operation.

General Scott was extremely elated over the success of the landing, as evident by his report: "The colors of the United States were triumphantly planted ashore, in full view of the city and its castle, and under the constant fire of both, in the afternoon of the 9th instant.... The whole army reached shore in fine style, and without direct opposition, accident, or loss."[3]

Scott's first step toward Mexico City had been taken and, surprisingly, everything went off without a hitch. In fact, one officer was so confident of their superiority he worried that the enemy would not challenge them in battle. In fact, the only views of anyone were those of the crowds of civilian spectators watching the proceedings from the top of the wall out of canon range and of visiting merchant seamen seen clinging to the rigging of their ships who were also enjoying the spectacle playing out before them.

In Washington, the president received Scott's encouraging message with mixed emotions. Although Polk was elated to know the army had a successful start in their drive to Mexico City, at the same time he was quite concerned over the political ramifications Scott's success could have on his presidential bid against a Democratic opponent. His concerns were well-founded, since General Taylor was already being mentioned in some circles as a possible choice for the White House position. Always weighing every move on a political scale, Polk could not rule Scott out as another potential Whig candidate. Under the present situation, Polk thought, Scott's success could spell even more political trouble for the party in the upcoming election.

Unfortunately, severe storms moved into the area as well that week, delaying the transfer of the animals, supplies, and artillery for several more days. In the meantime, reconnaissance reports convinced Scott that storming the city walls protecting Veracruz was out of the question. Instead, batteries of siege guns, some with gunners provided by the navy, were set up about two miles outside the perimeter of the city. Despite having to fight against the dense chaparral, rugged terrain, soft sand dunes, and swarms of insects, all three divisions furnished enough infantry to form an arching seven-mile siege line running parallel to the landside stretch of the city walls. Together with the ships of the Home Squadron on the oceanside, Veracruz was virtually surrounded. As an extra measure to induce a quick surrender, the water supply to Veracruz was shut down, rail links were cut, and all roads were closed. Veracruz was now totally isolated, and to make matters even worse, the inhabitants were about to be victims of Scott's artillery.

But General Scott had a problem. The large-caliber guns he was expecting, the big guys that could really destroy the Mexican will to fight, never showed up. Extremely frustrated, Scott had no choice but to sit in his headquarters and silently fume. When word of Scott's problem reached Commodore Conner's flagship, he immediately offered to loan a number of heavy guns from his ships to reinforce Scott's firepower and the gunners to man them. Although it was a blow to Scott's huge ego, he swallowed his pride and agreed to Conner's generous offer. It was yet another example of Conner's sense of duty and, coincidentally, occurred shortly before he was scheduled to turn over his command to Cdre. Matthew C. Perry.

General Scott, however, was too impetuous to wait for the naval guns to arrive. With his own artillery poised and primed, Scott gave General Morales, commanding around four thousand troops, one last chance to surrender before the attack commenced. Morales respectfully declined. Dispensing with any further courtesies, on the evening of March 22, 1847, Scott's artillery began their bombardment. The shells from the mortars and howitzers, as well as the broadsides from the ships, rained down on the city all that night and throughout the following day, relentlessly pounding the city's hapless inhabitants. The Mexican batteries were quick to retaliate, however, firing ineffectively at the American side. With both sides trading shells, the scene took on the appearance of a surreal exhibition of firepower as the air filled with smoke and the stench of gunpowder burned the nostrils. By the evening of the twenty-third, the navy's big 32-pounders were also in place, dragged from the beach by around two hundred sailors. The bombardment continued unabated. By this time the American firepower consisted of ten ten-inch mortars, four 24-pounders, two eight-inch howitzers, three 32-pounders, and three eight-inch Paixhans (French guns that fired explosive shells), each specifically positioned under the direction of Capt. Robert E. Lee.

The bombardment continued throughout each day and well into each night. Finally, on March 25, a white flag was spotted and a message delivered from Gen. José Juan Landero y Coss requesting negotiations on terms for capitulation. Under pressure from foreign representatives to surrender, General Morales had withdrawn from his command to avoid being disgraced. General Scott readily accepted the offer to talk and as a result representatives from both armies met to discuss the terms of the surrender of not only Veracruz but also San Juan de Ulúa. After long hours of bargaining, the two sides reached a somewhat liberal agreement that only required the troops to lay down their arms with pledges not to fight again. The generous terms of the surrender were attributed to Scott's desire to secure the friendship and cooperation of the Mexican people during the volatile period expected ahead. With the formalities completed, the agreement was signed and on March 29 the Americans occupied Veracruz. With some 12,000 troops on hand, Scott's losses in this battle were relatively tiny, with 13 killed and about 55 wounded.

Leaving troops behind to maintain his supply base, within the week General Scott began to organize his new drive into the rough and mountainous interior west of Veracruz. Despite Scott's vast military experience, chiefly from the War of 1812 and fighting the Indians in the Black Hawk and Seminole wars, many of the challenges and problems he had to deal with in this expedition would be new to him. For instance, he never had led such a large army into combat before, his extraordinary amphibious landing was a first in the country's history, and he never had to take his army over such a long distance and in such horrid conditions or to protect his extended supply line while at the same time maintaining a fighting force capable of carrying out the mission. But to the subordinate generals on his staff, although he might not be capable of solving all the problems, they knew Scott's massive ego was the driving mechanism that reassured them of his capacity to accomplish the ultimate goal before them.

When all the formalities of the surrender were over Scott was ready to move on. However, unable to secure sufficient quantities of wagons and animals to transport his huge quantities of supplies, he was begrudgingly forced to dispatch his forces piecemeal. Therefore, on April 8, 1847, General Twiggs received the honor of being the first to march his division out of Veracruz to the National Highway, one of the two roads directly linked to Mexico City. Patterson's division would follow the next day and finally the troops under General Worth. Scott's plan remained the same, to follow the highway through Cerro Gordo, Jalapa, and Puebla before he could make a stand before Mexico City.

In the meantime, Santa Anna left San Luis Potosí for a brief visit to Mexico City. It was here that he first learned that General Scott had taken Veracruz and was now advancing toward Mexico City. Disappointed over this terrible news, Santa Anna remarked, "However shameful it may be to admit this, we have brought this disgusting tragedy upon ourselves through our interminable in-fighting."[4]

As happened so many times in the past, during times of trouble when outside agitators threatened the sovereignty of Mexican soil the citizens of Mexico City were overjoyed to see the Savior of the Motherland was there to save them. To the throngs who came to greet him, Santa Anna made a pledge that he would protect them and their beloved city from the American invaders. Standing before them, from the balcony of the palace Santa Anna proudly pledged that his duty was to sacrifice himself in defense of the country.

With the reassuring shouts of support from the jubilant masses still echoing in his ears, Santa Anna rode out of Mexico City on the third of April to plan his strategy for driving the Americans out of Mexico once and for all. Two days later his coach reached his new hacienda of El Encero, located on the outskirts of Veracruz. Purchased by Santa Anna in 1842, the sprawling eight-acre ranch was a stunning example of Mexican architecture and a fitting residence for El Presidente to carry on his aristocratic lifestyle. Away from the constant political bickering he despised so much, Santa Anna began working on his plans to save the homeland once again.

Unfortunately, the lack of funds to maintain his troops was a major problem, as it always was. It frustrated Santa Anna tremendously that funding for his army was always the impediment to his plans. No matter how much he pleaded, the state legislatures had no money for the army and likewise with the town councils. This sad situation only reminded him of the interminable infighting between political factions seeking power that had now crippled the government; in-fighting that he had engaged in many times himself. Highly aggravated over the government's miserable financial condition and his inability to get financial backing, once again Santa Anna decided to fund the army the best he could out of his own resources. Consequently, he provided his own cattle to feed his men, as well as the produce gathered from his farms. He even paid for the materials necessary to make their ammunition.

Leaving the lavish comforts of his hacienda, Santa Anna rejoined his army at San Luis Potosí and prepared to make a gallant stand at the small town of Cerro Gordo, about 60 miles west of Veracruz. The Mexican general selected this location because he correctly assumed his enemy would be marching toward the town along the National Highway. Better yet, he also knew the rugged mountainous terrain in that area would significantly restrict their advance and would force the Americans to stay within the confines of a narrow stretch of highway. Having since replenished his army with over twelve thousand more volunteer troops, Santa Anna arrived at Cerro Gordo and dispersed his men and artillery across the National Highway, confident that his excellent knowledge of the area and his superior field position would reign supreme. With two towering hills protecting his left flank, steep cliffs and a river to shield his right, his battlefield position was well chosen and was perceived as near impregnable, or so he thought. His engineers recommended fortifying one of the hills on his left flank called Atalaya Hill, a defensive strategy Santa Anna refused to take seriously. He was convinced Scott's attack would concentrate on a frontal assault from the road. Once his two-mile roadblock of troops and artillery was in place, the Mexicans confidently waited for Scott's army to march into their trap.

As expected, many of the American troops, especially those unaccustomed to marching for hours under the intense glare of the Mexican sun, found it unbearable to continue without frequent stops to rest. Exacerbating the march was the fact that many of the troops could not keep up with the rest of the army and straggled far behind. As a result, the march was slow from the frequent pauses to tend to the collapsing men or to rest where roadside shade was available. Relief was found occasionally when the army came to a river crossing and, reminiscent of the migrating herds on the Serengeti, hundreds of the men enjoyed themselves immensely frolicking in the cool, refreshing water.

Nevertheless, despite the hardships, by mid–April of 1847 Scott's strung-out army regrouped about three miles east of the Mexican position at Cerro Gordo and a council of war was called to discuss the assault strategy and the movements of the troops and artillery. At this meeting the engineers who had reconnoitered the area, namely, Capt. Robert E. Lee and Lts. P. G. T. Beauregard, George B. McClellan, G. W. Smith, J. G. Foster, and Z. B. Tower, disclosed that Santa Anna's entrenched positions were spotted several days earlier at the base of Atalya Hill. Also discussed was the existence of a concealed, overgrown trail they found that ran along the crest of Atalya. If cleared of the heavy brush, they claimed, the road could easily get the army around Santa Anna's left flank. Once the order was given to utilize this approach, a labor force was dispatched to clear away the thick brush and trees to expose the trail. Incredibly, all the work on the hill went unchallenged. It seems Santa Anna was so convinced that Scott would be concentrating his forces on a frontal attack that he not only disregarded the reports from his sentries about hearing movements on the hills but also shrugged off a brief confrontation that occurred near Atalya as only a diversionary tactic.

Once the road was cleared, the next task for Scott was to haul several pieces of his artillery over the top of Atalya to the opposite side, a massive 24-pounder being the largest. Dragging a massive gun this size up the six-hundred-foot hill and down the other side was not an easy task by any stretch of the imagination. It took a team of five hundred men to begin the pull at around 9:00 p.m. with additional teams on standby to take over the ropes as each team tired from sheer exhaustion. It took six hours to finally get the guns into position primed and ready to fire on the unsuspecting troops still sleeping a short distance away. "Artillery was let down the steep slopes by hand," recalled Grant, "the men engaged attaching a strong rope to the rear axle and letting the guns down, a piece at a time, while the men at the ropes kept their ground on top, paying out gradually, while a few at the front directed the course of the piece. In like manner the guns were drawn by hand up the opposite slopes. In this way Scott's troops reached their assigned positions in rear of most of the entrenchments of the enemy unobserved."[5]

The movement of the troops was set to commence in the early morning hours of the seventeenth and would entail a three-prong assault. The first phrase called for General Twiggs to take his troops up the newly cleared path and to quietly circle around Santa Anna's left flank. Once in position Twiggs was ordered to simply occupy the ground in that sector until the following morning. Meanwhile, a brigade led by Gen. James Shields was ordered to follow Twiggs to the crest of the hill and General Worth would follow Shields.

The following day, April 18, the attack would be set in motion. While Twiggs cut off Santa Anna's escape route to the National Highway, the second phase required the brigade of General Shields and General Worth's division to attack Santa Anna's left flank with artillery. The third phase kicked in once Santa Anna's left was breached. At that point, the infantry was to advance along the highway and trap the main body against the river. At the same time, as a diversionary tactic, a third force led by General Pillow would strike a nest of three Mexican batteries positioned between Santa Anna and the river, just where Santa Anna expected Scott to attack. Unfortunately, General Patterson remained in his tent recuperating from an illness.

On April 18, 1847, the American offensive began shortly after Mexican reveille was heard. While General Twiggs cut off Santa Anna's escape route, the American artillery on the hills began to rain iron on the surprised Mexican forces below. Santa Anna veterans, not the kind of troops to be easily intimidated, returned round after round of grape and canister, which kept the Americans pinned down temporarily. At the same time, General Pillow's attack had gone terribly wrong. Not only was he late in launching his attack, but also when he did he permitted his men to be fully exposed to all three pieces of Santa Anna's artillery and they paid dearly for that mistake. Concentrated blasts of canister from the three guns were like oversized shotgun blasts that cleared away large swaths of troops in one mighty explosion. Pillow's men, consisting of two Pennsylvania and two Tennessee regiments, had no recourse but to run for cover or retreat to the rear.

In time, the fighting on the left flank grew more intense as General Worth's infantry charged into Santa Anna's fighters. The fighting at this point was so close, so fast, and so furious that hand-to-hand combat was the only way to defend oneself, with the bayonet being the weapon of choice. Overwhelmed by the superior numbers and the punishing assault on their left, the Mexican army broke as U.S. forces swarmed into them. Retreating before the onrushing troops, the now-panic-stricken Mexicans fled on foot in a wild and disorganized rout, Santa Anna among them. The Mexican artillerists who had just decimated General Pillow's forces saw they had no way out but to surrender, as did approximately three thousand of Santa Anna's troops.

In about three hours the action was over and the task of paroling the prisoners began. Scott had little choice in making the decision to parole so many of the enemy when having enough food to feed his own men was already a growing problem. Later, in a letter written by one of the despondent Mexicans he said, "It was an unmitigated disaster. As a defeat that is both complete and shameful; everything has been lost, nothing saved, absolutely nothing; not even hope."[6]

While the unpleasant duty to bury their 63 fallen soldiers commenced, General Patterson, now fully recovered from his sickness, led a detachment in pursuit of Santa Anna and a group of soldiers who they learned were riding toward Jalapa, only a short distance away. During the process of their search, members of the 4th Illinois Infantry came upon what looked like a recently abandoned campsite. While conducting their search of the camp the men were shocked to find a wooden leg, undoubtedly once belonging to the Savior of the Motherland himself. Evidently, they surmised, Santa Anna must have panicked when he heard that Patterson's search party was in the area and in his haste to retreat left the wooden and cork leg behind. (The leg is presently on permanent display in the Illinois State Military Museum.)

With all the loose ends cleaned up around Cerro Gordo, Scott marched his men back onto the National Highway. The army lumbered on, easily occupying Jalapa a few days later. The city was a welcome relief for the worn-out troops, a place where they could catch their breath and enjoy the spectacular weather.

Not so for General Scott, however. While at Jalapa, Scott would have to confront issues he seldom had to face before. Having to deal with unruly and undisciplined soldiers was not really a new problem for Scott or, for that matter, any commander but was an ongoing distraction throughout the military. With such a large number of raw volunteers entering the army, however, Scott had the foresight to prepare for the rowdy behavior he was sure to encounter. He handled it by issuing a Martial Law Order before he left for Mexico that made such infractions as rape, murder, assault, robbery, desecration of churches, and destruction of private property, among several other crimes, court-martial offenses subject to military court trials. A guilty offender could be punished by the lash, hard labor, imprisonment, branding, and even death. This edict applied not only to the American soldier but also to any Mexican citizen, as well as American civilians in Mexico.

Another problem he never had to deal with before arose when Scott learned he was losing a large portion of his army. As you may recall, shortly after Polk's War Bill passed through Congress in May of 1846 General Scott busied himself assembling an army, many of whom were 12-month volunteers. For these four thousand or so individuals the year was just about over, and now the volunteers demanded to be released from duty and returned to their homes. General Scott agreed to their release and General Patterson was ordered to escort the departing volunteers to the coast.

Scott recognized full well that in terms of manpower strength against Santa Anna his army would always be the underdog, that he would never be able to obtain any form of parity with the three-to-one advantage Santa Anna enjoyed. It was for this reason that Scott consistently stressed the importance of encouraging good public relations with the Mexican citizens of the cities under American occupation. He insisted that the public officials, the merchants, and the ordinary folks be treated fairly and with all the respect possible. He wanted life in the towns he occupied to return to normal as quickly as possible. Scott always made the case to civic leaders that with their cooperation with his forces the war would end sooner and with less devastation. After all, he insisted, the last thing he wanted was to suffer the wrath of the townspeople he just had vanquished. As he remarked at Cerro Gordo, "The people, moreover, must be conciliated, soothed, or well treated by every officer and man of this army, and by all its followers."[7]

The general-in-chief painfully acknowledged that as the army advanced and his manpower resources dwindled his supply line became more and more difficult to maintain. He was also unable to sufficiently garrison the cities and outpost he occupied along the way and it was getting more complicated to get sufficient quantities of reinforcements, a need he thought crucial for the next battle. Consequently, Scott had little choice but to recall each of his detachments and to cut ties with his base at Veracruz.

He was also having problems getting food and supplies from Veracruz. The longer he extended the distance between his army and Veracruz the more trouble he had. It seems the wagon trains from Veracruz were consistently attacked by robbers, angry citizens, or the Mexican troops. Scott's options were rather limited. He could guard the entire route, which was impossible to do, or dispatch cavalry units to escort the trains, which was too labor-intensive and not very practical. His army was now forced to live off the land.

There was also the problem of his highly inflated ego. When word reached the

White House that Veracruz had surrendered, President Polk was ecstatic. Calculating that Mexico's senior officials might be ready to capitulate, Polk decided to dispatch an emissary to Scott's army who would be invested with full authority to independently negotiate the terms of surrender on behalf of the U.S. government whenever the occasion arose. The cabinet dutifully agreed and Nicholas P. Trist, the chief clerk at the State Department and a man of outstanding qualifications, was selected to take on this role. On its face, the selection of a little-known bureaucrat for such a responsible position seemed a bit irresponsible to most observers. But Trist was not your average run-of-the-mill government clerk. He was fluent in Spanish and was well versed in the Latin American culture, from serving as U.S. Consul in Havana. He had studied law under Thomas Jefferson and was even a cadet at the West Point Academy. Furthermore, he was the highest-ranking professional officer in the State Department. And so it was that on May 6, with a secret draft of a treaty in his pocket, Trist walked ashore at Veracruz en route to Scott's headquarters, a confrontation neither of them was looking forward to.

General Scott was properly notified by letter from Secretary of War Marcy, which stated that Trist was clothed with such diplomatic powers as would authorize him to enter into arrangements "with the Government for the suspension of hostilities." And in the event he made known in writing that a contingency had occurred in consequence of which the president was willing to cease further active military operations, "you will regard such notice as a direction from the President to suspend them till further orders."[8] Needless to say, Scott's huge ego got the better of his sensibilities. To think, he fumed, a mere civilian clerk had the power not only to negotiate for peace with the Mexican government but also to give the cease-fire order to the general-in-chief. He was absolutely livid that again Polk was trying to discredit and humiliate him. Scott could not contain his anger any longer and in a letter to Trist acidly responded, "I see that the Secretary of War proposes to degrade me, by requiring that I, as the commander of this army, shall defer to you, the chief clerk of the Department of State, the question of continuing or discontinuing hostilities. I beg to say to him and to you, that here, in the heart of a hostile country, ... it would be impossible to withdraw this army without a loss ... which army, from necessity must soon become a self-sustaining machine cut off from all supplies and reinforcements until, perhaps, late in November.... I say, in regard to those critical circumstances, this army must take military security for its own safety...." Continuing his tirade in no uncertain terms, he reminded Trist that as general-in-chief he demanded all proposals for the suspension of hostilities be referred to him personally because "the safety of this army demands no less, and I am responsible for that safety until duly superseded or recalled."[9]

Disgusted with the current state of affairs with his new "partner" and with only around six thousand men left in his command, Scott decided it was time to resume his advance toward Mexico City. First, however, Scott had some unfinished business to attend to.

The enmity between Scott and Trist continued even from the time Trist arrived at Jalapa on May 14. In fact, the bitterness that had built up between the two had reached the point where they refused to meet each other when Trist first arrived. Instead, they communicated their insults via written letters. Scott was so upset he did the unthinkable for a soldier of his standing. To Marcy he wrote, "Considering the many cruel disappointments and mortifications I have been made to feel since I left Washington, or the total want of support and sympathy on the part of the War Department which I have so long experienced, I beg to be recalled from this army the moment that it may be safe for any person to embark at Vera Cruz, which I suppose will be early in November."[10] Obviously, Scott's request to be recalled was denied.

Following his defeat at Cerro Gordo, Santa Anna returned to Mexico City, where he arranged a meeting that was held on June 20, 1847. As he joined his generals in the Archive of the Mexican Ministry of Defense, the military hierarchy discussed the present state of military affairs and the government's responsibilities for supporting the army. During the course of their discussions, a surprising number of candid opinions were expressed by the generals to Santa Anna, many about the lack of a unified national spirit over the country's problems. They complained how factionalism had caused irreparable damage to Mexico unnecessarily and only incited civil wars. Even now, they lamented, as the enemy approached the gates of the capital city groups were still plotting against one another to the detriment of the country. The lack of support from the legislatures for the army's needs was also addressed, as was disenchantment with the press over their consistent message of gloom and doom instead of gathering support for the army. Despite all the problems talked about, at the end of the meeting Santa Anna asked the generals to vote on whether they preferred continuing the war or surrendering. The vote was unanimous for continuing to fight the war. But first Santa Anna had to raise another army.

What followed was a campaign to inspire the citizens of Mexico City with a sense of pride in their country and to awaken them to the fact that the enemy was about to enter the gates to their grand city. Focusing on the need to raise thousands of volunteers, he declared it was their obligation to defend the country, to rally to its defense and to fight for its salvation. Although he may have been quite sincere, his plea received mixed reactions. To many in Mexico City, Santa Anna was still their hero and the Savior of the Motherland. To others, however, he was always, is now, and will always be a corrupt and incorrigible dictator.

As for General Scott, after his resignation was denied he divided his army and departed Jalapa piecemeal with General Worth and some four thousand troops being the first to leave for Puebla on May 6, on a march of some 60 miles. General Scott and the rest of his smaller army would soon follow with a separate march to Perote, where a small garrison was left behind to care for the sick and wounded, and a third garrison traveled to Jalapa, where Scott established his headquarters. However, a month later Scott realized his mistake and became quite concerned over the large distance separating his forces. Consequently, in the first week of June he called his forces to reunite in Puebla.

13

Scott's Drive to Mexico City

By June of 1847, Gen. Winfield Scott and the American army were camped across the fields of Puebla, the second-largest city in Mexico. To their pleasant surprise, when General Worth's forces arrived they were well received by the citizens who came out to greet them. It seemed like the entire citizenry was there, since so many people lined the newly paved street watching intently as the troops marched toward the main plaza. Many of the soldiers were amazed at the sight of the macadamized main street leading into the city, the first they had ever laid their eyes on. The suspicious Mexicans were just as amazed at the casual behavior of the gringos as they strolled through the marketplace, a far cry from what the Mexicans were led to believe about the evil devils from America.

So far everything had gone reasonably well for Scott, and as he contemplated his next move he was pleased with the way his volunteers had performed. His amphibious landing on the sand-dunned beach at Veracruz went smoothly, his army was victorious in two consecutive engagements with a minimum of fatalities, and his sick and wounded were convalescing in Perote. At this point, he mused, his only real problem, besides the civilian upstart named Trist, was a manpower shortage. Scott estimated his losses to be considerable, if not catastrophic, due to battlefield deaths, sicknesses, incapacitated wounded, desertions, and the recent disastrous loss of some four thousand men whose enlistment term had expired.

As far as his relationship with Trist was concerned, in time Scott and Trist finally reconciled their differences when they realized they both had to cooperate with each other and to work together for the good of the country. This was made abundantly clear when, astonishingly enough, a message arrived in June from Santa Anna addressed to Trist asking to negotiate a peaceful solution to the war. There was, of course, one glaring condition. Santa Anna demanded a $10,000 down payment immediately and $1 million after the treaty was consummated in writing. Since Scott had the money, Trist initiated a meeting with Scott at his headquarters, where they cordially discussed the offer by Santa Anna. At that point, Scott went through a bit of soul-searching in which he rationalized to himself and to his staff that their role in this unseemly bribery scheme was well worth any potential problem if it meant ending the terrible bloodshed, and of course

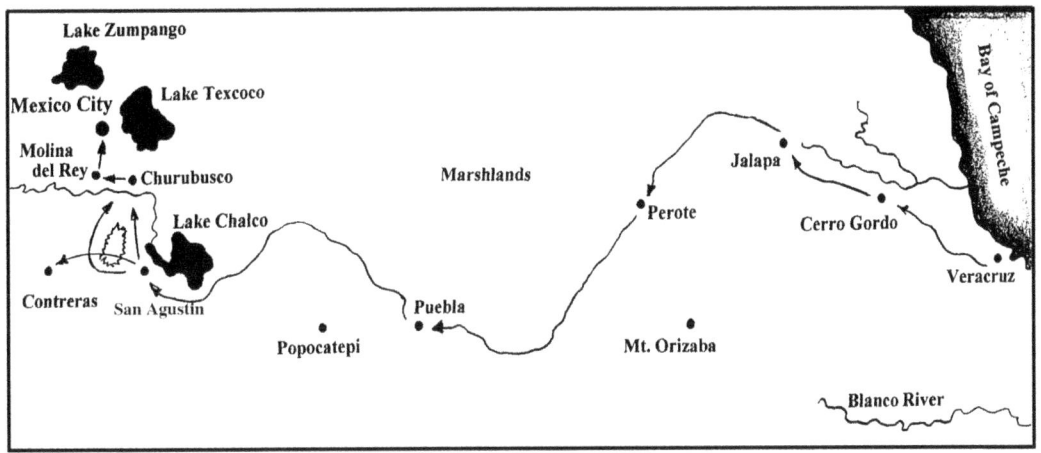

Scott's Advance to Mexico City

there was the glory and prestige for everyone that was certain to follow. Countering the suggestion from one of his staff on the appearance of impropriety, Scott remarked, "The overture, if corrupt, came from parties already corrupted."[1] Satisfied with the halfhearted acquiescence of his generals, Scott made arrangements with British go-betweens to have $10,000 transferred from his military account to Santa Anna. Unfortunately, it was soon learned, and quite embarrassingly so, that a new law in Mexico forbade under penalty of treason anyone, including the president, from offering to negotiate with the United States.

Nevertheless, to the chagrin of Scott and Trist, the transfer of funds was made and General Santa Anna pocketed the $10,000. Together with remnants of his destroyed army, he rode southward, where he undoubtedly used the money to scrape together enough men to help defend the nation's capital, a gambit only Santa Anna could carry out and get away with.

After three months at Puebla the American troops were reasonably rested, spirits were high, the food had been adequate, reinforcements had finally arrived, and Scott was growing more impatient each day to get on with his campaign. His new reinforcements numbered nearly seven thousand men, troops under the commands of Gen. Gideon J. Pillow and Gen. Franklin Pierce, the future fourteenth president of the United States. Consequently, as a result of these reinforcements, Scott reorganized his much larger army into four divisions. In addition to Generals Worth and Twiggs, the other two divisions fell under Generals Pillow and Quitman.

During those same three months Santa Anna, seemingly perpetually tireless in his desire to defend his country, managed to raise about twenty-five thousand volunteers and somehow found the means to feed, clothe, and equip most of them. And with the experience gained from years of managing a number of different armies, he began to fortify the strategic points in and around Mexico City.

With only around 70 miles left to reach Mexico City, on August 7, 1847, some fourteen thousand American troops marched out of Puebla along with their rumbling artillery, their long train of clattering wagons, and their wish that at Mexico City the war would finally end. As they tramped along the hot and dusty highway, anticipation ran high among the American troops that at Mexico City better times were coming. Around their campfires they had listened to the many stories about the beauty of Mexico City, the crown jewel of the republic, and they were eager to see it for themselves.

Still following the National Highway, soon the army was camped a mere 20 miles from the eastern entrance to the walled city. Fortunately, an earlier reconnaissance by Captain Lee and confirmed by other sources disclosed that Santa Anna had a sizable force and several pieces of artillery dug in along a small mountain located directly ahead called El Peñón. The new batch of Mexican soldiers, anxiously watching for the telltale cloud of dust, eagerly anticipated the arrival of the American forces. Relying on Captain Lee's expertise once again, General Scott dispatched his engineering staff to scout the surrounding area for a way to bypass the Mexicans and avoid a confrontation he didn't want. Several days later, Lee's suggestion of an alternate route, seconded by a number of Scott's commanders for its suitability for moving the artillery and wagons, was agreed to, and for the first time the American army would leave the highway and circle around toward the southern approach to the Mexican capital.

The southern approach to Mexico City was dominated by an enormous lava field surrounding Mount Zacatepec called the Pedregal. Covering approximately 15 square miles, the oval obstruction of volcanic boulders, deep fissures, and sharp ridges was about 5 miles wide and was entirely outlined by the only road available for gaining entry into Mexico City from the south. Like entering a huge rotary circling the mountain, on August 18 Scott's bedraggled army arrived at its most southeasterly point, at the town of San Agustín de las Cuevas.

When informed that the American army was approaching from San Agustín, Santa Anna surmised that Scott would follow the road to the right side of the Pedregal, which was the most direct route to Mexico City. To offer resistance to Scott's army in this direction Santa Anna ordered a detachment of troops to garrison a hacienda called San Antonio that was also located near the same road the Americans would travel. Furthermore, in case Scott decided to advance along the left side of the Pedregal, Santa Anna reacted quickly to impede the American advance on that section of the road as well by moving several thousand troops to the opposite side of the lava flow to the town of San Angel. In addition, Santa Anna ordered Gen. Gabriel Valencia, Santa Anna's archrival and the commander of the Army of the North, to a position a short distance ahead of San Angel so that Valencia would have first crack at the approaching American army. It seems Valencia was not pleased with his position and demonstrated his reputation as a maverick subordinate and an officer difficult to deal with by unilaterally ordering his four thousand men to a different location. He ignored Santa Anna's order and took his men closer to the town of Contreras, a position directly in line with San Agustín but on the left side of the Pedregal and several miles beyond his previously assigned location.

Scott's goal was to reach the small village of Churubusco, where a bridge over the Churubusco River would lead to Portales and then directly to the southern gates of Mexico City. Since the shortest route was along the right side of the lava flow, Santa Anna's assumption was correct. Scott ordered General Worth to advance his forces toward Churubusco, but it wasn't long before Worth was on the receiving end of heavy musketry and cannon fire from the well-fortified hacienda. Such was the blitz from the

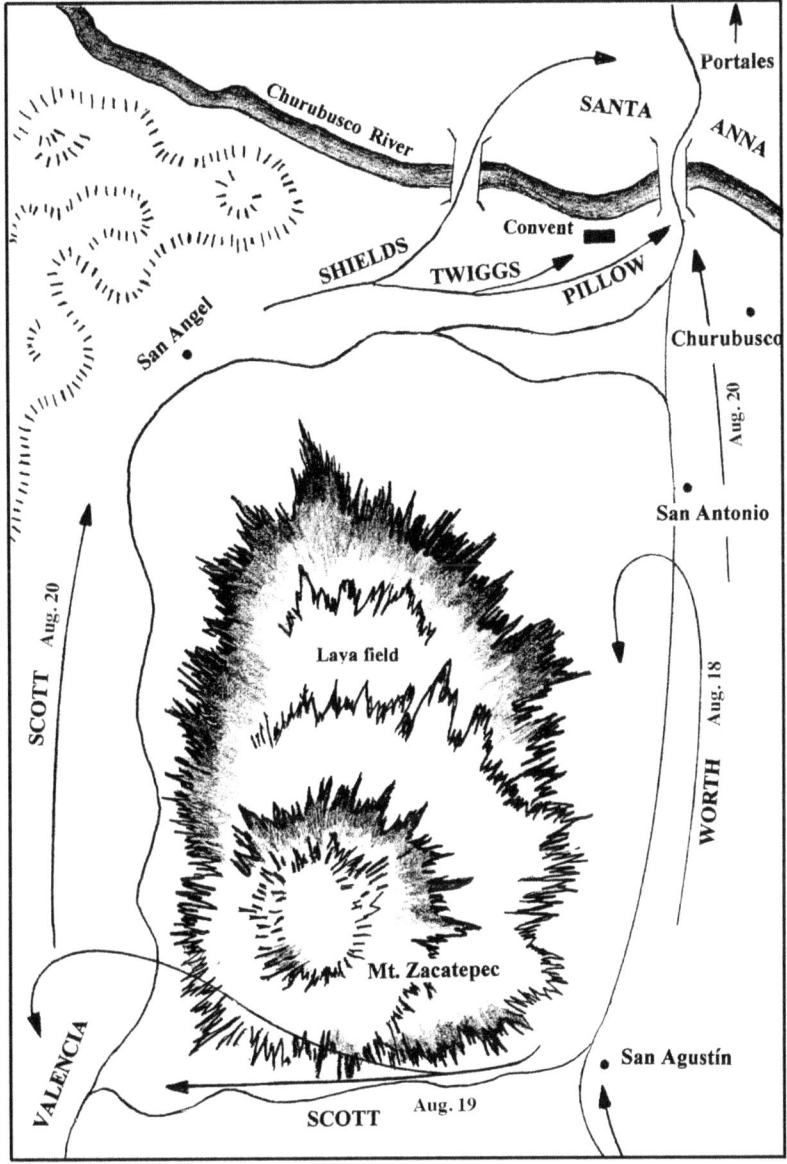

Battle of Churubusco

hacienda that within a very short time the assault forced Worth to backtrack toward San Agustín. Reported killed in the attack was Seth Thornton, the officer captured in the ambush across from Matamoros back in April of 1846, the episode that had triggered the war.

While General Worth advanced down the right side of the lava field, Scott also ordered Captain Lee and a body of dragoons to check out a narrow trail that crossed the Pedregal parallel to the road on the left side to see if it was impassable or if it could be used to support the army and the artillery. Returning later that day after being fired upon by Mexican troops hidden behind the black boulders, Lee informed Scott that the path over the Pedregal could indeed be made suitable with a little work. It was obvious to everyone by now that Santa Anna had a large body of troops and artillery positioned off the road ahead near the town of Contreras.

The following day Scott held a council of war. Despite the risks, he said to his staff, he decided to advance along the left side of Mount Zacatepec, but instead of following the existing road that was guarded by General Valencia, the army would use the route scouted by Captain Lee across the lava flow. On that basis Scott ordered several hundred men from General Pillow's command to begin preparing the crude road while the division of General Twiggs would provide the defensive coverage. If still unable to get by San Antonio, General Worth would bring up the rear some time later, with General Quitman remaining at San Agustín in reserve.

As the raging glare of the Mexican sun reached its fiercest early that afternoon of the nineteenth, just as the roadwork was completed on the downside of the Pedregal, the American forces came under an artillery attack from Valencia's batteries. To counter the Mexican firepower, two batteries of field guns and howitzers were brought up and returned fire from the road in Valencia's front as well as from the lava field but were unable to sustain their position for long and were forced to retreat. As Valencia's batteries continued to fire indiscriminately on the lava flow, that evening four American infantry brigades managed to work their way across the Pedregal undetected and gained a position through a ravine that led to the rear of General Valencia's command. With reinforcements arriving to strengthen the outnumbered and outgunned Americans, the troops quietly maneuvered into position for their upcoming attack. Lying awake in the cold rain that night, many of the men were fearful that most of them would not survive. Orders had already been given to discontinue the use of their guns after the first volley, since the steady rain would in all likelihood render their powder useless while they reloaded. Instead, most of the men would be forced into using their bayonets. In the meantime, having learned of the situation at Contreras, Santa Anna, who was still at San Angel, sent a message that ordered Valencia to withdraw his forces back to San Angel, another order the general refused to obey.

Around 5:00 a.m. on August 20, the final preparations were in place for Scott's troops to attack. On a given signal, a diversionary cannonading commenced from the road on the left of the Pedregal into Valencia's position. While the attention of the Mexican troops was drawn to their enemy directly ahead, in the early morning mist and cold rain the American infantry struck. It was a tremendous display of courage as Scott's troops, now reinforced to about forty-five hundred, sprang into action and pounced on the unsuspecting Mexicans. In what became known as the Battle of Contreras, Valencia's troops were caught completely by surprise by the sudden attack on their rear and in less than 20 minutes the Mexicans were sent fleeing for their lives. Relating what he saw that morning, one officer reported:

> We saw a devil of a hubbub in their camp, the men running to arms, the mounting of horses & c. It was a complete surprise. We received a volley from the enemy's infantry thrown hastily out to oppose us. We did not return a shot but stood up as if they were throwing apples instead of lead at us. We marched towards them still under heavy fire of musketry, for some twenty or thirty yards, than halted. During all this time we had not

fired a shot and men were dropping in our ranks at every moment. I admire the coolness of our men during this trying time even more than their headlong impetuosity after the word charge was given. When we deployed into line of battle, we gave them a volley, and then made a head long rush.[2]

At this point, the men rushed in with bayonets fixed, relentlessly stabbing every enemy soldier still standing or using the butts of their rifles to render blows to the enemies' heads. When it was over about eight hundred of Valencia's men were captured and seven hundred killed, while the rest, including General Valencia himself, escaped into the surrounding territory. In the meantime, Santa Anna and his troops had withdrawn from San Angel to provide more reinforcements at Churubusco.

When he received reports of Valencia's humiliating defeat, Santa Anna was absolutely outraged that his general had consistently disobeyed his orders. Indeed, Santa Anna was so upset over the general's arrogance and disrespect that without hesitation he ordered Valencia shot on sight. The decision to rid his army of Valencia was not that difficult for Santa Anna to make. The two were known to be political enemies for years, especially after Santa Anna learned that Valencia was plotting to overthrow him for the presidency.

As a consequence of Valencia's defeat Santa Anna called in all of his remaining forces, including the defenders at the hacienda and the force at El Peñón, to concentrate and strengthen his position around Churubusco. As a result, a heavily entrenched force was now scattered around the bridge, while more reinforcements also garrisoned the nearby and already well-fortified Franciscan San Mateo Convent. There Santa Anna, confident in the ability of his army to dominate the field, waited to do business with the approaching Americans. However, Scott knew that once he survived this impediment to his advance the road ahead led directly to the southern causeway and the gates into Mexico City.

Continuing their steady advance toward Santa Anna's position at Churubusco, Scott stopped to survey the deadly fortifications just ahead of him. At a council of war, Scott and his generals discussed their options and the strategy to overcome the challenges expected from Santa Anna's desperate efforts to survive. With no other recourse but to fight or retreat, Scott ordered General Twiggs to make an all-out attack on and around the walled convent where about two thousand Mexican troops, supported by some seven or eight pieces of artillery, were poised for battle. In parallel with Twigg's attack, General Pillow was directed to assault the nearby heavily fortified bridge spanning the Churubusco River, a position being held by approximately three thousand troops with their ample share of artillery along the riverbank as well. Also, Scott had information that a second, adjacent and undefended bridge was open and could be easily crossed. Consequently, he dispatched two brigades under Generals Shields and Pierce with orders to push ahead across the bridge, hold the road to Portales and attack the Mexican troops attempting to escape from the vicinity of the bridge. At the same time, General Worth would clear out any remnants of resistance remaining at the San Antonio hacienda and then reinforce Pillow at the bridge. The result would be a two-prong pincers movement that would trap Santa Anna's forces in the middle. Capt. Ulysses S. Grant, a member of General Garland's brigade of Worth's division, relates that drive in his memoirs:

We moved out at once, and found them [Mexican troops] gone from our immediate front. Colonel N.S. Clarke's brigade of Worth's division now moved west over the point of the Pedregal, and after having passed to the north sufficiently to clear San Antonio [a hacienda], turned east and got on the causeway leading to Churubusco and the City of Mexico. When he approached Churubusco his left brought on an engagement. About an hour after, Garland was ordered to advance directly along the causeway, and got up in time to take part in the engagement. San Antonio was found evacuated, the evacuation having probably taken place immediately upon the enemy seeing the stars and stripes waving over Contreras.[3]

Unfortunately, Gen. Franklin Pierce was unable to participate in the movement of his troops after his horse fell and he was severely injured.

Around noon of August 20, the Battle of Churubusco was under way. It was arguably one of the bloodiest confrontations of them all. Mercifully lasting only three hours or so, it was also the most decisive. Sizing up the situation confronting the Mexicans, Scott wrote, "The whole remaining forces of Mexico—some 27,000 men—cavalry, artillery, and infantry, collected from every quarter—were now in, on the flanks or within supporting distance of, those works, and seemed resolved to make a last and desperate stand; for if beaten here, the feebler defenses at the gates of the city—four miles off—could not, as was well known to both parties, delay the victor an hour... the assailants were resolved to win. Not an American—and we had less than a third of the enemy's numbers—had a doubt as to the result."[4]

Although Scott's men initially gave way at both the convent and the bridge, despite being defended by thousands of Mexican troops the bridge was the first to fail, falling to the swarming Americans who counterattacked and overwhelmed the Mexican defenders. At first, Pillow's outnumbered troops, supported by several pieces of artillery, were unable to gain a foothold there and were on the verge of withdrawing when two brigades from General Worth's division arrived to provide the final and deciding push. As predicted, the close-contact action that followed at the bridge was so rapid that after the first few volleys most of the men had little time to stand back and reload for another shot. As a result the battle became one of hand-to-hand combat.

When the resistance began to collapse in that sector, General Worth turned his attention to the chaotic scene at the convent only some three to five hundred yards away, defended mostly by hardened Mexican regulars. General Worth's tenacious division entered the fray to assist the struggling forces under Twiggs, who were being raked over by a steady onslaught of cannon fire, canister, and musketry and were about to withdraw. Finally rallying the men to regroup, the combined American divisions were able to close out the battle there as well in less than a half hour.

The surrender of Mexican forces at the convent as presented in Scott's official report to Secretary Marcy states:

> The fortified church or convent, hotly pressed by Twiggs, had already held out about an hour, when Worth and Pillow—the latter having with him only [one] brigade—began to maneuver closely upon the tete du pont (strong field-work), with the convent at half gunshot, to their left.... Finally, twenty minutes after the tete du pont had been carried by Worth and Pillow, and at the end of a desperate conflict of two hours and a half, the church or convent—the citadel of the strong line of defense along the rivulet of Churubusco—yielded to Twiggs' division, and threw out, on all sides, signals of surrender. The white

flags, however, were not exhibited until the moment when the 3d Infantry, under Captain Alexander, had cleared the way by fire and bayonet, and had entered the work.... The immediate results of this victory were—the capture of 7 field pieces, some ammunition, one color, three generals, and 1,261 prisoners, including other officers.[5]

Meanwhile, the brigades under General Shields had their hands full trying to cope with the fleeing Mexican troops. Without the proper resources to support the brigades, they were severely restricted from adequately turning back the fleeing Mexicans. Consequently, most of them were able make good their escape to Portales, along with the likes of Santa Anna.

Notwithstanding the brevity of the struggle, the casualties were extremely high for both sides. On the one hand, Scott reported his losses at slightly over 1,000 troops, of whom 139 were killed. Santa Anna's casualties, on the other hand, were estimated to be about twice that number.

In his remarks to Marcy, General Scott was truly gratified over the superb accomplishment of his troops and proudly said, "My thanks were but freely poured out on the different fields—to the science and abilities of generals and other officers—to the gallantry and prowess of all—the rank and file included. But a reward infinitely higher—the applause of a grateful country and government—will, I cannot doubt, be accorded, in due time, to so much merit, of every sort, displayed by this glorious army, which has now overcome all difficulties—distance, climate, ground, fortifications, numbers."[6]

Earlier that afternoon, General Santa Anna, in despair and assuming the worst, withdrew from Portales and obtained refuge behind the gates of Mexico City along with thousands of his demoralized soldiers.

By this time, Scott's men, as well as the Mexican soldiers, were in desperate condition. Scores of his weary troops were unable to continue, sick from sheer fatigue and the lack of food. Fully realizing the prospects of a severe and exhausting fight to overcome the Mexican's last-ditch stand, Scott ordered his army into bivouac until further notice. And in an attempt to prevent the horrors of that final assault, the general-in-chief prepared a letter for Santa Anna asking for the surrender of the city. Safely ensconced in the Palace of the Montezuma, Santa Anna was also distressed over the terrible losses his army had just suffered at Contreras and Churubusco and was also seeking a way to bring a halt to the fighting. Fearing that an attack on Mexico City was imminent, in reality Santa Anna wanted desperately to stall for time so that he could rest his troops, improve the fortification of the city, and rebuild another army capable of defending the capital city.

Before Scott's letter could be delivered, however, on August 21 a Mexican officer appeared at the entrance to the American camp under a flag of truce with a verbal message for General Scott. Speaking on Santa Anna's behalf, the emissary expressed the general's desire for a possible truce as a foundation for further negotiations. The one-year halt to hostilities, he suggested, would enable parties from both sides to meet and to discuss ways to head off the loss of more lives.

Unwilling to agree to such an extended truce, Scott respectfully declined but said he would be more receptive to a short-term armistice. Not wanting to lose this opportunity for a peaceful ending of the war, Scott decided to send Santa Anna a carefully worded reply written to give the appearance that the United States was actually the one seeking a truce. That same day, Santa Anna's minister of war forwarded a written reply to Scott that accepted the proposal to discuss an armistice.

Interestingly enough, it was quite obvious that General Scott knew by now that Mexican law explicitly forbids any Mexican citizen, even the president and general, from initiating peace negotiations with Americans. This was the reason Santa Anna communicated his proposal verbally instead of in a written document.

Nevertheless, with both parties agreeing to hold talks, the meeting was held on August 22. It was attended by two generals from the Mexican army and three from Scott's army, namely, Gens. Franklin Pierce, John A. Quitman, and Persifor F. Smith. This turn of events greatly pleased General Scott, who thought things were finally going his way toward a peaceful settlement of the war and the positive notoriety it would bring. It also pleased Santa Anna, who needed more time to rebuild his army and to prepare for Scott's attack. Although both generals were pleased for totally opposing reasons, Scott's officers were outraged that after all the hardships and sacrifices suffered by the army their leaders were going to talk rather than advance into Mexico City for the final showdown. "There was much muttering and grumbling throughout the army," lamented one officer, "when it was known that these were to be the fruits of all our fatigue and fighting."[7]

At the meeting, the delegation of generals agreed to establish an indefinite cease-fire that could be terminated by either side with 48-hour notice. Called the Tacubaya Armistice, it further stipulated that neither army could gain reinforcements or strengthen its fortifications within 90 miles and would be effective on August 24. Also, prisoners were to be exchanged and the wounded attended to. Finally, in exchange for not interfering with traffic coming in or leaving Mexico City, the Americans could obtain supplies from the city in the meantime.

In his typical fashion, however, despite the truce and its rules, Santa Anna continued to fortify the city.

By September 6 Scott learned that Santa Anna had continued to supplement his fortifications of the city, a distinct violation of their agreement. Scott was also quite disturbed over the verbal abuse his men were receiving when in the city picking up supplies. Unable to get a reasonable response from the general on the meaning of his defiance of the truce, Scott, now totally flustered and extremely angry over this lack of good faith, promptly notified Santa Anna that he was declaring the armistice over. And so the war was on once again.

Without the slightest sign of concern over the resumption of the war, within the walls of Mexico City Santa Anna could be seen carrying on his usual round of activities as he drilled his troops in the plaza, scurried deliberately through the city streets, argued with vendors, and held meetings with his staff as well.

At a council of war, Scott and his staff discussed the layout of the land before them and the strategy for gaining access to Mexico City. Entrance to Mexico City from the south, they agreed, could be obtained by capturing the gates at the end of four long elevated causeways. Bordered by marshes, each causeway led directly to a stone gatehouse manned by armed troops guarding admittance to the city through the gates. Contemplating the different ways he could gain access to the city, Scott was also considering the feasibility of entering Mexico City from the western side, over just two long stone

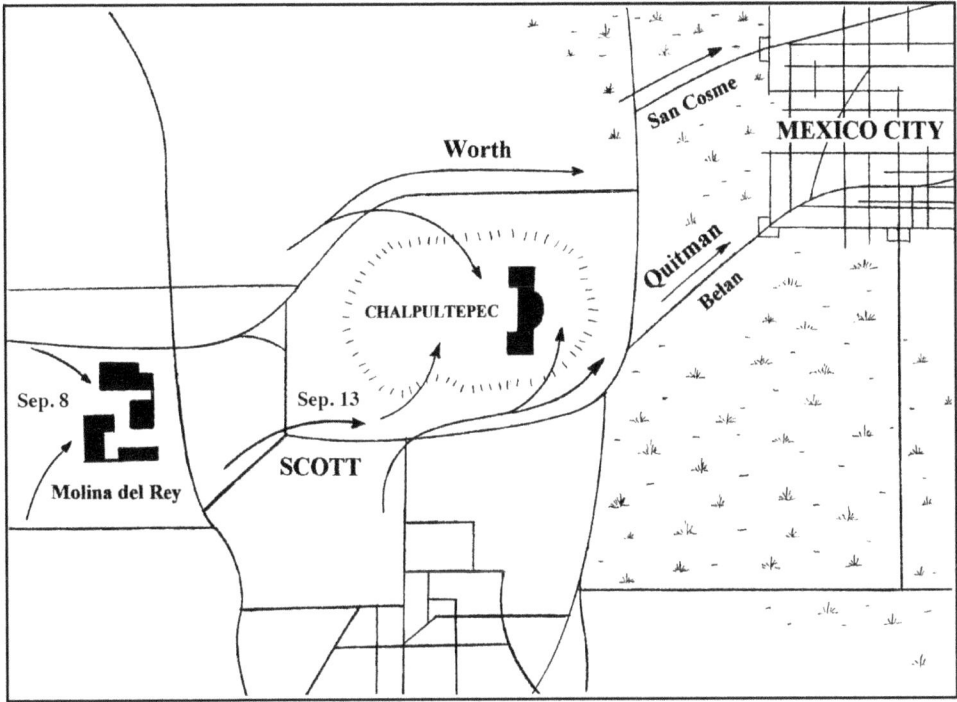

The Battle for Mexico City

causeways called the San Cosme and the Belan Causeways. However, besides being bordered on both sides by the same wide expanses of watery marshes, access to the two western causeways would be much more difficult since the army would have to first confront a number of Mexican troops meticulously protecting a two-hundred-foot high ridge called Chapultepec. Also, on the crest of the ridge stood an old yet regal palace built by the Spaniards for their colonial viceroys and now a national treasure. As it was sacred to their culture and to the history of their beloved capital, the Mexicans would protect it at all costs.

Examining their maps and reconnaissance reports, the officers were also aware of a group of buildings at a place called Molina del Rey, which was located a short distance from the base of Chapultepec. The buildings were nothing more significant than a dilapidated flour mill, a black powder warehouse, and an old foundry, each connected by walls and courtyards, and the decision to launch an offensive toward Molina del Rey first was largely influenced by the reconnaissance reports that located a number of Mexican troops garrisoned there and the fact that it was only a mile or so from the American camp. Besides, Scott thought it would be a relatively minor diversion for his troops until the rest of his scattered forces arrived for their main drive. In that regard, the only U.S. troops taking part in this assault would be General Worth's reinforced division of about thirty-five hundred men.

Moving toward the Mexican works in the very early hours of September 8, General Worth's men found more than they had bargained for. Santa Anna had cleverly shifted a number of brigades into Molino del Rey, supported by batteries and four thousand cavalrymen. What Scott thought would be a mere skirmish turned out to be a tough and hard-fought battle. After a two-hour exchange of musket fire and artillery, the Mexican fortitude weakened and they finally backed away. Although the Americans had won the battle, their losses were staggering. Over one hundred were killed and nearly seven hundred were out of action, almost a quarter of Worth's force. In the final analysis, it was a battle that won nothing except perhaps further demoralization of Santa Anna's army and to insult the victors.

Several days later, Scott called for another meeting with his generals and engineers. The discussion concerned the same question as before. Should they advance to the city gates from the southern sector or from the western side, via the defensives at Chapultepec? During the previous meeting, they had discussed the daunting prospect of assaulting the seemingly impregnable Chapultepec. About eight hundred troops guarded the palace, commanded by ex–vice president Gen. Nicolás Bravo, including a number of young teenage military cadets, many of whom would pay the ultimate price in their first action against an enemy. But despite the opinions from most of his staff that favored the southern route, Scott made the final decision; they would initiate their assault on Chapultepec and then attack the western gates into Mexico City.

Perhaps for the first time, their grossly inferior numbers and their weakened condition instilled a question of confidence in their ability to carry this demanding effort to fruition. From outward appearances, scaling the steep ridge in the face of enemy gunfire was perceived as a Herculean task, one about which Scott would later remark, "I have my misgivings."[8]

On the morning of September 12, the American army was now at full strength. The generals put aside their apprehensions, and with a mighty roar Scott's artillery began its bombardment of the Mexican works. The shelling of the palace would last the entire day and well into the night, employing batteries of siege guns, howitzers, and mortars. It wasn't long before the palace walls, now heavily pockmarked, would begin to crumble. The following day, beginning at dawn, the shelling continued unabated. Several hours later, around 8:00 a.m., the shelling suddenly ceased, huge clouds of smoke slowly drifted away and all was eerily quiet, a clear signal to the Mexicans that a manned assault was imminent.

In a three-prong attack, the American divisions rushed toward their target, each force scrambling headlong over a different route, each one charging up the ridge toward the same ultimate objective. Surprisingly, the onrushing assault to the summit of Chapultepec was swift and brief as each body of troops pressed forward with unrelenting fervor. Unable to contain the incoming American tide, the Mexican soldiers defending the palace walls quickly withdrew to the relative safety of the palace itself. Soon scaling ladders were brought up and the Americans scampered over the walls, gaining a foothold in the palace courtyard in less than 30 minutes. The ensuing carnage was absolute. The American troops, now fighting in hand-to-hand combat, offered no mercy to the Mexicans defending the palace. The young cadets fighting for the very survival of their treasured palace were nearly annihilated.

After two hours of the one-sided slaughter, General Bravo called for a retreat. However, of those troops still remaining, six young cadets ranging between 13 and 19 years old refused to give up. Instead they continued fighting until the last minute, when all six committed suicide by leaping to their deaths. General Bravo was one of the very few fortunate enough to survive the slaughter. Today the six cadets are honored as national heroes with an impressive marble monument at the entrance to Chapultepec Park.

Within moments of the battle and to the absolute horror of the Mexican citizens below, the American flag was seen hoisted to its lofty perch and now waved lazily from atop Chapultepec. At that point they knew their city would be next to feel the wrath of the invading American forces.

Following the fall of Chapultepec, two divisions, Worth's and Quitman's, raced down the causeways, and by the end of the day, after the same fierce and merciless fighting, the gatehouses into Mexico City were captured. That night, finding his army demoralized and dispirited, Santa Anna decided to withdraw his forces from the city. Retreating once again, the once proud army silently marched their final ten miles to the nearby town of Guadalupe Hidalgo.

No longer encountering military resistance, in the morning of September 14, 1847, General Scott, dressed in his finest uniform, rode triumphantly into the Grand Plaza escorted by a brigade of dragoons. Amid the deafening cheers from the troops fortunate enough to witness this momentous event, the band began playing "Hail Columbia." Then, in a stirring gesture, Scott dismounted and magnificently strode into the National Palace of Mexico as the Stars and Stripes were raised above the cheering throng in the plaza below.

Among the spectators that day were 30 of their fellow soldiers watching the proceedings from the crest of a nearby hill. They were some of the many American deserters who had renounced their allegiance to the American flag during the course of the war and had fought with the Mexican forces. Each prisoner stood on a mule-drawn wagon with a noose around his neck intently watching the flagpole in the Grand Plaza. When Old Glory reached the top of the pole Col. William Harney gave the signal to the mule drivers to drive away from the scaffolding. Called the San Patricio Battalion, the prisoners were emigrants from a number of countries, mostly Irish, who were captured at the Battle of Churubusco. The men have continued to be honored and revered as heroes in Mexico to this day.

Two days later, disgraced and humiliated, Santa Anna resigned from the presidency, and in October he was relieved of his command and court-martialed. He was ultimately banished to Jamaica in 1851.

In Washington meanwhile, Polk was having second thoughts about keeping his peace negotiator, Nicholas Trist, in Mexico. Polk feared that Trist's continued presence in Mexico might be construed as a sign that the United States was eager for a peaceful solution and, worse yet, that Trist, in a bold attempt to exert his own will, might even be willing to negotiate terms favorable to the Mexican government as he previously suggested to Polk. Under this perception, Polk asked Secretary of State Buchanan to withdraw Trist from Mexico at once and insisted that from then on any overtures from Mexico for a peace should be forwarded through the commanding general of the army to Washington.

In the meantime, in Mexico City, General Quitman was named military governor and Scott instituted martial law, and by mid–October the city was relatively calm and peaceful. Reinforcements would soon arrive and even treaty negotiations between the new Mexican president, Manuel de la Peña y Peña, and Nicholas Trist were taking place. The following month, Trist became aware that he was being recalled and that he no longer had the authority to negotiate the terms of the peace treaty on behalf of the United States. However, he thought the Peña government sincerely wanted an end to the war and being such a proud people the Mexicans would never suffer the humiliation of approaching Washington for new talks. Under the current circumstances, Trist found himself in an enormous quandary. On the verge of winning a peace and all the concessions Polk desired, Trist felt he could not permit this opportunity to slip through his nation's fingers. Without Polk's authorization, therefore, and with the urging of Scott and Peña, in December Trist decided to stay at the bargaining table. Informing the president by letter, Trist, unfortunately, not only wrote that he was staying on to finish his job but also took it upon himself to castigate Polk for using an unlawful war to invade and occupy Mexico. If that language weren't bold enough, he indirectly suggested that he and General Scott would rescue Polk and his administration from this awful predicament.

The letter from Trist arrived at the White House, and quite understandably Polk could hardly contain his fury after reading it: "His dispatch is arrogant, impudent, and very insulting to his Government, and was personally offensive to the President. He admits he is acting without authority and in violation of the positive orders recalling him. It is manifest to me that he has become the tool of General Scott and his menial instrument, and that the paper was written at Scott's instance and dictation. I have never in my life felt so indignant, and the whole Cabinet expressed themselves as I felt."[9]

True to his word, Trist continued his unauthorized negotiations over the next two months. Finally, on February 2, 1848, the terms were agreed upon and the Treaty of Guadalupe Hidalgo was signed. While Trist represented the United States, the Mexican signatories were Don Luis G. Cuevas, Don Miguel Atristain, and Don Bernardo Conto. Ratification of the treaty by the U.S. and Mexican governments was all that remained.

Despite the fact that the treaty contained more than he had asked for when he sent Trist to Mexico last April, Polk was not happy with this sudden turn of events. He was infuriated that he had no recourse but to honor such a defiant and dishonorable man as Trist by accepting a treaty he had negotiated without the proper authority.

Nevertheless, Polk knew he had no other choice but to send the treaty to the Senate for ratification. The people were fed up with the war and wanted it to end. Besides he mused, if he rejected the treaty to push for more concessions, Mexico would certainly not concede, Congress would not support the continued fighting of his army, and without war supplies the army would have to be withdrawn, all with nothing gained.

Consequently, the treaty was received at the Senate on February 23. Senate Whigs who were vehemently opposed to "Mr. Polk's War" from the beginning and were equally against taking the territorial spoils of that war now found themselves in a catch-22. If they voted against the treaty they would be voting for extending the war, and if they voted for the treaty they would be unwilling participants in the land grab that they totally abhorred. Still others, like Jefferson Davis, now a U.S. senator, argued that the treaty was not legally binding since it was negotiated by an unauthorized civilian. The frenzied and salivating hawks in the administration, however, all expansionists in their own right, were clamoring for even more territory. Mexico was on the verge of collapse, they argued, a perfect time to take the entire republic, a scenario that Polk was inclined to agree with. Nevertheless, following intense and spirited debate the Treaty of Guadalupe Hidalgo was finally ratified on March 10 by a vote of 38 to 14. The Mexican Senate subsequently approved the treaty on May 19, 1848.

On June 12, 1848, amid gun salutes by both nations and witnessed by thousands of thrilled Mexican citizens, Old Glory was lowered and the Mexican tri-colored flag was raised once again over the Grand Plaza. The American army, represented by the division under General Worth, then proudly marched out of Mexico City for the last time.

By virtue of the treaty Mexico agreed to the Rio Grande boundary west to the Pacific and to cede thousands of miles of northern territory to the United States. To appease the Whigs who were against a perceived American grab of Mexican land from the beginning, Polk agreed to pay the Mexicans $15 million in cash for the ceded land and $3 million for American damage claims against Mexico. The war itself cost an estimated $97 million, but besides the money the United States lost about 14,000 lives out of some 105,000 who served, 11,000 from disease and exposure alone, reputed to be the highest death rate of any war in our history. Only about 1,700 died in actual combat.

Once back in the United States, Trist proposed the impeachment of Polk in a letter to the House of Representatives in August of 1848. Not surprisingly, because Trist was acting in an unofficial capacity, he was refused payment for his services from the date he received his notice of recall. And as a final reprimand, because of his insubordination he was forced to wait until 1870 for the money he was owed.

When Polk took office in 1845, the United States had not been enlarged for some 25 years. With the victory over Mexico, 525,000 square miles more were added, land now consisting of California, Nevada and Utah, most of New Mexico and Arizona, and parts of Colorado and Wyoming. When this was added to the land area gained from the annexation of Texas and the Oregon Territory treaty, the United States, under Polk, had grown by 1.2 million square miles, to nearly double its previous size.

In the United States, the war was a victory for the proponents of expansionism to be sure, but in the greater scheme of things it triggered an enormous period of internal strife and social and political divisions and brought to the forefront a new and bitter struggle the country had to deal with called territorial sectionalism.

As for Santa Anna, he remained in exile until 1853, when he was allowed to return to Mexico. Still unchanged and unrepentant, incredibly he succeeded in returning to power once again. And true to form, a year later he was charged with such offenses as embezzling government funds for his personal use and selling more Mexican territory to the United States, in this case the Gadsden Purchase and decreed himself dictator for life. Stripped of his power, he then fled to Cuba.

He was a man who caused great turmoil in the country he claimed to love. Over the years he lost hundreds of thousands of square miles of Mexican territory from the wars he lost and stole untold millions of dollars for his own extravagant lifestyle while the country went bankrupt. Although tried in absentia for treason, Santa Anna was still offered amnesty in 1874. Two years later, Santa Anna died in his beloved Mexico penniless, crippled, and shunned.

His obituary merely remarked, "General Antonio Lopez de Santa Anna died in this city on the 21st inst. However he may have been condemned by parties, his career formed a brilliant and important portion of the History of Mexico, and future historians will differ in their judgment of his merits. General Santa Anna outlived his usefulness and ambition, and died at the ripe age of eighty-four. Peace to his ashes."[10]

Epilogue

Following periods of armed conflict, border raids, and skirmishes with Mexico between 1835 and 1848, the American army, both regulars and volunteers alike, headed home for good. Celebrations were in order in just about every major city of the United States. Parades along flag-draped streets, endless speeches, barbeques, and fireworks welcomed back the heroes who had endured so much hardship. To some, it had been a fight for democracy and political freedom; to others, the soldiers had fought for a political ideology called expansionism.

The Mexican civilians and their embittered army, however, had nothing to celebrate. Despite the odds against them, they were a proud people unwilling to simply negotiate their beloved nation away to the United States or to any foreign power. As remarked by peace negotiator Nicholas P. Trist in an 1847 letter to Secretary of State Buchanan, "however helpless a nation may feel, there is necessarily a point beyond which she cannot be expected to go under any circumstances, in surrendering her territory as the price for peace." Instead the Mexicans chose to fight to the death to uphold the sacred honor of the motherland.

But, when all the fighting was over and the semblance of peace restored, what became of the men mentioned within these pages? The following is a brief summary of their accomplishments, failures, activities, and deaths.

Col. Juan N. Almonte: After serving as minister to the United States, Almonte resigned in 1845 and returned to Mexico shortly after President Polk was sworn in. Almonte then served as minister to Great Britain the following year and was reappointed to the United States once again in 1853 under Santa Anna's last term as president. In 1856 Almonte was transferred back to Europe once again, this time as minister to England, France, and Spain. Much of his time in Europe was spent conspiring to reintroduce the monarchy back into Mexico with aspirations of taking the throne for himself. As a result, he returned to Mexico with the French troops in 1862, in the so-called French Intervention. Appointed as envoy to France by Maximilian I, the emperor of Mexico and the only monarch of the Second Mexican Empire, Almonte was named "supreme chief" of

Mexico by Maximilian in 1864. After the execution of Maximilian, Almonte fled to Europe, where he died, in France, on March 21, 1869, at the age of 65.

Gen. Pedro de Ampudia: Following the war he commanded the Army of the East. In 1854 he was appointed general-in-chief and governor of Nuevo Laredo, and four years later he took part in the War of the Reform supporting Benito Juárez, a powerful Mexican politician. Ampudia died on August 7, 1868, three months after Juárez became Mexico's twenty-sixth president. Ampudia was laid to rest in the distinguished cemetery Panteón de San Fernando in Mexico City.

Gen. Juan José Andrade: In April of 1836, when Gen. Vicente Filisola received Santa Anna's order to retreat from Texas, he notified Andrade, who marched out of the Alamo with his troops and joined Filisola's forces at Goliad for the trek back to Matamoros. However, after assuming leadership of Filisola's command Andrade was ordered by General Urrea to return all the troops back to Goliad. Ignoring Urrea's orders, Andrade continued the retreat, arriving in Matamoros on June 18, 1836. Following his return he became commandant general of Mexico and in 1843 he began serving as the governor of the Department of Sinaola. A year later he passed away in the city of Mazatlán.

Gen. Mariano Arista: In June of 1848 he became Mexico's minister of war. Three years later he was declared the constitutional president of Mexico by the Mexican congress, succeeding José Joaquín de Herrera. Following Arista's attempt to institute stricter regulations and discipline in the army and fiscal stability to the country, the ensuing conservative revolt persuaded him to retire in January of 1853. As a result he was forced into exile and died aboard a steamer off the coast of Portugal two years later at the age of 53.

Gen. José Joaquín de Arrendondo: Shortly after Mexico gained her independence from Spain in 1821, he surrendered his command and went into retirement in Havana, Cuba, where he died in 1837.

Empresario and General Stephen F. Austin: After the first presidential election in the Republic of Texas, Pres. Sam Houston selected Austin as the country's first secretary of state. Three months later, on December 27, 1836, like his father before him, he succumbed to pneumonia. He was 43 years old. The "Father of Texas" is buried at the Texas State Cemetery in Austin.

Gen. Isidro Barradas: After capitulating to Santa Anna at Tampico in September 1829, Barradas was informed that when he arrived back in Spain he would be arrested for his decision to surrender his army in return for his safe release. Furthermore, he would be returned to Cuba to stand trial and face sure execution. Consequently, Barradas changed course and sailed to Paris, where he lived in squalor for the rest of his life, the result of lies, jealousies, and injustices from his own in-house enemies. He died in Marseille, France, in 1835 at the age of 53.

Gen. Nicolás Bravo: One of the few survivors of the Battle of Chapultepec on September 13, 1847, General Bravo was taken prisoner and later paroled to his hacienda in Guerrero, where he died in April of 1854 from a supposed poisoning.

Gen. Edward Burleson: Over the three years following the 1836 Battle of Jacinto he held commands in the first militia created by the Republic of Texas and successfully defeated Mexican insurrectionists with the Texas 1st Infantry Regiment. He also served as a representative in the Texas Second Congress and was elected to the Senate in the Third Texas Congress. Burleson also engaged in Indian battles, defeating the Cherokee in 1839 and the Comanche in 1840 in the Battle of Plum Creek. The following year he was elected vice president of the republic, but he failed in his 1844 bid to defeat Anson Jones for the Texas presidency. While serving as senator in Austin, Burleson died of pneumonia in 1851. He was 53 years old.

Anthony Butler: After his failed attempted to negotiate a purchase agreement for Texas, Butler was recalled to Washington in 1836 and took up residence in Texas. Two years later he was elected to the Texas House of Representatives. Moving to the North during the outbreak of the U.S./Mexican war, on April 28, 1850, he lost his life in the Mississippi River trying to save passengers trapped on the burning steamboat *Anthony Wayne*. He was in his early sixties.

Lt. Francisco Castañeda: Following his failure to obtain a loaned cannon from the townspeople of Gonzales, he remained garrisoned in San Antonio de Béxar, from where he fought in the Battle of Concepción in October of 1835 and the siege of Béxar that December. After the Treaty of Velasco was signed in May of 1836, ending the Texas rebellion, Castañeda surrendered the Alamo to Texas forces before accompanying the retreat of the Mexican army back to Mexico. With the rank of captain, in September 1842 to take part in an effort to retake Texas he returned to San Antonio, where he received a mortal wound in the Battle of Salado Creek on September 17, 1842.

Gen. José Maria Castro: Soon after Commodore Stockton's entry into Los Angeles, Castro traveled to Sinaloa, Mexico, where he took up residence for two years before returning to California in 1848. Several years later he returned to Mexico and was appointed governor and military commander of Baja California. His demise came in February 1860 at the age of 52 when he was assassinated by a bandit.

Capt. George Collingsworth: Returning to Matagorda after his victory at Goliad in October 1835, he was elected collector of customs for the port two months later. He resigned from the army the following year and was elected collector of the revenue for the county of Matagorda in 1839 and for the port of Calhoun in 1841. In four years he became customs collector for the entire Aransas District. In 1847 Collingsworth became a surveyor, in which capacity he served until his death in 1866 at the age of 66.

Cdre. David E. Conner: In 1847, soon after his tour of duty ended during the siege of Veracruz, he left seagoing service and became commander of the Philadelphia Navy Yard. Ill heath, however, limited his service until his death in 1856 at the age of 64.

Gen. Martin Perfecto de Cos: Following the end of the conflict, General Cos served as commanding general and political chief of the Tehuantepec Territory, a post he held until his death in Veracruz in October of 1854.

Col. Jefferson Davis: After recuperating from a foot wound received at the Battle of Buena Vista, Davis returned to the U.S. Congress as a Mississippi senator. In 1853, Pres. Franklin Pierce appointed Davis as his secretary of war, but he returned to the Senate when Pierce lost his reelection bid. He resigned his Senate seat when Mississippi seceded from the Union in January of 1861, taking the rank of major general and commander of the Army of Mississippi. The following month, however, he was chosen by a Constitutional Convention to serve as provisional president and in November elected as president of the Confederate States of America, serving in that capacity throughout the Civil War. At the end of hostilities in April 1865 Davis made an attempt to elude capture by the Union army only to be apprehended in Irwinville, Georgia, the following month. Released from a two-year incarceration, Davis served for a time as the president of the Carolina Life Insurance Company but soon spent most of his time writing and giving speeches around the country. In December 1889 he was in New Orleans when he became ill and within weeks died at the age of 81. His body is interred at Hollywood Cemetery in Richmond, Virginia. His U.S. citizenship was restored in 1978 by an act of Congress.

Empresario Green DeWitt: In 1835, as the Texas Revolution was beginning to break out, DeWitt traveled to Monclova, Mexico, in search of more land for a settlement colony. While there, however, he contacted cholera and died on May 18, 1835, and was buried in an unmarked grave.

Capt. Philip Dimmitt: He settled in Refugio after the Texas Revolution and in 1841 he built a trading post on a newly purchased ranch on the Aransas River. In July of that year, he and several associates were kidnapped by Mexican troops and brought to Matamoros. His abduction was ordered by the Mexican government in retaliation for writing and framing the Goliad Declaration of Independence while he was in La Bahia. Responding to the outrage from concerned citizens, that September Texas president Mirabeau B. Lamar made a failed attempt to stop Dimmitt's execution by a firing squad or years of imprisonment. Dreading the idea of spending the rest of his life in a "loathsome dungeon," at the age of 40 he took his own life with an overdose of morphine.

Gen. Vicente Filisola: After resigning his command to Gen. Juan Jose Andrade, Filisola retired from the military and moved to Saltillo. Brought before a court-martial, he was exonerated in June 1841. In his remaining years he wrote several accounts of the Texas Revolution and published a defense of his role in the conflict. He died in Mexico City in 1850, a victim of the cholera epidemic. He was 61.

Gen. Jose Maria Flores: On January 11, 1847, after resigning his command to Gen. Andrés a Pico, Flores left California and traveled to the Mexican state of Sonora in northwest Mexico. He died there in 1866 at the age of 48.

John C. Frémont: After his resignation from the army and still keenly interested in the future of the railroad, the following year he organized a failed expedition to find an adequate route for a road from St. Louis to San Francisco. Returning to California, he was elected one of the first two senators from 1850 to 1851 and as a Free Soil candidate won the nomination as the first presidential candidate for the Republican Party in 1856 in a losing bid against James Buchanan. Frémont later became the governor of the Arizona

Territory but was forced to resign after several years due to his lack of interest in the position. When the Civil War broke out he honored the call by serving as commander of several departments in a somewhat undistinguished military career. In 1864 he was nominated for president once again but abandoned the campaign shortly afterward and soon became the owner of the Southwest Pacific Railroad. His new venture lasted for less than a year, until the state of Missouri repossessed it when Frémont was unable to make the payments. Now destitute, he moved to Staten Island, where he was forced to live a meager lifestyle merely on his wife's earnings. At 77 years of age and suffering from peritonitis (inflammation of the thin tissue that lines the inner wall of the abdomen) he died in New York City in 1890 and was interred in the Rockland Cemetery in Sparkill, New York.

Lt. Archibald Gillespie: In 1848 Gillespie was promoted to captain and married the daughter of President Jackson's Treasury secretary, William J. Duane. At that time Gillespie became the marine commanding officer at the Washington Naval Yard and was subsequently ordered to serve in Pensacola as commander of the Marine Guard. However, because of health problems from the hot and humid weather he was reassigned as the senior marine officer with the Pacific Fleet. Before he began his new duties, in October 1854, he was charged with swindling money from his fellow officers. Gillespie, now facing a court-martial, abruptly resigned, and to make matters worse, his wife left him. With his life falling apart, he returned to the Sacramento, California, area, where he managed to eke out a living by working on small, obscure jobs. He died while visiting San Francisco on the fourteenth of August, 1873, at the age of 63.

Capt. Ulysses S. Grant: Following the war with Mexico Grant was assigned to various remote posts where the excruciating boredom was relieved only by excessive dependency on alcohol. Adding to his depression was the fact that his salary was not sufficient to support a wife and a son at home in St. Louis. Unable to live up to the standards expected of a West Point officer, to avoid the humiliation of being discharged from the army he resigned in 1854. Over the next six years, Grant auctioned off his farm and worked at various odd jobs until deciding to return to Galena, Illinois, to work as a clerk in the family store.

When the Civil War began he responded to Lincoln's call for volunteers, serving as a colonel in the Illinois infantry. By virtue of his previous army experience, in July of 1861 he was promoted to brigadier general and two months later received his first command. His reputation and winning ways throughout the war so impressed President Lincoln that in 1864 Grant was honored with the highest military rank of lieutenant general. As general-in-chief of the armies of the United States and despite extremely heavy casualties, Grant's tenacity against a much-weakened Southern army forced Confederate general Robert E. Lee to surrender in April of 1865. Back in civilian life, Grant tried his hand at politics when President Johnson appointed him secretary of war. Four years later he became the eighteenth president of the United States. Following his second term Grant went on a world tour and soon after spent the last remaining years of his life writing magazine articles and his memoirs. Suffering from throat cancer, in 1885 he died at the age of 63. Along with his wife, Julia, beside him, he lies in the General Grant National Memorial, popularly known as "Grant's Tomb," in New York City.

Sam Houston: After serving as president of the Republic of Texas from 1836 to 1838 and again from 1841 to 1844, Houston was elected to the U.S. Senate from the new state of Texas, serving until 1859, when he took the governor's seat in Texas. When Texas seceded from the Union in 1861 Houston, a Unionist, refused to recognize the legitimacy of such a move. Consequently, the powerful legislature evicted Houston from the governor's office when he refused to take the oath of loyalty to the Confederacy. The following year he moved to Huntsville, Texas, and was an active member of the Masonic Lodge. In 1863 Houston developed pneumonia and died in July at the age of 70. He was buried in Huntsville, Texas.

Col. Frank Johnson: Angry that General Houston was retreating from Gonzales in 1836, Johnson quit the fight and returned home to Johnson's Bluff. For the next three years he managed a plantation, until he became bankrupt. At that point he abandoned his wife (and his creditors) and left home, wandering around the country taking on odd jobs. In 1847 he returned home and remarried his ex-wife. Following her death, he ran a livestock operation, but now penniless in 1861 he moved to Indianapolis, where he spent most of the Civil War. He returned to Texas in 1871, living in Austin and finally Round Rock, where he lived as a recluse, researching and writing about Texas history. During his last research trip, he died of cancer in a hotel room in Aguascalientes, one of the 31 states located in North-Central Mexico, in 1884. He was 85 years old.

Gen. Stephen W. Kearny: After serving as military governor of California in 1847, he traveled to Washington, D.C., where he was praised as the conqueror of California and received a brevet promotion to major general. He traveled to Mexico, where he briefly served as military governor of Veracruz and of Mexico City. Unfortunately, in Veracruz he contacted the dreaded yellow fever and at 54 succumbed to the disease the following year after returning to his home in St. Louis. His body is interred in Bellefontaine Cemetery in St. Louis.

Capt. Robert E. Lee: When the war with Mexico ended, Lee returned to his in-laws' plantation in Virginia. He spent the next two years managing the homestead, in total disrepair since the death of his wife's father. Out of his element, in 1859 he reentered the military, being assigned to a remote outpost in Texas until he was called to end the slave insurrection led by John Brown at Harper's Ferry in (West) Virginia. Having made an enormous impression on President Lincoln, when the Civil War began Lee was the president's first choice to lead the Union army. Lee, being a loyal Southerner, chose to join the Confederate army instead and to fight for the honor of his home state of Virginia. Consequently, over the last three years of the war Lee led the Army of Northern Virginia mostly against the Union's Army of the Potomac. In 1865, however, the lack of manpower, food, supplies, clothes, and ordnance had reduced the Confederate army to a mere shadow of its former glory. Under these circumstances, the war of attrition had finally caught up to Lee, who had little choice but to surrender his army. Returning to Virginia after the war, Lee accepted the position of president of Washington College, now Washington and Lee University, a position he held until his death. In September of 1870, at the age of 63, Lee suffered a massive stroke. In Lexington, Virginia, two weeks later Lee died of pneumonia. He was laid to rest beneath Lee Chapel at Washington and Lee University.

Gen. Manuel de Mier y Terán: The year after General Mier y Terán and Santa Anna repulsed a Spanish invasion of Tampico, the former was promoted to commander of the Eastern Interior Provinces with headquarters near Matamoros. During his tenure, he gained additional notoriety for his oversight of the Anahuac Disturbance in 1831. However, as the problems increased from the Texian colonization effort, as well as the volatile political situation in Mexico City, the general, who was subject to bouts of depression, grew increasingly despondent. Finally, relenting to the stresses of his illness, Miery y Terán committed suicide by falling on his sword behind a church in Tamaulipas, in northeastern Mexico, at the age of 43. His body was interred in the same tomb with Emperor Iturbide until 1938, when the emperor's body was moved to Mexico City.

Col. James C. Neill: Following the Battle of San Jacinto the new Republic of Texas granted him a league of land for his service and for the terrible wound he received to his hip from a Mexican canister blast. However, despite his painful injury, he remained active in the military. He led a campaign against hostile Indians in 1842 and two years later he accepted an appointment as an Indian agent. In 1845, still suffering from his injured hip, he was granted a pension of $200 a year as compensation but died before the year was over at 55 years of age.

Gen. Andréas Pico: After California was granted statehood in 1850, Pico became an American citizen. The following year he was elected to represent Los Angeles in the California State Assembly. In 1858 he received the rank of brigadier general in the California militia, and he was elected as a state senator in 1860. In 1862, when heavy debts forced him to sell half of his landholdings to his brother he retired. Pico died in Los Angeles in 1876 at the age of 66.

John K. Polk: Upon leaving the White House in 1849, Polk went on a goodwill tour of the southern United States. Already weak and in ill health from the stresses of the presidency, he is reported to have contacted cholera in New Orleans. He died at the age of 53 three months after leaving office and is buried in a tomb on the grounds of the Tennessee State Capitol.

Gen. Antonio de Padua Maria Severino López de Santa Anna: Rejected by his country after the war, Santa Anna lived for a few years in Jamaica and Colombia. In April of 1853 he went back to Mexico and in his own inimitable fashion regained power for the last time. Living up to his corrupt reputation, however, he was removed from power a year later and fled to Cuba. By 1859, Santa Anna was living on Staten Island, New York, where he became involved in a venture to replace the rubber in carriage tires with chicle, a base for chewing gum. Although his attempt failed, his associate eventually successfully used the product to market the popular chewing gum called Chiclets. From 1867 to 1874 Santa Anna lived in Cuba, the Dominican Republic, and Nassau. By the time he returned back to Mexico during a general amnesty in 1874, he was 80 years old, partially blind, and crippled. Despite the lavish lifestyle he afforded his wife, Dolores, she refused to help him financially in his hour of need. Instead, he managed to live on only the 200 pesos a month he was given by two of his children. Shunned by the Mexican government, ignored by the public, and living in squalor, he died two years later in Mexico City. His body was buried in the Panteón del Tepeyac Cemetery near Guadalupe Hidalgo.

Gen. Winfield Scott: Widely respected and highly praised after the war, Scott was bestowed with the rank of lieutenant general, at that time a title only held by George Washington. Taking advantage of Scott's popularity, in 1852 the Whig Party nominated him in an unsuccessful bid for the presidency against Franklin Pierce. When the Civil War broke out in April of 1861, Scott was 74 years old and in failing health. Due to his infirmities, he relinquished his field command to Gen. Irvin McDowell. While Scott was serving as general-in-chief and the president's military adviser in Washington, D.C., his advice at the beginning of the war, called the "Anaconda Strategy," established the basic strategy used by the administration throughout the conflict. However, political pressures ultimately led to his retirement in November of 1861. He then visited Europe for a short time, wrote his memoirs, which were published in 1864, and was the recipient of several honorary degrees from such prestigious universities as Harvard, Columbia, and Princeton. While at West Point, New York, in May of 1866 Scott died of natural causes and was buried at the West Point Military Academy. He was 80 years old.

Cdre. John D. Sloat: After handing over his command to Cdre. Robert F. Stockton, Sloat commanded the Norfolk Navy Yard for four years. In 1855 he was one of the driving forces behind the attempt to design and construct the *Stevens Battery,* the first ironclad vessel authorized by the government, a project that failed due to lack of funding. Sloat was also a participant in the planning of the first U.S. Navy facility on the Pacific coast, named Mare Island Naval Shipyard. Retiring in December of 1861, Sloat died six years later in New Brighton, New York, at the age of 81.

Commodore Robert F. Stockton: Once the dispute with General Kearny was settled Stockton went back to sea for several years and resigned from the navy in 1850. The following year, as a Democrat representing New Jersey he was elected to the U.S. Senate. To satisfy his business aspirations, he resigned from politics in 1853 to become the president of the Delaware and Raritan Canal Company, a position he held until his death. During the Civil War he served as a delegate to the unsuccessful Peace Conference of 1861 to resolve the secession crisis and was selected to lead the New Jersey Militia when Confederate forces under Robert E. Lee invaded Pennsylvania in 1863. When Stockton's wife died in 1863 he sold all his land and retired from public life. He died in Princeton, New Jersey, on October 1, 1866.

Gen. Zachary Taylor: Considering the hero's welcome he received at New Orleans on his return to the United States in 1847, Taylor's immediate future had already been determined. Nominated on the Whig ticket for president of the United States, he won the 1848 election against Lewis Cass, the Democrat, and Martin Van Buren, who represented the Free Soil Party. On July 4, 1850, the 65-year-old president welcomed the opportunity to get a break from the current issues and attended a celebration at the Washington Monument. During the day he reportedly consumed large quantities of fruits, including cherries, and drank cold beverages reported to be either milk or iced tea. Soon he became ill with a digestive ailment and died five days later from "bilious cholera," as diagnosed by his doctors. Clinical analyses of his exhumed remains in 1991 concluded his cause of death was most likely severe gastroenteritis. After serving only 16 months, Taylor was laid to rest in a mausoleum in Louisville, Kentucky.

Nicholas P. Trist: In 1848, when Trist returned to Washington, D.C., after negotiating the Treaty of Guadalupe de Hidalgo, instead of being honored for his accomplishment, he was immediately castigated for his insubordination and dismissed from service. To add insult to injury, the administration refused to pay him wages earned after his recall in 1847 and to reimburse him for any of his expenses. Trist moved to West Chester, Pennsylvania, and for the following 22 years he worked in various administrative jobs for the Philadelphia, Wilmington, and Baltimore Railroad, until 1870, when President Grant appointed him the postmaster in Alexandria, Virginia. The following year, thanks to the intercession of Sen. Charles Sumner, the government finally agreed to pay Trist the $14,559.90 he was owed. Following a stroke, his death occurred in 1874 at the age of 73.

Gen. David E. Twiggs: Twiggs served in a number of departments until 1857, when he was appointed to command the Department of Texas, a post he held until the opening of the Civil War. His responsibility was mostly to secure the border between the United States and Mexico. However, when Texas seceded from the Union Worth, a states' rights advocate, refused to wage civil war on American citizens. Consequently, he surrendered his command to the Confederate forces in a pre-arranged and staged attack at San Antonio by Col. Ben McCulloch. As a result, Twiggs gave up all federal installations in Texas, including all the forts and the Federal Arsenal at the Alamo, and any other government property such as horses, wagons, mules, cash, and supplies, excluding U.S. troops and their weapons. By order of President Buchanan, Twiggs was discharged from the army for "treachery to the flag of his country" in March of 1861. Soon after, he joined the Confederate army as a major general and was assigned to command the Confederate Department of Louisiana. However, due to his advanced age and ill health he retired in October of 1861 and died in Augusta, Georgia, of pneumonia in July 1862, at 72. His body lies in Twiggs Cemetery in Augusta.

Col. Domingo de Ugartechea: After General Cos's defeated army withdrew from Béxar, Ugartechea was commissioned to command the reserve troops. However, when Santa Anna ordered a withdrawal of all Mexican forces from Texas after the loss at San Jacinto Ugartechea and his command traveled to Matamoros, where he participated in a failed attempt to persuade Native Americans to initiate war with Texas. Remaining a dedicated supporter of the centralists' policies, he helped put down a federalist disturbance in February of 1839 but was killed defending Saltillo the following May.

Gen. José Urrea: Although General Urrea was against the Mexican withdrawal from Texas following the 1836 loss at San Jacinto, he nevertheless grudgingly followed Santa Anna's orders. A year later Urrea was given the command of the departments of Sinaola and Sonora. When Santa Anna returned to Mexico to lead the army in the Pastry War, Urrea relinquished this position to fight a losing battle against Santa Anna in the 1838 uprising called the Battle of Mazatlán. After fleeing to Durango, Urrea was captured in 1839 and sent to prison. Upon his release he initiated several more failed coups in an attempt to revive his reputation and his military career and led a cavalry division in the war against the United States. He died in 1849 of cholera at the age of 52.

Gen. Gabriel Valencia: While serving in the U.S.–Mexican war, the 49-year-old general was killed in 1848 while trying to defend the National Palace against U.S. forces.

Capt. Ira Westover: On March 19, 1836, Captain Westover was one of the unfortunate troops captured at the Battle of Coleto by Mexican general José Urrea. As a result, six days later Westover was shot along with the other captives in the Goliad massacre.

Gen. John E. Wool: For his services at the Battle of Buena Vista General Wool was recognized by the U.S. Congress with a congressional sword. He was then promoted to commander of the Eastern Department as well as the Department of the Pacific and was instrumental in settling the Indian wars in Oregon in 1855–56. During the first year of the Civil War it was General Wool's efforts that secured the all-important Fort Monroe, Virginia, for the Union forces. Wool followed up a year later by occupying the Norfolk Navy Yard after the Confederates withdrew from the base and was assigned to regain control of New York City during the riots in July of 1863. A month later, General Wool retired, holding the distinction of being the oldest army general in the Civil War. Living in Troy, New York, he died at the age of 85 in 1869.

Gen. William J. Worth: In 1848, following the war with Mexico, Worth was approached by a group of Cuban businessmen whose goal was to overthrow the Spanish colonial government in Havana. After listening to their scheme, Worth agreed to accept $3 million to lead an invasion force of some five thousand army veterans to carry out their scheme. However, before the plot could be carried out, the army transferred Worth back to Texas. The following year the 55-year-old commander of the Department of Texas contacted cholera in San Antonio and died. His body was placed in a tomb constructed in Worth Square on a traffic island at the intersection of Fifth Avenue and Broadway at 25th Street in New York City.

Notes

Chapter 1
1. Moses Austin, carrollscorner.net, History of Mine A Breton.
2. Barker, chapter 3, p. 22.
3. Ibid., p. 24.
4. The Land Act of 1820.
5. Cole, p. 131.
6. J. Smith, *War with Mexico,* Vol. 1, p. 62.
7. Cole, p. 132.
8. Barker, Papers II, Oct. 2, 1833, p. 1007.
9. Henderson, p. 89.

Chapter 2
1. Gilliam, p. 412.
2. Ibid., p. 425.
3. Ibid., p. 426.
4. Fowler, pp. 123–24.

Chapter 3
1. Winders, p. 54.

Chapter 4
1. *The Quarterly of the Texas State Historical Association*, Vol. XI, p. 1.
2. Davis, p. 156.
3. Smithwick, p. 114.
4. *The Quarterly of the Texas State Historical Association*, Vol. XI, p. 2.
5. Hoyt, p. 56.
6. Todish, p. 26.
7. Hardin, p. 89.
8. Williams, p. 32.

Chapter 5
1. Crockett, p. 7.
2. Chariton, pp. 11–12.
3. Johnson, p. 401.
4. Ibid.
5. Ibid.
6. De Zavala, p. 34.
7. Ibid., p. 39.
8. Ibid., p. 38.
9. Cole, p. 133.

Chapter 6
1. Davis, p. 234.
2. Hardin, p. 163.
3. Scheina, p. 88.
4. Hardin, p. 189.
5. Brands, p. 467.
6. Gilliam, p. 119.
7. Henderson, p. 132.
8. Eisenhower, p. 6.

Chapter 7
1. *Biographical Encyclopedia of Texas*, p. 13.
2. Ibid.
3. Henderson, p. 121.
4. Calore, p. 169.
5. Merk, pp. 42–43.
6. Ibid, p. 42.
7. Holt, p. 169.

Chapter 8
1. Page Smith, p. 200.
2. Executive Document No. 60, *Messages of the U.S. President*, May 28, 1845, p. 80.
3. Livermore, p. 271.
4. J. Smith, *The Annexation of Texas*, p. 468.
5. Nevin, p. 23.
6. Holt, p. 220.
7. Executive Document No. 60, *Messages of the U.S. President*, January 13, 1846, p. 91.
8. Ibid., April 26, 1846, p. 141.

9. Fowler, p. 254.
10. Ibid.
11. Executive Document No. 60, *Messages of the U.S. President*, May 13, 1846, p. 774.
12. Ibid., August 16, 1846, p. 785.
13. Fowler, p. 256.

Chapter 9

1. Montgomery, pp. 134–35.
2. Grant, p. 44.
3. Montgomery, pp. 155–56.
4. Ibid., p. 14.
5. Ibid., p. 152.
6. Ibid., pp. 147–48.
7. Giddings, p. 148.
8. Haynes, p. 202.
9. Grant, p. 55.
10. Executive Document No. 60, *Messages of the U.S. President*, October 13, 1846, pp. 355–56.
11. *Letters of Zachary Taylor*, p. 67.

Chapter 10

1. Grant, p. 57.
2. Executive Doc. No. 60, *Messages of the U.S. President*, January 15, 1847, p. 863.
3. Ibid., January 26, 1847, p. 864.
4. Eisenhower, p. 186.
5. Scheina, p. 57.
6. Ibid., p. 59.

Chapter 11

1. Adams, p. 746.
2. Ibid., p. 747.
3. James Buchanan and John B. Moore, p. 277.

4. Sherman, pp. 51–52.
5. Ibid., p. 74.
6. Ibid.
7. Ibid., pp. 75–76.
8. Magoffin, p. 67.
9. Brockmann, pp. 215–16.
10. Bayard, p. 152.

Chapter 12

1. Carney, p. 9.
2. Grant, p. 59.
3. Eisenhower, p. 253.
4. Fowler, p. 265.
5. Grant, p. 63.
6. Fowler, p. 269.
7. Carney, p. 30.
8. McMaster, Vol. VII, p. 511.
9. Executive Doc. No. 60, *Messages of the U.S. President*, May 7, 1847, p. 960.
10. Ibid., June 4, 1847, p. 994.

Chapter 13

1. J. Smith, *The War with Mexico*, Vol. II, p. 390.
2. Nevin, p. 185.
3. Grant, p. 70.
4. Official Report of Scott, August 28, 1847.
5. Ibid.
6. Ibid.
7. Nevin, p. 202.
8. J. Smith, *The War with Mexico*, Vol. II, p. 154.
9. Bourne, p. 166.
10. Williams, p. 114.

Bibliography

Adams, Ephraim Douglass. *English Interest in the Annexation of California*. 1909.

Barker, Eugene C. *The Life of Stephen F. Austin*, Kindle ed. Seattle: Mockingbird Books, 2012.

Bauer, K. Jack. *Zachary Taylor: Soldier, Planter, Statesman of the Old Southwest*. Baton Rouge: Louisiana State University Press, 1985.

Bayard, Samuel J., and Robert Field Stockton. *A Sketch of the Life of Com. Robert F. Stockton: With an Appendix: Comprising His Correspondence with the Navy Department Respecting His Conquest of California: and Extracts from the Defense of Col. J. C. Fremont, in Relation to the Same Subject: Together with His Speeches in the Senate of the United States, and His Political Letters*. New York: Derby & Jackson, 1856.

Biographical Encyclopedia of Texas. New York: Southern, 1880.

Bourne, Edward Gaylord. *The Proposed Absorption of Mexico in 1847–48*. 1900. Annual Report ... for the Year 1899, 1: 155–169.

Brands, H. W. *Lone Star Nation: The Epic Story of the Battle for Texas Independence*. New York: Anchor, 2005.

Brockmann, R. John. *Commodore Robert F. Stockton, 1795–1866: Protean Man for a Protean Nation*. Amherst, N.Y.: Cambria Press, 2009.

Buchanan, James, and John Bassett Moore. *The Works of James Buchanan Vol. VI*. Philadelphia: J. B. Lippincott, 1908.

Calore, Paul. *The Causes of the Civil War: The Political, Cultural, Economic, and Territorial Disputes Between North and South*. Jefferson, NC: McFarland, 2008.

Carney, Stephen A. *The Occupation of Mexico, May 1846–July 1848*. Washington, D.C.: U.S. Army Center of Military History, 2005.

Chariton, Wallace O. *Exploring the Alamo Legends*. Dallas: Wordware, 1990.

Cole, Donald B. *The Presidency of Andrew Jackson*. Lawrence: University Press of Kansas, 1993.

Crockett, Davy. *A Narrative of the Life of David Crockett*. Philadelphia: E. L. Carey and A. Hart, 1834.

Davis, William C. *Lone Star Rising: The Revolutionary Birth of the Texas Republic*. New York: Free Press, 2004.

De Zavala, Adina. *History and Legends of the Alamo: And Other Missions in and Around San Antonio*. 1917.

Eisenhower, John S.D. *So Far from God, The U.S. War with Mexico 1846–1848*. New York: Random House, 1989.

Fowler, Will. *Santa Anna of Mexico*. Lincoln: University of Nebraska Press, 2007.

Giddings, Luther. *Sketches of the Campaign in Northern Mexico: In Eighteen Hundred Forty Six*. New York: Putnam, 1853.

Gilliam, Albert M. *Travel Over the Table Lands and Cordilleras of Mexico During the Years 1843 and 44; Including a Description of California ... and the Biographies of Iturbide and Santa Anna*. Philadelphia: John W. Moore, 1846.

Grant, Ulysses S. *Personal Memoirs of U.S. Grant*. Cleveland: World, 1952.

Hardin, Stephen L. *Texian Iliad*. Austin: University of Texas Press, 1994.

Haynes, Sam W. *Soldiers of Misfortune: The Somervell & Mier Expeditions*. Austin: University of Texas Press, 1990.

Henderson, Timothy J. *A Glorious Defeat, Mexico and its War with the United States*. New York: Hill and Wang, 2007.

Holt, Michael F. *The Rise and Fall of the American Whig Party: Jacksonian Politics and the Onset of the Civil War*. New York: Oxford University Press, 1999.

Hoyt, Edwin Palmer. *The Alamo: An Illustrated History*. Dallas: Taylor, 1999.

Johnson, Francis W. Eugene C. Barker, and Ernest William Winkler. *A History of Texas and Texans*. Chicago: American Historical Society, 1914.

Livermore, Abiel Abbot. *The War with Mexico Reviewed*. Boston: American Peace Society, 1850.

Magoffin, Susan Shelby. *Down the Santa Fe Trail and into Mexico; The Diary of Susan Shelby Magoffin, 1846–1847*. New Haven: Yale University Press, 1962.

McMaster, John Bach. *A History of the People of the United States from the Revolution to the Civil War*. New York: D. Appleton, 1927.

Merk, Frederick, and Lois Bannister Merk. *Manifest Destiny and Mission in American History: A Reinterpretation*. Cambridge: Harvard University Press, 1995.

Messages of the President of the United States, With the Correspondence, Therewith Communicated, Between the Secretary of War and Other Officers of the Government, on the Subject of the Mexican War. Washington, D.C.: Wendell and Van Benthuysen, 1848.

Montgomery, H. *The Life of Major General Zachary Taylor*. Buffalo: Derby and Hewson, 1847.

Nevin, David. *The Mexican War*. Alexandria: Time-Life Books, 1978.

Nofi, Albert A. *The Alamo and the Texas War for Independence, September 30, 1835 to April 21, 1836: Heroes, Myths, and History*. Conshohocken, PA: Combined Books, 1992.

The Quarterly of the Texas State Historical Association Report, Vol. XI, 1907.

Scheina, Robert L. *Santa Anna: A Curse Upon Mexico*. Washington, D.C.: Brassey's, 2002.

Sherman, Edwin A. *The Life of Rear Admiral John Drake Sloat, Of the United States Navy, Who Took Possession of California and Raised the American Flag at Monterey on July 7th, 1846*. Oakland: Carruth & Carruth, 1902.

Smith, Justin Harvey. *The Annexation of Texas*. New York: Baker and Taylor, 1911.

_____. *The War with Mexico*, Vol. I and II. New York: Macmillan, 1919.

Smith, Page. *The Nation Comes of Age: A People's History of the Ante-Bellum Years*, Vol. IV. New York: 1981.

Smithwick, Noah, and Nanna Smithwick Donaldson. *The Evolution of a State, or, Recollections of Old Texas Days*. Austin: Gammel Books, 1900.

Taylor, Zachary, and William K. Bixby. *Letters of Zachary Taylor, from the Battlefields of the Mexican War: Reprinted from the originals in the Collection of Mr. William K. Bixby, of St. Louis, Mo.: With Introduction, Biographical Notes, an Appendix, and Illustrations from Private Plates*. Rochester, N.Y.: Genesee Press, 1908.

Todish, Timothy J., Terry Todish, and Ted Spring. *Alamo Sourcebook, 1836: A Comprehensive Guide to the Alamo and the Texas Revolution*. Austin: Eakin Press, 1998.

Williams, Amelia W., and Michelle M. Haas. *The Alamo Defenders: A Critical Study of the Siege of the Alamo and the Personnel of the Defenders*. [Rockport, TX.?]: Copano Bay Press, 2010.

Winders, Richard Bruce. *Sacrificed at the Alamo: Tragedy and Triumph in the Texas Revolution*. Abilene: State House Press, McMurry University, 2004.

Winfield Scott: Official Report on the Battles of Contreras and Churubusco (1847). 2000.

Index

Alamo 36, 44, 50, 54, 57–59; Battle of 59–63
Almonte, Col. Juan 16, 73, 74, 90, 163
Ampudia, Gen. Pedro de 96, 102, 107, 120, 164; Battle of Monterrey 108–13
Anaya, Gen. Pedro María de 118
Andrade, Gen. Juan José 63, 76, 164
Annexation, reaction to 90, 91, 94–95
Anti-Americanism 13, 53, 56, 94
Apodaca, Juan Ruiz de 18
Arista, Gen. Mariano 97, 102, 104, 105, 107, 164
Armijo, Manuel 133
Arredondo, Gen. José Joaquín de 5, 6, 18, 164
Arrillaga, Gen. Mariano Paredes y 93, 94
Atristain, Don Miguel 160
Austin, James 4, 6
Austin, Moses 3–6, 30
Austin, Stephen F. 4, 5, 14, 30, 38, 46, 80, 82, 164; Béxar campaign of 41–46; contract 6–9, 10; death 81; Gonzales affair 32, 34, 35; imprisonment 15–16

Bancroft, George 100, 128
Barradas, Gen. Isidro 25–26, 164
Barrágin, Gen. Miguel 28, 53
Bastrop, Baron de 5
Bear Flag Revolt 127
Beason, Benjamin 69
Becerra, Manuel 7
Benton, Thomas H. 86, 125
Bernard, Dr. J.H. 63
Béxar, San Antonio de 5, 31, 35, 37; Austin's advance to 41–44; Battle of 48–50

Bonham, Col. James B. 60
Bowie, Jim 42, 43–44, 45, 63; at the Alamo 58, 59
Bragg, Lt. Braxton 92, 121
Brávo, Gen. Nicholas 23, 158–59, 164
Brazos Island 106
Brown, Maj. Jacob 102, 106
Brown, Maria, children of 3–4
Brown, Milton H. 87
Buchanan, James 124
Buena Vista, Battle of 118–22
Burleson, Gen. Edward 32, 67, 73, 165; Béxar campaign 46–47, 50, 51
Burnet, David G. 61, 68, 71, 72, 80; and Santa Anna 73, 74
Burnham, Jesse 69
Bustamante, Gen. Anastasio 53; French Pastry War 77, 78; presidency 12–13, 14, 27
Butler, Anthony 12, 165
Butler, Gen. William O. 109, 111, 112, 117

Caldwell, Col. Matthew 85
Calhoun, John C. 84, 86
California, interest in 124; see also Polk, James K.
Carson, Kit 126, 133, 134, 135
Casa Mata, Plan of 22
Castañeda, Lt. Francisco 43, 53, 165; Battle of Gonzales 32–33
Castro, Gen. José Maria 126, 127, 129, 130, 165
Cerro Gordo, Battle of 141–44
Churubusco, Battle of 153–55
Cincúneque, Gen. Ignacio 18, 19
Clarke, Col. N.S. 154
Clay, Henry 89
Clements, Joseph D. 32
Coleto, Battle of 64–65

Collingsworth, Capt. George 37, 38, 47, 165
Concepción, Battle of 43–44
Condelle, Col. Nicholas 36, 37, 50
Conner, Cdre. David E. 95, 97, 106, 139, 165
Conto, Don Bernardo 160
Contreras, Battle of 150–53
Convention of 1832 14
Convention of 1833 15, 17, 42
Convention of 1836 60–61, 68
Cordoba, Treaty of 20
Corro, José Justo 76
Cos, Gen. Martín Perfecto de 31, 34, 53, 72, 75, 165; Alamo campaign 54, 62; defends Béxar 42–46, 48–51; reinforces Mexican garrisons 36, 37
Coss, Gen. José Juan Landero y 141
Costilla, Miguel Hidalgo y 18
Crockett, Davy 58, 63
Cuernavaca, Plan of 28
Cuevas, Don Luis G. 160

Davis, Col. Jefferson 120, 122, 160, 166
DeLeon, Martin 10, 38
DeWitt, Evaline 33
DeWitt, Green 10, 13, 30, 31, 32, 166
DeWitt, Sarah 33
Dickinson, Susanna 67
Dimmitt, Capt. Philip 37, 38–40, 51, 52, 57, 59, 68, 166
Doniphan, Col. Alexander 132, 133

Edwards, Haden 10
Expulsion, General Law of 24

177

Fannin, Col. James W., Jr. 32, 43, 45, 51, 52, 60, 64, 68; Battle of Coleto 65
Farías, Valenín Gomez 14, 16, 117, 118; ouster 28
Ferdinand VII, King 20, 21, 25
Filisola, Gen. Vicente 54, 55, 56, 72, 73, 75–76, 166
Flores, Capt. José María 131, 166
Fort De La Barra 25
Fort Lipantitlan 36, 37, 38; capture 39–40, 56
Fowler, Will 26
Frémont, John C. 125, 130, 135–36, 166–67; Bear Flag Revolt of 126–27
French Pastry War 76–78

Gaona, Gen. Antonio 63, 70, 71, 75
Garcia, Inés de la Paz 23, 78
Garland, Col. John 111–12
Giddings, Joshua R. 87
Gillespie, Lt. Archibald 167; California mission 124–26, 130, 135
Goliad, Battle of 35–38; massacre at 65
Gonzales 10, 31, 42; Battle of 31–34; Houston retreat from 68–71
Gonzáles, Don Rafael 30
Grant, Dr. James 51–52, 57, 58, 64
Grant, Capt. Ulysses S. 92, 167; quotes 103–4, 113, 116, 138, 143, 153–54
Guerrero, Gen. Vincente 12, 20, 22, 24, 25, 26; death 27

Harney, Col. William S. 159
Harrison, William H. 83
Herréra, José Joaquín de 20, 92, 93, 94
Houston, Gen. Sam 15, 57–58, 64, 67–68, 74, 168; Battle of San Jacinto 72–73; calls for volunteers 61, 67; consultation delegate 42–43; Matamoros campaign of 51, 52; named army commander 46, 61; presidency 80–81; retreat 68–71; seeks Texas annexation 86, 87

Iguala, Plan of 20
Immigration laws 8, 9, 13
Iturbide, Gen. Agustín de 7, 8; rise and fall of 7, 19–20, 21–23

Jackson, Andrew 15, 53, 66, 68, 75; interest in Texas 10–12; supports Texas statehood 82, 87
Johnson, Col. Francis (Frank) W. 47–48, 49, 51, 64, 168

Johnson, Henry 88
Jones, Anson 91
Jones, Comm. Thomas Catesby 129

Kearny, Gen. Stephen W. 106, 136, 168; California trek 133–35; Santa Fe expedition 131–33

Lamar, Mirabeau B. 80, 81
Larkin, Thomas O. 124, 125
Lee, Capt. Robert E. 141, 143, 150, 152, 168–69
Liñán, Gen. Pascual 19
Lincoln, Mary T. 127
Linn, John J. 37
Long, James 5, 38, 47

Mackenzie, Comm. Alexander Slidell 100
Macomb, Gen. Alexander 99
Manifest Destiny 90
Mansfield, Maj. Joseph K.F. 96, 109
Marcy, William L. 91, 95, 113, 116
Martínez, Lt. Col. Antonio Maria 5–7
Matamoros, campaign 16, 36, 40, 51
McCulloch, Benjamin 119
Mervine, Capt. William 131
Mexico City, capture 155–59
Mier y Teran, Gen. Manuel de 13, 25, 86, 169
Milam, Col. Benjamin 38, 54; Béxar campaign of 42, 44, 47, 49
Miller, Dr. James 15
Molina Del Rey, Battle of 158
Monterrey, Battle of 108–13
Montgomery, Capt. John B. 129, 130
Moore, Col. John H. 32, 33
Morales, Gen. Juan 139, 140
Músquiz, Ramón 14, 31

Negrete, Gen. Pedro Celestino 23
Neill, Col. James C. 33, 48, 49, 51, 169; at the Alamo 57–58, 67
Nobel, Lt. Ben 59
Nuñez, Col. Gabriel 73

O'Riley, James 39

Palo Alto, Battle of 103–4
Paredes, Gen. Mariano 78, 100
Patterson, Gen, Robert 109, 114, 117; at Cerro Gordo 141, 144
Pedraza, Manuel Gomez 24
Peña, Manuel de la Peña y 160
Perry, James F. 15
Perry, Cdre. Matthew C. 140

Pico, Gen. Andreas 129, 130, 135, 169
Pierce, Gen. Franklin 138, 153, 154, 156
Pillow, Gen. Gideon J. 138, 144, 152, 153, 154
Poinsett, Joel 11–12
Polk, James K. 89, 118, 146, 169; advocate of Manifest Destiny 90, 92–93; clandestine plan 100; interest in California 93–94, 123–24; Nicholas Trist episode 159–60; opinion of generals 99, 106, 116, 140; strategy 115–16
Ponton, Andrew 31, 32
Powell, Elizabeth 75
Prieto, Guillermo 26

Quitman, Gen. John A. 112, 156, 159

Resaca de la Palma, Battle of 104–5
Rincón, Col. José Antonio 18
Robinson, James 46
Romero, Col. José María 62
Runaway Scrape 68
Rusk, Gen. Thomas J. 66, 74, 80

Salado, Battle of 85
Salas, Gen. Mariano 101, 117
Salomón, Col. José Mequel 25
San Jacinto: Battle of 72–73; treaty 74
San Pascual, Battle of 135
Sandoval, Col. Juan López 37, 38
Santa Anna, Gen. Antonio López de 65, 77, 144, 147, 159, 169–70; Alamo 59–63; attack on Zacatecas 29; Buena Vista 118–22; Cerro Gordo 141–44; character 22, 24, 27–28, 170; Churubusco 153–55; Contreras 150–53; death 162; early years 17–21, 22; French Pastry War 76–78; march to Béxar 54–57; marriages of 23, 78; opposition to 29, 30, 36, 78–79; plans 16, 35–36, 67; presidential elections of 14, 27, 78, 117; San Jacinto 72–73; surrender of Mexico City 155–59; Tampico 25–26
Scott, Gen. Winfield 99, 116, 147, 155–56, 170; acquires army 116–17; Cerro Gordo 143–44; Churubusco 153–55; Contreras 150–53; final drive to Mexico City 155–59; Trist affair 146–48; Veracruz 137–41
Sequín, Josef Erasmo 6, 7, 15
Sesma, Gen. Joaquín Ramírez y

54, 59, 62, 123; pursues Houston 70, 71
Shields, Gen. James 143, 153, 155
Sims, Harold D. 24
Slidell, John 93–94
Sloat, Cdre. John D. 115, 124–25, 170; occupation of Monterey 127–30
Smith, Henry 46, 51, 80
Smith, Justin H. 12
Smith, Gen. Persifore F. 156
Spanish Texas 5–7
Stockton, Cdre. Robert F. 86, 135, 136, 170; occupies Los Angeles 130–31
Sutter, John A. 125

Tacubaya Armistice 156
Tampico, Battle of 25–26
Taylor, Gen. Zachary 97, 115, 117, 170–71; advance to Corpus Christi 91–92; assigned to Rio Grande 95–96; Buena Vista 118–22; Monterrey campaign 107–14; Palo Alto 103–4; Resaca de la Palma 104–5; returns to Washington 122
Terrell, Kate 73

Texas, Republic of 76; annexation 81–82, 83, 85–88, 91, 94–95
Thomson, Waddy 84
Thornton, Capt. Seth 97, 102, 108, 151
Todd, William L. 127
Tolsa, Gen. Eugene 70
Tornel, José María 56
Torrejón, Gen. Anastasio 96, 97, 108
Tosta, Maria Dolores de 78
Travis, Col. William B. 63, 68; at the Alamo 58, 59, 60, 63
Trist, Nicholas P. 171; complaints from Scott 146–47, 148; feud with Polk 159–60, 161
Turner, Henry S. 135
Twiggs, Gen. David E. 106, 109, 111, 117, 171; advance to Mexico 138, 141, 143, 144, 153, 154
Tyler, John 90; presidency 83; Texas annexation 86, 88

Ugartechea, Col. Domingo de 31, 58, 171; defense of Béxar 36, 44, 46, 48, 49; Gonzales episode 31, 33, 35

U.S. Congress, war declared by 98
Upshur, Abel P. 86
Urrea, Gen. José de 56, 64, 75, 76, 171–72; Battle of Coleto 64–65

Valencia, Gen. Gabriel 150, 152–53, 172
Van Buren, Martin 82
Vásquez, Gen. Ráfael 84
Veracruz, Siege of 137–41
Victoria, Guadalupe 8, 10, 19, 20–21, 22, 23

Westover, Capt. Ira 39–40, 172
Wharton, William H. 15, 61
Woll, Gen. Adrian 85
Wool, Gen. John E. 118, 119, 120, 133, 172
Worth, Gen. William J. 143, 144, 150, 152, 157, 159, 161, 172; Battle of Churubusco 154; Battle of Monterrey 109–11, 112; Siege of Veracruz 138, 139, 141

Zacatecas 30, 36; Battle of 29

www.ingramcontent.com/pod-product-compliance
Ingram Content Group UK Ltd.
Pitfield, Milton Keynes, MK11 3LW, UK
UKHW050523150426
521?PUK00026B/1768